PRAISE FOR
THE EMPATHETIC CLASSROOM

"*The Empathetic Classroom* is a refuge for educators. Supporting mental health in the classroom starts with the teacher, and this well-researched, comprehensive guide belongs in every educator's library. It takes readers on a thoughtful journey to understanding emotions while providing practical, actionable activities to create an emotionally healthy environment—for both teachers and students!"
—**Kelley Peel**, author, teacher, and counselor

"As a psychologist specializing in emotional regulation for parents and caregivers, I am thrilled to see these principles and strategies applied to educational settings. This book is an invaluable resource for teachers and school administrators, offering practical tools to create emotionally safe learning environments and responsive curricula for students. I'm excited to witness the innovative ways education will evolve with this essential resource at hand."
—**Dr. Amber Thornton**, clinical psychologist and author of *A Parent's Guide to Self-Regulation*

"*The Empathetic Classroom* is a roadmap for creating classrooms rooted in empathy and care that support both student and educator mental health. Munro-Schuster highlights practical strategies teachers can use to foster student growth, mental health, and positive classroom dynamics—approaches that are simple and effective for educators at any level."
—**Kiran Bhai**, program director of Making Caring Common at Harvard Graduate School of Education and former school counselor

THE EMPATHETIC CLASSROOM

How a Mental Health Mindset Supports Your Students —and You

Maria Munro-Schuster, M.A., M.S., LCPC

Copyright © 2025 by Maria Munro-Schuster

All rights reserved. No part of this book may be reproduced or transmitted in any form or by any means, electronic or mechanical, including photocopy, recording, or any information storage and retrieval system, without the prior written consent of the publisher, except for purposes of review, in which brief passages may be quoted, or to photocopy dedicated reproducible pages for single-classroom use.

Free Spirit, Free Spirit Publishing, and associated logos are trademarks and/or registered trademarks of Teacher Created Materials. A complete listing of our logos and trademarks is available at freespirit.com.

Library of Congress Cataloging-in-Publication Data
Names: Munro-Schuster, Maria author
Title: The empathetic classroom : how a mental health mindset supports your students-and you / Maria Munro-Schuster, , M.A., M.S., LCPC.
Description: Minneapolis, MN : Free Spirit Publishing, 2025. | Includes bibliographical references and index.
Identifiers: LCCN 2024045257 (print) | LCCN 2024045258 (ebook) | ISBN 9798885549431 paperback | ISBN 9798885549448 ebook | ISBN 9798885549455 epub
Subjects: LCSH: Teachers–Mental health | Students–Mental health | Empathy–Study and teaching | Educational counseling
Classification: LCC LB2840 .M86 2025 (print) | LCC LB2840 (ebook) | DDC 371.1001/9--dc23/eng/20250404
LC record available at https://lccn.loc.gov/2024045257
LC ebook record available at https://lccn.loc.gov/2024045258

Free Spirit Publishing does not have control over or assume responsibility for author or third-party websites and their content. At the time of this book's publication, all facts and figures cited within are the most current available. All telephone numbers, addresses, and website URLs are accurate and active; all publications, organizations, websites, and other resources exist as described in this book; and all have been verified as of January 2025. If you find an error or believe that a resource listed here is not as described, please contact Free Spirit Publishing.

Disclaimer: The content of this book is intended for consultation purposes only. This book is not meant to be used, nor should it be used, to diagnose or treat any psychological condition. As a licensed professional, you are responsible for reviewing the scope of practice, including activities that are defined by law as beyond the boundaries of practice in accordance with and in compliance with your profession's standards.

Edited by Alison Behnke
Cover and interior design by Mayfly book design

Printed by: 68348
Printed in: USA
PO#: 16999

Free Spirit Publishing
An imprint of Teacher Created Materials
9850 51st Avenue North, Suite 100
Minneapolis, MN 55442
(612) 338-2068
help4kids@freespirit.com
freespirit.com

Dedication

To SB, for all the small details that make life good.

CONTENTS

List of Activities viii

Foreword by Cassie Nastase, Nick Covington, and Chris McNutt,
    Human Restoration Project ix

Introduction: Taking a Leap 1

Chapter 1: Before All Else, Attune 19

Chapter 2: Know Your Unique Triggers 32

Chapter 3: Build a New Relationship with Emotions 51

Chapter 4: Validate the Emotion, Understand the Behavior 66

Chapter 5: Your Classroom as a Refuge 82

Chapter 6: Form a Secure Attachment 97

Chapter 7: Support the Change Process 113

Chapter 8: You Can Play 124

Chapter 9: Trauma Awareness 138

Chapter 10: All About Power in Schools 161

Chapter 11: How to Navigate Boundaries 184

Chapter 12: Responding to Your Intrusive Thoughts About Teaching . . 194

Conclusion: Finding Solid Ground 209

Acknowledgments 223

Appendix 225

   Warning Signs of Suicide 225

   How to Find Your Own Mental Health Professional 226

Recommended Resources 231

References 233

Index 237

About the Author 244

LIST OF ACTIVITIES

Note: These reflections and activities are for your own use—alone, with students, or with fellow educators. None are intended to be handed out to students for their independent use.

For Teachers and Students: Self-Attunement 22

For Students: The Classroom System 29

For Teachers: Identifying My Triggers 45

For Teachers: The Observation Point 49

For Teachers: Emotional Mapping 61

For Students: The Empty Chair 80

For Students and Teachers: Re-Envisioning Our Spaces 92

For Students: Self-Care Jar 95

For Teachers: Identifying My Attachment Tendencies at School 110

For Students: Insight Survey 112

For Teachers and Students: Visualizing Change 122

For Teachers: Explore Your Playful Side 134

For Students: Gifting Improv Game 136

For Teachers: Noticing Cues 155

For Students: Getting to Know My Nervous System 157

For Teachers: My Power Associations 176

For Teachers: Noticing My Communication Patterns 178

For Students: Role Cards 181

For Teachers: What Are My Priorities? 192

For Teachers: Working with My Intrusive Thoughts 205

For Educator Groups: Discussion Questions 219

FOREWORD

by Cassie Nastase, Nick Covington, and Chris McNutt, Human Restoration Project

What does it mean to live a good life?

What does it mean to live in a thriving community?

How would you want others to describe you when you're thirty years old?

If you asked these questions of the young people in your life, in your classroom, what do you think they would say? When we talk to students in the course of our work with schools, here's what they tell us:

> *"A happy life is one where most days are enjoyable. Of course, there will be tough days, but overall, you find joy most of the time."*

> *"Being surrounded by people you love and who love you makes life fulfilling. With love, life feels pretty good."*

> *"I want to be someone kind and trustworthy, someone people feel comfortable turning to when they need to talk."*

Yet as powerfully as young people communicate their goals, ambitions, and visions of the future for themselves and for their communities, when we really listen, we also hear that they don't always see how school fits in:

> *"Most of what we do in class doesn't really prepare us for our future."*

> *"I feel like I've just coasted through school my whole life. I'm lucky I could do that, but I've never really been excited to go to school—ever."*

> *"School should be a place that helps people grow and become functional members of society. I'm not saying it's completely failing at that, but it often feels like it is. We're just living to be a percentage, chasing a grade."*

When we ask these same young people to use one word to describe school, *boring*, *okay*, and *mid* top the list. In fact, it turns out that the majority of the words students use to describe school are negative. A national survey of over 21,000 students found that the most common words they used to describe their feelings at school were *tired*, *stressed*, and *bored* (Moeller et al. 2020). And these challenging feelings are not harmless. The childhood risk of suicide increases dramatically during the school year (Black 2022). Not only are teachers more likely than ever to have students in their classrooms diagnosed with anxiety and depression, they are more likely to be diagnosed themselves (Agyapong et al. 2022). Among U.S. professions, teachers report the highest rates of burnout—even higher than healthcare workers (Marken and Agrawal 2022).

There's clearly something in the educational environment that kids and adults alike are responding to, and it's taking a physical, mental, and emotional toll. It can feel as if small fires are breaking out everywhere. Some of them are immediately seen and felt, while others quietly smolder. Extinguishing these fires is a necessary and sensible first step, but it's not enough on its own, and the fatigue of constantly fighting each new outbreak is a serious contributor to teacher burnout. As educators—and as humans—we are at a point where we must courageously explore the root causes in our school communities in order to find sustainable preventative practices and long-term solutions.

The Empathetic Classroom is a guide for those seeking to chart this course. At its heart, this book reminds us of the central humanity that connects us all. Through an honest examination of the effects of measurement, control, and competition in education, a more humane path emerges. Beginning with introspection and building toward authentic integration in the classroom and beyond, Maria Munro-Schuster provides layered strategies for connection. She offers therapeutic self-reflection activities and prompts for educators and colleagues, the psychological theories underpinning these practices and mindsets, guidance for applying them to your work with students, and scalable activities for classroom implementation. And throughout, she aligns classroom strategies with the mantra "I must put on my own oxygen mask before I can help you with yours." True and lasting connection begins with reconciling our own humanity—our thoughts, feelings, and behaviors; our past; and the experiences of everyday life that

The Empathetic Classroom

fuel our classroom purpose. By building a practice of self-reflection, we are better able to foster meaningful connections with others.

This path requires courage and vulnerability. Delving into our personal histories, understanding our cognitive biases, and investigating our response to triggers are not tasks most people eagerly take on. However, those who do will reap significant benefits: improved mental well-being, stronger relationships, and greater job satisfaction (Keng et al. 2011). And as neuroscientist Mary Helen Immordino-Yang's research on learning, emotions, and the brain reveals, not only do emotional connections play a crucial role in fostering deep learning and engagement, but "when educators fail to appreciate the importance of students' emotions, they fail to appreciate a critical force in students' learning. One could argue, in fact, that they fail to appreciate the very reason that students learn at all" (Immordino-Yang 2016, 40).

Maria Munro-Schuster's call to consider the mundane over measurement is essential to improving the current state of education. This proactive approach acknowledges that we are all learners and that all of humanity has something to gain from this mission. We can create school climates that are no longer so arid that a single spark or gust of wind sets everything ablaze. And in doing this, we may find that the fires are less frequent, more manageable, and less destructive.

At Human Restoration Project, our hope is that this becomes a collective movement among educators, striving to create oases of understanding that prioritize thriving communities and good lives built around our shared humanity. As one insightful student shared with us:

> *"I think what makes a thriving community is a general sense of empathy, at least trying to understand what something looks like from somebody else's perspective. Because you're looking past what you don't agree with in that person and finding things that you can connect with so that you can collectively push toward something better."*

Let's build a more connected classroom and a more empathetic future. Together, we can restore humanity to education.

Note: All student quotes have been paraphrased from actual focus group conversations.

References

Agyapong, Belinda, Gloria Obuobi-Donkor, Lisa Burback, and Yifeng Wei. 2022. "Stress, Burnout, Anxiety and Depression Among Teachers: A Scoping Review." *International Journal of Environmental Research and Public Health* 19 (17): 10706. doi.org/10.3390/ijerph191710706.

Black, Tyler. 2022. "Children's Risk of Suicide Increases on School Days." *Scientific American*, August 22, 2022. scientificamerican.com/article/childrens-risk-of-suicide-increases-on-school-days.

Immordino-Yang, Mary Helen. 2016. *Emotions, Learning, and the Brain: Exploring the Educational Implications of Affective Neuroscience.* W. W. Norton & Company.

Keng, Shian-Ling, Moria J. Smoski, and Clive J. Robins. 2011. "Effects of Mindfulness on Psychological Health: A Review of Empirical Studies." *Clinical Psychology Review* 31 (6): 1041–1056. doi.org/10.1016/j.cpr.2011.04.006.

Marken, Stephanie, and Sangeeta Agrawal. 2022. "K–12 Workers Have Highest Burnout Rate in U.S." *Gallup*, June 13, 2022. news.gallup.com/poll/393500/workers-highest-burnout-rate.aspx.

Moeller, Julia, Marc A. Brackett, Zorana Ivcevic, and Arielle E. White. 2020. "High School Students' Feelings: Discoveries from a Large National Survey and an Experience Sampling Study." *Learning and Instruction* 66: 101301. doi.org/10.1016/j.learninstruc.2019.101301.

INTRODUCTION: TAKING A LEAP

I had no plans to become a teacher. Similarly, I had no intention of becoming a counselor. As is the case for many people, there was already a seed growing within me long before I took notice. My own odd introduction to the teaching world was as a moose.

Consider the scene: I was a shy thirteen-year-old, and I had heard through the grapevine that there was a moose costume available to anyone who wanted to talk about the risks of smoking to grade-schoolers. Having long given up hope of winning the popularity jackpot, I threw caution to the wind. Something compelled me to order the moose. I was a gangly kid weighing less than a hundred pounds, and this moose arrived in a box the size of a golf cart. From the moment I put the bobbling brown head on my shoulders and looked in the mirror at my massive brown snout, cartoonish eyes, and floppy antlers, I knew I could do anything as a moose.

I spent weeks perfecting my loping moose-like walk, saying "Hello, everybody!" in my deep moose-y voice, and learning how to blow my nose like any good health-conscious moose would. And yet, when it came time to walk into my first classroom of second graders as "Mo," I initially felt as if I might pass out from sheer terror or heat exhaustion.

"A moose!" said two dozen little voices at once. Someone asked if they could hug me. Another kid gently pulled my tail. Little fingers reached out to touch my fuzzy brown tufted fur. I didn't realize I would be such a tactile experience! All eyes were on me as they waited for me to speak. After what felt like a long beat of silence, my new moose voice emerged. "Hello, everybody! My name is Mo," I said.

Almost instantly my fears disappeared. I felt something I'd never experienced before—I began to connect with both the whole group *and* each individual, all at once. There was so much I noticed from behind my big goofy eyes—who smiled, who looked terrified, who was curious yet cautious. I soon realized I couldn't just go on autopilot and teach my lesson. I had to consider *who* I was teaching. If what I was going to say or do would make any difference, I would have to focus not only on the lesson but on the individuals.

Twenty years later, sans moose costume, I sat in a circle with my eighth grade English class, waiting for someone—anyone—to speak. All eyes were downcast, as if counting the gray flecks in the carpet. School had just started a few weeks ago, and something about this year felt different. I didn't know if it was me, my students, or pretty much everything about life as we knew it. It was 2019, and my students looked at me with the exhaustion of a bunch of sixty-year-olds.

Though I could identify with many of the stressors my soon-to-be high schoolers were experiencing—parents, peer interactions, social pressures, concerns about the future—their burdens were also unique to their generation. Many of them grew up as digital natives, habitually exploring a world apart from the physical one, often on their own. As well-meaning as many of their caring adult figures were, these kids had exposure to sights, sounds, and feedback that most of us "elders" were unprepared to address. In part because of this, my students were keenly aware of the boiling tension of a world that was experiencing seismic political shifts; they were navigating differing views on identity and culture; they were witness to violence captured on the phones of teens like themselves—and sometimes directed at their fellow teens; and they were trying to figure out what the future meant for them if the climate changed. Little did we know that we were also mere moments away from a global pandemic.

Not to mention, amidst all of this, their fourteen-year-old human brains were still using the amygdala (an emotion-oriented region of the brain) for much of their processing rather than the planning- and decision-oriented prefrontal cortex. No wonder the world beyond the classroom—the one I *thought* I was preparing them for—looked like an awful lot to handle.

And so I finally decided to pose a question that had been sitting in my gut. It was not related to the text we were supposed to be discussing.

"Raise your hand if you feel unseen."

A few chairs squeaked as bodies shifted. Several hands started to cautiously slide up, and some eyebrows arched in surprise at seeing a hand raised across the circle where they hadn't expected it. Even the one kid who talked all the time had his hand up.

In that moment, I faced a choice: address this monumental need and wade into an unknown depth of muddy water with my students, or keep on keepin' on. I was feeling my own anxiety creep up that year, so keeping to the playbook felt safe and convenient. But I also realized that encountering the unknown together might help us all live more freely.

Why We Need a Mental Health Mindset in Classrooms

I was not alone in facing a mounting crisis. The Centers for Disease Control and Prevention's (CDC) Division of Adolescent and School Health was among the first to report what I believe many teachers were already feeling deep in their bones: students were drowning. The CDC's *Youth Risk Behavior Survey Data Summary and Trends Report 2013–2023* found that in 2023, more than 40 percent of school-age individuals experienced feelings of sadness or hopelessness for at least two weeks. Students reported decreased interest in familiar activities, increased use of alcohol and drugs, and increased experiences of violence. Two in ten students considered attempting suicide, and one in ten students did make an attempt. Groups that were most affected included LGBTQ+ students and girls. Prevalence was high in students across all racial and ethnic groups.

The glimmer of hope within the CDC's report came as a call to action: Student hopelessness decreases when they feel connected to the adults in their schools (Steiner et al. 2019). That's an easy fix, right? Teachers tend to be naturally caring individuals, after all, so the solution is already at work. We simply need to connect *more*. The flawed assumption here, though, is that to *care* about someone is to know how to *connect* with them. Caring is the output of one. Connection, on the other hand, requires maintained output and reception from a whole community of people.

While care and connection are not identical, they are closely related. The trait of caring about others is foundational for learning the concrete skills and constructive strategies inherent in connection. These are the skills that mental health professionals learn so they can create a safe and secure relationship with their clients, and they are the skills this book guides you to practice in your classroom so that both you and your students can find your feet on steadier ground.

Introduction: Taking a Leap

Your Mental Health Responsibilities as a Teacher

You are not alone in addressing student mental health. Developing a mental health mindset and implementing it in the classroom does not (and must not) equate to providing therapy, and it does not replace the need for trained mental health professionals. Educators and the mental health community must work collaboratively in our current high-need environment.

Educators and parents are on the front line of children's mental health, so deepening our own understanding of human connection is of the utmost importance to providing access to the support students may need. Prominent scholarship on teachers' mental health responsibilities suggests an emphasis on teachers as *promoters* of mental health, *collaborators* with other mental health professionals to implement targeted interventions, and *supporters* who refer students who indicate higher levels of need (Franklin et al. 2012). If and when issues arise that go beyond your role, it's crucial to seek the support of a counselor at your school or another mental health professional.

> *In most states, educators are mandatory reporters. This means it is your legal responsibility to immediately report any indication of a child's abuse or neglect, by any person, to the authorities. You do not need to see evidence of these acts; you only need to suspect them. Review your state's requirements and laws and visit childwelfare.gov for more information on how to report child abuse and neglect.*

A New Way to Teach

It was that school year in 2019, with that class of eighth graders, when I decided I would consider mental health—that of my students and myself—above all. I couldn't see the point in discussing a beloved book if students couldn't feel their own heartbeats or notice the warmth in their own hands. They were disconnected from their own minds and bodies, and from each other. Their expressions exposed their constant fear of judgment at the slightest misstep. They were afraid to laugh too loudly or to accidentally let a tear roll down their cheek. How could we learn and grow if we did not address our humanity?

That year of teaching also brought to the surface something else I couldn't ignore anymore—a desire to dig deeper into the world of mental health. To me, it seemed something had been missed in my foundational education courses, and I wanted to know how mental health training could change my experience of teaching and interacting with young people. I returned to the classroom, this time as a student in a two-year graduate counseling program.

When I reflect on my years as a teacher, I can now see the towering stack of mental health issues I faced every day. I remember ten-year-old Cade standing on his desk, crying and screaming like a tiger. The time I felt a hot slap across my face from eight-year-old Buck. Finding fourteen-year-old Sarah's artwork in my grading pile with black and red tears on a girl's face. Reading an essay about the death of a beloved dad by twelve-year-old Micah. Noticing my most talkative student fall silent when another classmate brought up suicide—and knowing his older brother died by suicide at the age the student is now. And I can remember feeling helpless.

The State of Mental Health Training for Teachers

Training for US teachers to address the skills of connection tends to fall short. On average, higher education teacher training programs require courses in child psychology and child development. They occasionally offer additional elective courses addressing topics such as trauma and student mental health. Even within pre-service training specific to mental health, the content often covers mental health concepts in broad terms rather than providing practical relational skills and practice (Brown et al. 2019). Think about what might look different in schools if educators were trained in what to do when a student believes they are a failure, or how to work with a student who has difficulties at home, or how to connect to a student who doesn't seem to care about school. All these situations have a significant impact on a teacher's ability to teach and on all students' abilities to learn.

More recent efforts to train teachers have been focused on suicide or crisis-related mental health concerns. Within US schools, it was only in 2007 that the nation's first model for suicide prevention training for teachers

Introduction: Taking a Leap

began in Tennessee after the Jason Flatt Act passed. With support from the American Foundation for Suicide Prevention, as of 2024, twenty-one states had passed a version of the act, which requires two hours of youth suicide awareness and prevention training each year. Since 2008, courses such as Mental Health First Aid have provided training for educators to "recognize and respond to signs and symptoms of mental health and substance use challenges as well as how to provide initial support until they are connected with appropriate professional help" (National Council for Mental Well-being, n.d.), and continuing education offerings now include a variety of well-being-related courses.

All these efforts are steps in the right direction. But while a crisis does need timely and skillful attention, focusing *only* on mental health crises can lead us to miss everyday interactions at school that also deserve our attention. A holistic mental health mindset is about how we take care of ourselves as teachers, how we regard our students, how we talk to and about them, how we address "problems," and how we manage our classrooms. These seemingly mundane aspects of a school day impact our students' and our own well-being in significant ways. Mental health awareness is not just for a crisis but about the details of everyday living.

Clearly, the work to make school environments sustainable and healthy places to go about being human is far from done. A 2017 report published in the journal *Children and Youth Services Review* showed that 85 percent of educators surveyed from both rural and urban schools felt they needed more mental health training (Moon, Williford, and Mendenhall). Specifically, they wanted to learn more about mental health disorders, behavior management, and social skills.

Teacher Mental Health Needs Attention Too

We've been made more aware of our students' needs, but there is also no shame in saying "What about me?" The 2023 RAND State of the American Teacher (SoT) survey asked teachers to report on indicators of well-being, including frequent job-related stress, burnout, lack of resilience, symptoms of depression, and difficulty coping with job-related stress. Out of the 1,439 K–12 teachers surveyed, 78 percent said they experienced at least one indicator and 52 percent reported two or more (Doan et al. 2023).

As educators, we have been impacted by similar forces as our students— our own personal histories, current challenges at home, health and

The Empathetic Classroom

financial stressors, and the larger social, cultural, and political systems that affect our lives. On top of all of this, we feel the weight of expectations to hold space for our students' emotional needs *and* adhere to high curriculum standards. As if teachers have superhuman capabilities!

The response to these challenging conditions can be seen in the ever-mounting reports of teacher shortages. The 2023 SoT survey also reported that one in four teachers were considering leaving the profession, a higher rate than other types of adult employment at the time. Black and African American teachers were even more likely to leave the profession. Rates of depression for teachers were higher than among the general population (Doan et al. 2023).

Much of this exodus has happened silently. The stigma around leaving runs deep in education, where "we do it for the children" is a rallying cry. Mere thoughts of pursuing a different life can bring feelings of shame and guilt, and such thoughts seem dangerous to voice for fear of falling from a pedestal teachers never asked to be on in the first place. And this is not to mention the grief that can occur alongside feelings of failure. Yet it is only natural to consider what one has given up to teach—nights, mornings, and weekends; the ability to provide for oneself and family beyond basic necessities; opportunities to experience other passions.

Foundational Relationship Skills

Today's teachers need a mental health toolbox to serve both themselves and their students. What I learned in my counseling program became the most valuable advice I could receive as a teacher. In training as a counselor, I discovered that many of the relationship skills and concepts from contemporary psychotherapy fit seamlessly into best practice teaching methods. And they make teaching more sustainable and enjoyable.

This book will walk you through foundational therapeutic concepts that you can use in your classrooms beginning today, including attunement, attachment, validation, play, power, emotions, and change. To learn how to become a counselor is to learn how to be in relationship. This is a significant part of what teachers do too. The moment to connect with our students and ourselves has never been so critical. I will show you how.

Increasing Self-Awareness

First, to learn to connect with another person is to learn to be skillfully aware of *yourself*. This means you not only notice something, but you also know how to go about understanding and caring for it. For example, I might be *aware* that I feel anger starting to creep into my chest when a student loudly announces how stupid they find the assignment I just spent all weekend excitedly concocting. What do I *do* with this emotional information, though? If I practice skillful awareness, I can see that what appears to be anger might be rooted in embarrassment, and I can respond more helpfully. Had I just stopped at "I feel angry," I would have missed something valuable.

To practice using awareness skillfully is also to notice that judgments or voices from your past may act as critics, telling you a thought, feeling, or reaction is bad or wrong. For example, in the scenario above, I might reflexively tell myself, *You shouldn't be feeling anger about a comment a student made!* If I do find my inner dialogue becoming critical, I have learned how to remind myself of why this judgment is showing up: *My past tells me anger is not a good emotion, but adult Maria knows that anger is a part of normal human emotions. I'm not bad because I feel anger.* It's amazing how this part of me quiets down when it feels heard!

In connecting with one or many students, you will need awareness of what is going on inside yourself at the same moment that you have awareness of what you observe in your students. Our interpretation of what is going on for someone else will always be colored by our own history. Maybe, when I reassess the student's critical comment, I realize I would never have been brave enough to openly criticize my teachers. So maybe I could try approaching my student with curiosity to better understand why they chose to give feedback in this way. After all, I do want to welcome feedback. Maybe I'll even provide some new opportunities for students to offer me feedback.

My intention in this book is to support curiosity about your own self-awareness. One way I do this is by showing you what awareness looks like for me, especially as it pertains to my role as teacher. Feel free to borrow my ideas, but don't feel there is only one way to go about it. I am suggesting you find your own rhythm. And know that it's not always tidy or pretty. In your bid for connection with your students, there will be missteps. I have my own fair share. As we remind our students, our mistakes can also be our opportunities to learn.

Taking Action

I will also show you what to *do* with this awareness as a teacher. Whatever you choose to do in a given instance, you'll benefit from knowing yourself better. This will require further introspection into yourself—your personal history of relationship to self and other humans, your thought and behavior patterns, what your emotions tell you, how your body feels, and what feedback you get from others about how you present in the world. This can seem overwhelming and uncomfortable at times, but I encourage you to not shy away. I've included activities in each chapter to support your exploration and to support your students in theirs.

Doing this self-work can dredge up things you'd rather keep from the light of day. When I begin work with new clients, I remind them that things might feel like they are getting worse before they get better. This may happen for you as you encounter and engage with the concepts in this book. The memories, hopes, traumas, and feelings we hold most closely have been tucked away deep inside for a reason. Sometimes, we do not like the parts of ourselves that we see when we inspect them closely, so we'd rather pretend they're not there.

If any of this sounds like you (and by the way, it is true of many people), I recommend keeping these ideas in mind:

- **Go at a pace that works for you.** If it feels overwhelming, pause. There is no reason to rush work on the self or to compare your progress to others. Some of the best realizations can come when we step away from something for a while and come back to it—something you have probably recommended to your students!
- **Be gentle with yourself.** Remind yourself that, while you are really experienced at some things, you may be a newbie at this work. When we are new to things, we tend to make more mistakes. So, prepare yourself for going through the emotion cycle that can come with mistake making—frustration, embarrassment, anger, annoyance, disappointment. When I was a new teacher and a new counselor I did not always say or do the right things, but I have learned that I am capable of *repair*.
- **Allow yourself to acknowledge your true feelings during this process.** Maybe you think something "should" make you happy or "should" make you sad—but try to ignore the

Introduction: Taking a Leap

"should" and to instead listen closely to what comes up in you when you encounter new or old parts of yourself. Our authentic emotions, no matter how out of place they might seem, are what we most need to hear from.

- **Reflect before sharing.** When we do work on the self, we sometimes want to tell others what we have learned. Be aware that sharing personal realizations with others can result in unexpected consequences. Some people might offer opinions, advice, or their own histories, or even respond in unsupportive ways to your introspection. I always ask my clients to think about what they are hoping for before they share an insight with others, and then I ask them to check back in with themselves on how they think a negative or unclear reaction might impact their perspective on what they wanted to share. When we are feeling more vulnerable, the chances to feel hurt also increase.

- **Keep in mind *why* you are on this journey.** Gaining comfort with our internal workings provides us with a path to be more resilient humans. You will learn to better interpret your body's cues. You will see how processed feelings can provide you with insights. Knowing your patterns and triggers will help you feel more prepared and less surprised. Feeling more settled with how you function can allow you to show up as you want in the world. This just feels better. And others will notice too.

- **Seek support if you need it.** In case the work suggested in this book or the circumstances of your own life lead to more questions or concerns, I've provided a guide in the appendix on how to go about finding a quality mental health professional who can support you in this process. I want you to find someone you feel comfortable with! And know this—you don't have to be at your lowest point in life to seek the support of a trained professional. There are many good reasons to talk to someone in a confidential setting, including the desire to learn more and make valuable connections about yourself; to better understand your role and patterns in relationships; to process old memories, thoughts, and feelings; or to work on skills that may have been missed earlier in life. Sometimes we need to just talk to someone to understand how we fit into the world, or we need someone to tell us we are worthy of love. When clients say to me, "My problems must seem so silly to you," I always reply that no, they are not silly to me, and that the small things are the stuff of life. If we give the small things attention, the big things are less likely to crop up.

Finally, I will show you how to make some well-informed leaps to what your students may be experiencing internally. This is a tenuous dance that occurs between teacher and student: *I get you, and I will also misunderstand you.* The methods in this book will help you meet the challenge in a way that gives room for you to be human and for authentic respect to grow between you and your students.

There's a good chance you're already showing up therapeutically for your students in some ways. My aim here is to remind you of that, to provide additional vocabulary and structure that help you continue doing what's already going well, and to highlight opportunities for internal or external growth. Teaching is like doing an eight-hour improv show 180 days of the year! Moments happen and then they are gone before you know it. You have had to learn to adapt to survive.

The Risks of Working with Emotions

There is risk in practicing the mental health thinking and doing suggested in this book. When you are more aware of your feelings and those of your students, you will undoubtedly face moments of uncertainty about what to think, do, or say. You might find yourself not knowing how to react or respond. That is okay. You are human if you don't have all the answers, and it is essential that students see that in their teachers as well as themselves. This book will guide you through these uncertain moments.

You might also have strong opinions about emotions. You might even be wrinkling your nose at some of the ideas presented here—and you may also see your students do the same. That is okay. Many people have formed an idea that feelings are problematic. Maybe you had a parent who seemed "overly emotional" yet didn't really seem to care about *your* feelings. Maybe emotions were a weakness in your household. Experiencing or expressing feelings may not have been safe or okay for you or your students at some point. Even how our brains are wired can impact our ability to process feelings. These are all realistic situations that can cause a person to dislike having or talking about feelings. As you work through this book's ideas,

Introduction: Taking a Leap

you can notice if such resistance arises, be curious about it, and remember that feelings are just another point of information among the many points we gather on others and ourselves. Having feelings is biological; knowing how to process and understand them is a skill learned with and from other humans.

Adopting a mental health mindset can affect your relationship with your students in ways you may not expect at first. I've noticed that with some students, and even my clients, using therapeutic language can have the opposite effect from what I intend. Statements like "be kind to yourself" or "practice self-compassion" can seem to gloss over very real and difficult experiences and can come across as invalidating. Words and phrases from psychotherapy are also now used more widely and more casually. Sometimes when we overuse language, students can grow tired of it. I've heard classes protest "mindfulness" attempts and joke about the "pointlessness" of social-emotional lessons. In our attempt to draw closer to our students, we can inadvertently push them away.

If emotion-oriented language does not work with your students, don't use it. It's not the language that can make your teaching more therapeutic— it's how you are showing up! As you're already aware, students are smart cookies and quick to read what seems genuine and what seems forced. You can use many of the ideas within this book without changing the language you use with your students, or even letting on that you are teaching therapeutically. Much of what I suggest is about aligning with your true self so you can show up genuinely with students. In the end, this just means that your students see and understand that you like yourself and you like them.

Do not feel alone in confronting your own messy emotional identity. An underacknowledged truth is that, as humans and teachers, we are all in recovery. We have all experienced the endless barrage of physically and psychologically harmful events and realities that have seemingly become routine: school shootings, the epidemic of suicide and self-harm, hate and violence toward human identities, our students' and coworkers' mental health crises, and feeling unheard, unwelcomed, and unvalidated—all while being underpaid. It is a well-studied idea in psychology that harm that occurs to us *from* relationship can be healed *through* relationship. This means that the journey of healing your own emotional wounds begins with surrounding yourself with a safe and supportive community.

The Empathetic Classroom

A slow but sure decrease in stigma around acknowledging the complexity of mental health—as well as increased conversation about mental health topics as a society—has enabled us to become better versed on these health issues than we were in the past. You may have your own therapist, or have friends who do. You may have contact with your school counselor and may even have social-emotional lessons happening in your classroom. These are all welcome changes.

About This Book

This book is written for educators in any setting, as well as pre-service teachers. It is meant for individuals whose time and energy need respect. Therefore, this is not an academic text. It is not professional mental health training. You do not need to read it from front to back. I try to balance practicality with details and examples that provide clarity to a subject for which teachers are afforded little time.

Each chapter opens with a vignette to help illustrate the main idea of that chapter. My examples may not apply directly to your teaching environment. If that's the case, know that the concept is of greater importance than the specifics of my examples. You may adapt the suggestions to be appropriate for the age and needs of your students.

The stories about teachers and students in this book allow you an opportunity to observe the dynamic emotional environment in the classroom from a bit of a distance. Some of these moments demonstrate our imperfections as humans. And some of the classrooms you read about might even look like your own. However, my intention in sharing these vignettes is not to suggest anyone is "bad" or "wrong," but to show how we all experience less-graceful moments, especially as educators under time and energy constraints, and that these experiences are opportunities to grow rather than feel shame. For many of these examples, I have created fictional scenarios, which open some chapters and begin with an asterisk. For others, several educators from around the country have graciously contributed their stories to this work to demonstrate how embracing therapeutic teaching, without changing who you are, can look. These true stories include the real first and last name of the educator and do not begin with an asterisk.

Throughout the book you'll also find reflections and activities for your own use and for use with students. These are opportunities to put the

Introduction: Taking a Leap   **13**

concepts into practice when you feel ready. To easily return to a specific activity, view the list at the front of the book. If a certain idea or activity is especially appealing or interesting to you and you'd like to learn more, I have included a list of recommended resources on page 231. Many contemporary psychotherapy books for laypeople include helpful activities like the ones you'll find in this book.

At the close of each chapter, I provide key points from its main ideas. My hope here is that you walk away from each new idea feeling like you can start to put it into practice in at least some small way.

Theoretical Foundation

The mental health information I share with you is based on counseling modalities and standards supported by the Council for the Accreditation of Counseling and Related Educational Programs and the American Counseling Association. I layer these therapeutic ideas over best-practice teaching methods and have adapted them for use in classrooms by educators. In other words, I don't advocate for anything that sound education research hasn't backed. There is no reason excellent pedagogy cannot also be empathetic.

You may have already encountered some of the ideas in this book in educational psychology or development courses. My addition to that knowledge base is to demonstrate how it can *look* and *feel* in your classroom. As many counselors do, I use an integrative approach and borrow from the areas of psychology that make the most sense in today's classrooms. The applications of psychology to education are endless, and I strive to provide both an overview of the concepts and an introduction to skills that address the urgency of teacher and student mental health.

Psychology is a science because its concepts are the result of studying human behavior. While this approach to understanding humans has led to new perspectives, insights, and approaches, like all lenses it is not all-encompassing, and it can have its biases. There are important details that can be lost when we *only* take a scientific view of humans. Humans around the globe learned how to connect with other humans long before the science emerged—psychologists did not invent or discover these methods. Taking from the best of modern psychology does not have to mean excluding the long-standing insights of so many cultures and individuals. Current, holistic psychotherapy practitioners should acknowledge and account for many ways of approaching the same situation. While there is still more progress

The Empathetic Classroom

to be made, mental health work today is often grounded in multicultural and social contextual viewpoints that have long been missing in the field's history. Today, most practitioners view their clients as the experts on themselves.

The Value of Doing Something Different

It can be tempting to think that the solution to our students' and our own mental health concerns is to delve into lists of symptoms, behaviors, diagnoses, and treatments, but as important as accurate identification and treatment of a condition is, placing emphasis on *only* this can result in looking right past the most essential of human needs: relationship.

Robin Walker, a marriage and family therapist who works primarily with children, reminds us that children in treatment are often tired of adults who only care about what is "wrong" with them. He challenges therapists to "do something different" with them from what they are experiencing in the rest of the world (2011). Walker describes the relationship between a child client and their therapist as "a relationship with a neutral and respected person that strengthens the child's sense of self and [their] efficacy in the world" (2011). And he finds that when there is careful attention to this relationship, a relief of symptoms follows.

In my counseling office, I might have to do something different when meeting a young client whose parent says they're not listening. Many young kids have no idea who I am or what they are doing in my office. Sometimes they think they are there because they are in trouble or "need fixing," and it's my role to undo these ideas (and sometimes talk with their parents about what therapy is and what it is not). I might look like a parent or a teacher, and so my work is to figure out what they are experiencing from adults in their world and try a new way of interacting with them. Maybe adults tend to talk *at* them rather than *with* them, and maybe I'll do something different by sitting in silence with them and drawing. From this alone, I often see a deep breath occur, as if they had been holding it in for a long time.

The role of teacher is not that of parent, friend, family, or stranger. And while it's also not that of a therapist, these two roles do share many attributes. So, in the classroom, I might need to do something different if I see that a student is shutting down whenever I talk to them. Maybe I am unaware that I am sending them the same message they have heard for years. Instead of talking to them about missed assignments and low test

Introduction: Taking a Leap   **15**

scores, I could ask them about basketball, since I see them playing with friends after school. I may not be good at basketball (in fact, I'm afraid of catching the ball), and I may not know much about it, but I can be curious about why *they* like basketball.

True connection takes time to develop. And there is no getting it perfect. The classroom environment is rich in possibilities, though, for teachers to genuinely and creatively get to know their students and to provide healing emotional experiences. How do we know when a person is on the path to wellness? When they can have what Walker calls a Genuine Experience of Self—which is the feeling of connection with and acceptance of one's true self (2011). Once they are settled within, a person is able to reach outward and connect with the world around them in a purposeful way.

Taking a Leap

Learning skills of connection helped me realize that I could teach and *also* actively notice and care for my nervous system all day long. Now, by noticing when my heart rate spikes, when my face flushes, when I feel numb, when my jaw tenses, or when my breath is tight, I can directly observe how this affects everything I say and do—and how it affects my students too. If I were to pick a metaphor for my teaching from before I learned these skills, I'd say I was a snowplow that just pushed on regardless of the conditions. I think I was afraid that if I slowed down, I wouldn't be able to get going again. But with my nervous system fully on my radar, I can use what I know about the *conditions* to determine how I approach each day in counseling, in teaching, and in the rest of my relationships going forward.

My goal in sharing what I've learned from my years teaching and my training as a mental health counselor is to help you feel more connected to the work you do and the students you encounter on the way. My hope is that as a teacher with a mental health mindset, you will have an even greater awareness of your own feelings and needs. And as a result, you'll have more tools (and energy!) for supporting your students. When students feel validated, understood, and respected by their educators, they can feel safe enough to learn. The empathetic classroom is one where burnout can be prevented. You already have this capability within you. This book is meant to honor what you already know and what you're already doing and expand on that from a mental health perspective.

So, what does a classroom with mental health in mind look, sound, and feel like? How do we integrate what we know about mental health into our teaching? What do we do if we don't always get it right? Let's dig in and be curious together.

Introduction: Taking a Leap

1

BEFORE ALL ELSE, ATTUNE

*By October, Ms. D had finally found her rhythm in the new school year. It was her second year of teaching, and at least this year she wasn't feeling the same urge to vomit before school each morning. Her sixth grade class was larger than last year—twenty-eight minds and personalities to get to know. But so far, she hadn't needed to meet with a single angry parent. She felt more excited now than she had expected. She was even able to enjoy the fall colors on the drive into school, mug brimming with her second cup of coffee, snuggling into the knit of a well-loved sweater.

As her mind started to transition to the plan for the day, she recalled it was a presentation day. Finally, a chance to take a breath! She envisioned sitting back in her rarely used chair, soaking in her students' discoveries. They were finishing a month-long study of their community's water systems. She was quite proud of herself for putting this unit together, complete with demonstrations, guest speakers, and even a facilities tour. This day would really be a celebration of every-one's efforts.

As she walked through the halls toward her classroom that morning, passing by her usually chatty students, she was met instead with silence and whispers. At the bell, students sauntered into her classroom in a far-too-orderly single file. Her attempt at a corny joke about a talking pumpkin fell flat and was even met with a glare by Cam, who always laughed at her jokes. Jackson, getting up to sharpen his already-sharp pencil, knocked over an open and newly filled water bottle all over Lily's packet of handouts for her presentation. "Damn it!" Lily screamed, turning tomato red and bursting into tears before

> throwing the whole stack into the air. Sammy fell out of his chair dramatically. Laughter erupted, and suddenly everyone was chatting like a million little starlings. Just as Ms. D was yelling at the class to quiet down, Principal Riley popped her head in to discuss a drawing she had found in the bathroom that morning. Ms. D felt her cheery morning float away like a distant dream.

As educators, we often develop finely tuned barometric pressure gauges that can sense when something is up. After a traumatic news event, the heaviness is clear in an unusual quietness and tired faces. When a blow-up occurs in the hallway between students, glances shoot across the room and little comments are passed just below your hearing abilities. Even when you don't know what is up, you know.

This is attunement. You are tuning into your students. You're getting on the same radio wave. This is an initial step for mental health professionals in working with clients too. In therapy, attunement is used to understand what clients are feeling—first to validate that what they are feeling is real, and then to support a shift in what they are feeling when they are ready. If we don't go there with them in their feelings, even just briefly, we are simply external critics. When we are viewing another human with judgments about their emotional state, we often miss opportunities to increase our understanding of why they feel the way they do.

We All Want to Be Wanted

In psychotherapy, empathetic attunement is a concept that came from the observations of a practitioner named Heinz Kohut in the 1970s. Originally, Kohut was a good old Freudian—he grew up in Vienna during Freud's significant work on psychoanalysis, and he couldn't ignore the appeal of the "talking cure." It was the early days of therapy as we know it, when clients would lie on long velvet couches and explore their unconscious thoughts and desires aloud to their psychoanalyst, who would do a lot of listening and note-taking.

At one point in his career, Kohut's therapeutic perspective was shaken by a client who wasn't afraid to offer him some much-needed advice: She noticed that he kept trying to offer an intervention each time she expressed a strong feeling. She didn't want an intervention—she wanted him to

The Empathetic Classroom

understand her! A valid point. But for Kohut, this was a revolutionary idea, and he began to try to see his clients' experiences through their perspectives rather than his own.

Through his no doubt very thick clinical goggles, Kohut (1984) established the theory that sometimes humans need what are called "corrective emotional experiences." For all of us to develop a sense of self, he suggested, we needed someone in the world to help us feel unique and wanted. He noticed that children who did not receive cues of empathy from their parents—smiles, hugs, nods, an open body posture—often landed on his therapy couch as adults, seeking the very emotional experience they craved from their parents. By empathetically attuning, he found that the foundations of a relationship could be rebuilt to be able to address the missing parts of self-development that are critical to experiencing well-being. Today we may not need a psychoanalyst to tell us why cues of empathy are so critical, but at the time, it was a significant shift in how patients were viewed and treated.

We now know that lack of empathetic cues from others can affect all people at all stages of life, no matter their upbringing. As adults, we can so easily be thrust right back into middle school when someone turns their back on us to talk to another person. Or we might feel our cheeks turn bright red if we are scolded in front of our peers. For students—even those who display what seems like a solid sense of confidence—a teacher's body language, facial expression, or tone of voice can increase a sense of belonging or instill a feeling of exclusion or abandonment.

Cues of Connection

When we teachers notice that something feels off in our classrooms, we can respond with empathetic attunement. This means we are attentive and responsive with our whole body—our eyes are checking in with all eyes in the room; our body language says, "I'm here to stay"; and even the tone of our voice becomes warm and steady. We might get quieter to show we are calm. We might sit in a desk at the same level as our students rather than stand above them. These are all cues to a student that no matter how they feel, we can handle it.

As a counselor, another way I provide attunement is to create *space* for my clients in the room. This is not just physical space—it is emotional space. That means I must quit talking! This includes not asking questions—which, to a dysregulated child or adult, can send signals of danger. Asking "why"

Chapter 1: Before All Else, Attune   **21**

creates an accusatory dynamic, even if this is not what you intend. If I am busy talking as a counselor, my mind is focused on myself and the "important" things I need to say. And as a teacher, if I am talking, my students are likely trying to decipher (or tune out) what I'm saying. In this common scenario, there is little room for cognitive or emotional processing. Most students only experience moments of quiet during the school day when they are focused on completing a task. But this type of quiet does not allow for processing either.

If you provide room for your students to process, even if just for two minutes, they will be able to integrate some of their earlier experiences (*I fought with my brother at breakfast this morning*) into their present (*now I feel tired and a bit sad*). By prioritizing students' internal attunement, you help students avoid feeling that they must attempt to attune to *your* needs. Often, students are masters of doing what they think their teachers want, rather than being their true selves. As one of my young clients shared with me, "I'm really good at smiling for adults, even when I don't feel good." You can support students in attuning to their own emotions by giving them the time to do it. Then *you* can attune to how they are really feeling.

For Teachers and Students
SELF-ATTUNEMENT

It's essential to support yourself and your students in checking in with the emotions that you bring to school. This activity allows for practice in noticing the connection between thoughts and emotions, and then provides an opportunity to care for the emotions. Your work is not to try to "fix" what is coming up for you or your students but to allow space to process it.

Essentially, this is a reflection activity. As such, if you are doing this with students, they may want their processing to be private. School can be a difficult place to maintain privacy. To help protect privacy, I like to

The Empathetic Classroom

ask the following questions aloud and suggest that students answer them internally. If you have the time after students reflect, you can welcome *optional* sharing with a few ground rules, including not commenting on what others share. You want to emphasize that the role of others is to listen.

I begin by asking students to find a way to sit or stand that allows them to relax. Some may want to close their eyes. After you ask each question, let students know you'll be quiet for some time so they can think, and allow at least thirty seconds. Reassure them that if nothing comes to mind or their mind wanders, that is okay. This is not an assignment.

- What's on your mind right now?
- What do you feel right now?
- Where do you notice the feeling in your body? It might be more than one feeling and more than one place in your body.
- What color or shape does the feeling have? What texture does it have?
- Imagine taking the feeling outside of your body and holding it gently in your hands. What do you notice about it now? Is it heavy or light? Did it change shape? Does it look bigger or smaller? Is there anything about it that is different from what you expected?
- What is one thing you could do today to care for this feeling?
- Before putting the feeling back inside yourself, if you choose, let the feeling change color or shape. Now let it go back into you in whatever way you would like it to. Maybe you imagine breathing it in, drinking it, or letting it soak through your skin.

Note: Students may need examples to help them answer some of these questions, especially when it comes to "caring for a feeling." You may suggest that we can care for sadness by listening to music, making art, or talking to a friend. We might take care of anger by telling the anger it's okay to be there. Maybe we'll yell when we get outside. We can take care of happiness by laughing more or doing something we love. We might take care of anxiety by making a list to keep in mind what we need to do or cleaning out our desk or locker. Give some ideas, then let students be creative. What they choose must work for them. By doing this you are showing them how to validate their feelings and identify helpful coping mechanisms.

continued

Chapter 1: Before All Else, Attune   **23**

In concluding this reflection, thank your students for taking the time to check in with themselves. Remind them that feelings can change over time, sometimes getting stronger, sometimes getting softer. You can provide a visual such as ocean waves to describe how we can observe our emotions changing. It can also help to think about letting ourselves ride the waves rather than trying to swim against them. This is also a good time to remind them that they can come to you with anything. From here, you can support students by listening to them or by providing a referral to an appropriate in-school resource.

Attuning to a System

Of course, you don't just have one student to attune to. You might have three dozen. How do you attune to a whole classroom with so many individual thoughts, feelings, and perspectives? And how can they learn to attune to each other? First, recognize that this group of individuals functions as a system when under your care. Just as families are a system, student bodies are a system. And systems are interconnected. You can help students explore and understand this idea using the Classroom System activity on page 29.

Now it's your turn. The next time you are about to start teaching, take a moment to attune to the whole system. To be able to attune to a group, you must begin by grounding yourself. This means pausing, noticing your belly breath moving up and down, and opening all your senses. Then find a spot in your classroom to step back and observe. Take a whole minute. If thoughts come to mind, or to-do lists, just ask them to step back for a moment while you are doing this.

- What do you see and hear?
- How did students enter the room?
- What does their posture tell you?
- Who is talking, and who is sitting quietly?
- Are they looking at you or away?
- How are they interacting with one another?
- Is there anything you are aware of that might impact the group's mental well-being today?

- Is there anything that may have impacted yours?
- Does your mood feel misaligned with that of your students?

While there may be individual outliers, there is almost always a general momentum to a group.

Next, locate your emotions. Using a feeling wheel like the one provided in figure 1.1 on page 31 can expand emotional awareness. Some people use feeling wheels like this one by starting in the center and then moving outward to more specific emotional experiences. I notice that many of my clients identify with the more specific emotions on the outer edge of the wheel, and then I ask them to follow the emotion to the center so they can familiarize themselves with their core emotions. It's sometimes surprising to see that a feeling might be rooted in something like *fear* or *love*, big ideas we tend to avoid.

You can interact with this wheel in whatever way works for you. I keep a laminated copy of it on my desk so that I can quickly look at it for myself or hand it to a client. The wheel is often a helpful tool to use with students because sometimes they can become overwhelmed by noticing feelings and this is something they can easily point at rather than having to talk.

Choose a feeling or two that most closely aligns with how you are feeling at the moment. Now locate one or two feelings that the group might be experiencing. Don't overthink it. Listen to your gut, or whatever part of you is intuitive. If you are wrong, you can adjust.

Is there a general sense of anxiety, excitement, anger, sadness, confusion? Name it internally and go there within yourself for a moment. How does this emotion tend to affect you? How is your own emotional state interacting with that of the group? For example, you might ask, *If I am feeling elated and the group is sending out signals of anxiety, how might this incongruence affect the day?*

Here's an idea of what Ms. D's internal dialogue might be as she uses a feeling wheel, reflects on what she's seeing in her classroom, and checks in with herself:

I'm picking up on some anxiety this morning, a bit more than usual. I know presentations are today, but they've had a whole month to prepare. I don't like what anxiety does to my students when they present. It feels like they become robots and just say what they think I want them to say instead of all the really interesting stuff I've seen them learn in the past month. I wish they could relax and have fun with their presentations and not worry about their grades.

Chapter 1: Before All Else, Attune

Okay, so she's identified anxiety. And maybe some frustration. She's making progress attuning to her students and herself in this moment. But her mind's initial response is to wish the feelings away. Wouldn't that be nice! She also knows that wishing something away doesn't work, and it won't serve her if she continues to wish for something to be different than it is. That mindset will create a disconnect between her and her students, as she'll likely experience and then express frustration as each presentation becomes more and more anxiety-ridden as students observe each other's fears modeled. But as Ms. D gets more practice attuning, she can learn, instead, to take a moment to *feel* her students' anxiety before responding. To feel greater empathy for her students' anxiety, she can also investigate her own relationship to anxiety.

Connect to Your Past

Speaking of anxiety, what do *you* remember about being a student? When I think back, I remember how challenging it was to figure out what my teachers really wanted. It felt like a guessing game. Sometimes I got it right, sometimes I got it wrong. I also felt like my performance might be judged on whether my teacher liked me. And I hated standing up in front of my classmates with my hand-me-down wardrobe—all-too-often a matching sweatsuit with cat print—on full display. What a helpless feeling! I now recognize that, in part, these were stories I was telling myself, rather than necessarily being truths, but my feelings were real. Becoming a robot sometimes felt like the only way I could survive presentation day.

When I take a moment to check in with my experience with anxiety, I also feel sadness. My fear was rooted in my desire for approval from others. Anxiety was the most obvious symptom of a deep fear that my teacher might not approve of the work that I had done (and had usually put a lot of effort into), a fear that my peers would think my clothes were weird (something I had no way to change), and a fear that the presentation would impact my grade, and therefore, the rest of my life.

That's a lot resting on little Maria's shoulders when she walks in the classroom that Tuesday morning. Her hands are cold and sweaty, and her stomach doesn't like the feeling of breakfast. To make it even worse, her friend was talking to someone else when her dad dropped her off, so she stood alone looking down at her feet and counting the minutes until the bell rang. It's in this state that she encounters her teacher, who's just hoping

The Empathetic Classroom

Maria will have some fun with her presentation and not worry about things so much.

By touching our own experiences of specific feelings and times in our life, we can remember that those feelings are as solid and as real as our hands. Students need support in validating the reality of their feelings so that they don't have to work even harder to suppress them. Letting anxiety come to the surface can allow it to begin to release.

Here's how Ms. D might address the mood in her classroom after reflecting on her own relationship to anxiety:

It seems like there might be some anxiety today about presentations. I can totally understand. I'm asking a lot of you in this work today. Getting up in front of everyone can be challenging. I feel anxious when I get in front of a group too. Even right now! Let's tell our nervous systems that everything is okay by getting up and shaking it off.

Ms. D might even crank up some tunes to get students out of their minds and into their bodies. By doing this, she is engaging with the natural energy that anxiety is so good at creating and putting it to work in a new and more helpful way. It's like finding a new role for anxiety rather than getting rid of it. Also, a tired body has a lot less energy for the effort that is needed to be anxious.

Another approach is to embrace your students' emotions with open arms. You go to the emotion with them and sit in it for a while rather than try to change it. If the emotion is anger, maybe you even "get mad" about something with them . . . after all, some things can be truly frustrating. As long as you can genuinely identify, it is okay to validate their emotional experience. When I am working with younger clients (and adults too), many find it relieving if I admit, "Yeah, being ignored at lunch really sucks" or "I'm feeling excited for you and your new puppy today! I totally want to see photos!" You might ask what is helpful to them when they are feeling anxious, angry, or sad. The point is not to suggest there is a one-size-fits-all approach to emotions but to expand their awareness of the options that are out there.

You can also let real emotions come to the surface in your classroom by showing your own humanity. In Ms. D's shoes, I might share a story about a time I was nervous and had to get up in front of a big scary group of people. I might talk about the time I was a moose and almost passed out from my nerves and heat. Or the time when, as a new teacher, I accidentally caught

Chapter 1: Before All Else, Attune

my shoe heel on my skirt and pulled it down in front of a class of my students and adult observers. (The adults laughed the hardest, by the way.) The key here is to help students avoid the assumption that everything was easy or went perfectly for you. When you share your experience, students can see that you, too, have your limitations and your fallibility, and in turn they will experience less pressure to perform perfectly.

Students can never have enough reminders that you accept and value them however they're showing up that day. We may often think that we have told or shown our students that we value them, but the nature of being human is to always test for and seek security. We can provide this through showing that we see them by attuning to them, even if we don't fully understand everything about them.

KEY POINTS

- Children and adults feel validated and seen when a person responds to them empathetically.
- By giving attunement, you are validating your students' emotional experience rather than ignoring it or hoping to change it.
- Empathetic attunement can be shown with tone of voice, facial expression, and body language.
- Allow your students to attune internally by providing "space."
- To attune to yourself or others, take a moment to be an observer: Notice facial expressions, body language, behaviors, who is speaking, who is silent, and how students are positioned in the room—alone, in a group, moving about.
- Reflect on what your senses tell you about the system (your students) at work: Name an emotional state of the system, empathize with the emotion, verbally validate the emotion, and provide an option to soothe and shift when students are ready.
- Support students in understanding how their classroom system works and in identifying strategies for caring for those within it.

The Empathetic Classroom

For Students

THE CLASSROOM SYSTEM

This hands-on activity is a way to demonstrate the idea of a human system and to help students *feel* how we all are connected and how we affect each other. Ask students to stand in a circle. Pass a ball of yarn from one person to the next, each person holding onto one part of it (including you), until it reaches the last person to form a taut circle of yarn. Ask the group to hold it without talking to one another and just see what they notice for one minute. Even if students are being very still, they will still feel movement in the yarn from the group. You can ask individual students to pull on their part of yarn a bit or to drop their piece or ask the whole group to step toward the center. All of this helps demonstrate different tensions.

Once you've tried a few scenarios with the yarn's tension, ask students to sit down in the circle. If you have older students, invite them to interpret the meaning of the yarn in relation to each other with the following questions:

- What did you notice while holding the yarn?
- What happened when someone dropped it?
- What happened when someone pulled it?
- What do you think the yarn represents?
- What might cause push and pull feelings in our class? (Note: You may have to remind students not to provide names but instead to use general examples.)
- How can we adapt as a group when something changes the mood or feel of our class? As individuals? (Note: This can be a great place to brainstorm group coping skills that you can write down and use when your class needs them.)
- What are things we can do when we feel tension?
- What can we do when we might be contributing to the tension?

continued

Chapter 1: Before All Else, Attune   **29**

If you have younger students, you may want to explain how the yarn is our connection to one another. When one person tugs, everyone can feel it. You might ask students if they have any ideas of what an example of a "tug" in the classroom might be. When one student drops the line, tension changes for everyone, so you may also ask what it looks like when someone feels less connected. You can share how one person's experience, no matter how subtle, is felt by the group. For example, when one student is sad, it affects the mood of the whole class—maybe in different ways, but everyone is changed by the change in one person. You could ask students what facial expressions or body language they might see if someone is feeling sad or disconnected. You may ask students to brainstorm what they might do if they see someone is not feeling connected or if they themselves are not feeling connected.

Adapted and used with permission from Katey T. Franklin, PhD, LSC, LCPC, 2022.

Figure 1.1 The Feeling Wheel

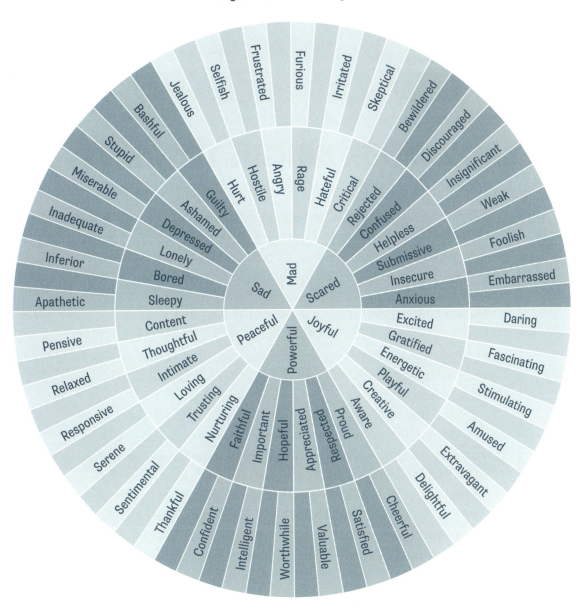

Colored Feeling Wheel by Feeling Wheel is licensed under a
Creative Commons Attribution-ShareAlike 4.0 International License.
Based on a work at https://www.tandfonline.com/doi/abs/10.1177/036215378201200411.

Chapter 1: Before All Else, Attune

2

KNOW YOUR UNIQUE TRIGGERS

*Bill discovered teaching after years of hating school. He was raised in a formal, high-income home in New England and, like many of his friends, he was sent to boarding school as a high school freshman. He never fully revealed to his family how awful these years were. He was bullied during his first two years and then turned to bullying behavior himself, just to survive. His father would have never forgiven himself for sending his son if he had known. Or he might have been too embarrassed to ever talk to his son again. Bill wasn't sure which outcome would happen, and he didn't want either of them—so he just kept it all inside.

After a life-changing meeting with a professor in college, Bill decided that the best way to bring about change to this environment he had come to hate was to become part of it and never allow what had happened to him happen to anyone else. He found a quaint private school in Vermont where he felt simultaneously at home and in unfamiliar territory. There was a farm and a small lake where students could swing off a rope during their afternoon break. Large trees where students could hole away in the strong branches and read dotted the grounds. Bill was greeted with a welcome song by the students on his first day, bringing tears to his eyes. Everything here was more relaxed and "earthy" than any school he had ever known. But the kids were familiar, reminding him of his young self.

The students fell in love with Bill. He was a big guy with a booming voice and loveable quirks, like his extreme dedication to all things wool, which the students capitalized on by delivering him ugly unpaired wool socks. And Bill felt love for his students as well.

A strange thing happened to Bill when he started to get to know seventh grader Sammy. He had heard multiple reports from Sammy's other teachers that he was failing his classes. He was quick to over-promise and underperform, it seemed. Bill decided to try taking Sammy under his wing. When Bill met with Sammy in his classroom, Sammy was a smooth talker and seemed to have it all figured out, Bill thought. After Sammy left that initial meeting, Bill realized that he too had been swept up in Sammy's elaborate stories, and that he'd never actually gotten around to addressing his concerns during the meeting.

After that, whenever Bill encountered Sammy in class or in the hall-ways, students and staff noticed a different Mr. Bill. He would follow closely behind Sammy and clap his hands to keep him moving. If Sammy started talking, he would cut him off mid-sentence. During staff meet-ings, Bill would often talk about Sammy and be sure to repeat how none of Sammy's stories should be believed. "He's full of crap," a red-faced Bill would proclaim.

Bill, too, started to notice the change in himself when he was around Sammy. He didn't like how he felt, but he didn't know why it was happening or what to do about it.

Anytime you bring passion and heart to something, you also bring your most vulnerable self. Not only are you vulnerable as a teacher, but you are also tired, overworked, and underpaid. Perfect conditions for a surprise attack by triggers. Experiencing a trigger in a place with people you care about, such as your classroom, can be a deeply unsettling experience.

If you decided to become a teacher, and if you have decided to stay a teacher, then I'm guessing you experience something that looks and feels a lot like love for your students. This could mean you take time out of your lunch to listen to a distraught student describe a painful family conflict. You might host an after-school gardening club. You're willing to make a joke at your own expense to take eyes off the student having a breakdown in front of their peers. There are myriad other small or grand gestures you embark on every single day to show that you care about each and every one of your students—even when the care is not reciprocated. Teachers are a unique kind of human. But, despite our care, we can encounter a different side of ourselves from time to time.

Chapter 2: Know Your Unique Triggers

The Body's Alarm System

A trigger can be a behavior, a sound, a smell, a time of day, a type of light, a word, a taste, a feel ... really anything that sparks a sensory cue within us and sends us back in time to an unpleasant or traumatic experience that occurred along with that sensory cue. This experience of being triggered is usually accompanied by a sudden mood shift to something that feels like irritability, anger, tiredness, sadness, or numbness. As a result of that emotion, our behavior also changes: We raise our voice, we change our posture, we turn away, we tear up. We do something that our students, family, or friends would consider uncharacteristic. To begin getting a sense of what *your* triggers are, try the Identifying My Triggers activity on page 45.

In some educational environments, teachers' triggered responses are considered justified and are normalized. Some schools may have a culture within the leadership or teaching staff that encourages swift repercussions for behavioral issues. Maybe anger, yelling, or other reactionary responses are regarded as appropriate ways to manage behavior. I remember thinking as a young teacher that the only way to get my class under control was to yell a burly, "Hey!" This is what I saw others do, and I imagine they learned it from teachers before them.

You have the right to your triggered response. However, here's my case for further examination of triggers: When our brain encounters a threat, our entire body goes through a physical change to prepare for the threat. Our brain is barraged with cortisol, our heart rate speeds up, our blood vessels constrict, our breathing becomes rapid. This stress response is useful when there is an actual threat, but if there is not, and if we do this to our systems several times a day, our ability to sustain and thrive in our role of teacher will be impacted. And that only covers the impact on you. While you're in the midst of this threat response, students are the receivers of it. A raised voice. A stony silence. Maybe a passive-aggressive comment. Walking away from a student. Students will interpret this as you telling them that *they* are the threat.

Think about the idea of repeatedly being told, *You are a threat. You are a problem.* Being on the receiving end of a threat response can bring up feelings of deep shame, which can then manifest in a variety of other mental and physical health outcomes. Clients of mine regularly share stories of being reprimanded by a teacher and the shame that has stayed with them. I imagine you too can remember a time of feeling shame, sadness, or anger in response to a teacher's actions.

How Triggers Show Up in Our Teaching

When I first started teaching, I probably would have told you I didn't have any triggers. I felt grounded and capable of handling the variety of student and parent interactions that occurred in a day. From my current perspective, I can now clearly see the ways I became triggered, and how difficult it was for me to act with compassion and reason when this occurred. I have yelled at students to get a certain behavior to stop. I have expressed deep disappointment in a choice a student made. I have pulled drumming pencils out of a student's unsuspecting grip. I have more confessions than are worth listing here that I, as loving and compassionate as I would purport to be, have succumbed to due to my unique set of triggers. This occurs for teachers young and old: A button is pushed, and suddenly a student no longer recognizes the teacher in front of them.

I remember being a ripe old senior in high school, held after class as a teacher wrote down how many years of education she had compared to my friends and me, clarifying her authority and expertise. Her face was red, she was shaking, and she slapped the board with a ruler. This was uncharacteristic of this English teacher I otherwise loved. The offense: My friends were laughing about a specific word. My teacher walked by, assumed it had to do with something she had said earlier, and told us she would talk to us after class. Because I felt wrongly accused in several ways and watched her lose it over something that hadn't actually happened, I never saw her the same way after that. I didn't feel safe around her anymore. When I think back on this today, I feel sad thinking about losing connection with her.

Sometimes the things our students do to set a trigger in motion are intentional. A student may want your attention and choose to try to get it by slamming the door as they leave the room. Sometimes the behavior will be morally or ethically wrong in your eyes. For example, you may feel strongly about the use of derogatory language or the way someone dresses. Sometimes you will have a student with a personality or character trait that just doesn't jive with yours. Maybe you really care about respect for others, and you have a student who seems to do whatever they can to show disregard for this value of yours. Often, it will be the same individual over and over again who pushes your trigger button.

The answer is not to try to stop their behavior, believe it or not—unless it has the potential to hurt someone. Their behavior serves a purpose they are likely not aware of. It might be to connect, to protect, to be noticed, to

Chapter 2: Know Your Unique Triggers   **35**

seek justice, to right past wrongs. Students who use a behavior like lying, such as Sammy in Bill's story, are likely seeking control in any form they can get it. This can be a sign of losing age-appropriate control in some other aspect of life. You, as an adult, get to take a step back from your interaction with them and notice what is at work. Here's an example of what Bill's internal dialogue might be like *before* he recognizes his trigger:

I really don't like how Sammy always blames his missing work on something else. He's so naturally intelligent—I just don't get it. I wish he would take some accountability. Instead, he concocts elaborate stories daily. If that's the game he wants to play, then I'll play it and show him.

Notice here that Bill is creating more work for himself to confront a behavior he doesn't want to deal with anymore. He's going to engage in Sammy's "game"—but good luck at winning that one! What Bill is really *engaging* in is a tug of war in which he is pulled into the very behavior he's trying to eliminate. This is a classic sign of a trigger. Bill is feeling the survival instinct of "fight" with this thinking. He wants to defend his territory and not back away. Other times, I see teachers disengage into a "flight" survival mechanism. *I'll just stop teaching and see if anyone notices.* Notice how there's something territorial here too, a defensiveness, even if it looks different. Defensiveness is another sure sign of a trigger. It signals that we perceive a threat to something we strongly believe needs protecting or upholding.

The Parts of Our Personality

These triggered responses are all signs that a stressed or traumatized part of our personality is taking the reins. Psychology research suggests that our mind sometimes splits into two central parts or roles: the "going on with normal life" part of our personality (our caring, organizing, analytical, or focused parts) and the "traumatized" part (the part that seeks a stress response of fight, flight, freeze, submit, or attach). Our mind believes it needs to do this to survive! When our traumatized part further compartmentalizes, this is known as *structural dissociation*. Each "part" of your personality is playing a role to protect you or help you adapt. Look at figure 2.1 and see if you can identify how you might compartmentalize or "show up" to others when you encounter a trigger. Can you trace this reaction back to an earlier experience?

A psychotherapy approach known as Internal Family Systems (IFS), developed by Richard Schwartz (2020), suggests that the parts of our

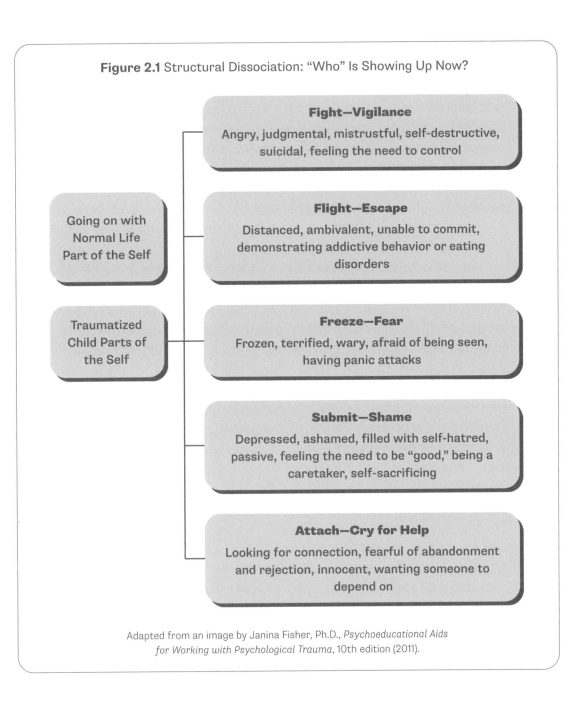

Figure 2.1 Structural Dissociation: "Who" Is Showing Up Now?

Adapted from an image by Janina Fisher, Ph.D., *Psychoeducational Aids for Working with Psychological Trauma*, 10th edition (2011).

Chapter 2: Know Your Unique Triggers

personality that might expand and take control when trauma occurs aren't trying to cause us problems; they are trying to help. This theory views each human as "a system of protected and wounded inner parts led by a core self" (IFS Institute, n.d.). IFS suggests that each of us has a core self that is calm, capable, creative, and compassionate. When something traumatizes or stresses our system, a part of us becomes wounded. Many of us are wounded in childhood when we are at our most vulnerable and our brains have not learned to process complex emotional events. Bullying, a parent yelling, witnessing a scary event, or experiencing the death of a loved one are just a few of the ways we can become wounded. And because our mind is a system, other parts try to come to the rescue.

Some of these parts become like firefighters and work to protect these wounded parts from ever being seen or from being hurt further. For instance, anger might play a firefighter role to keep others at a distance from seeing your sadness. Other parts become like managers and work to adapt to the needs of normal life. For instance, a planning part of you might be trying to adapt in order prevent anything from ever going wrong. Can you see your managers and firefighters at work? Can you identify what role each of your threat responses might be playing for you?

Often when a student encounters one of your threat responses for the first time and observes your change in mood, character, or behavior, it will stun them. Students are probably used to your caring confident parts showing up. They may be confused by a firefighter suddenly appearing—just as I was stunned by my normally kind and funny English teacher's lecture on her educational authority. Usually, students don't know that certain actions of theirs will elicit a response that is so strong—and so different from your typical behavior. For some students, your uncharacteristic response will send them running, and they'll opt not to poke the bear. Others may enjoy seeing your bear awakened. Creating a triggered feeling within another person can be a sense of power for some. For individuals who feel powerless, like some of our students, engaging in the trigger tug-of-war may become a new favorite pastime.

Recovery

To stop this push and pull feeling you might experience with your students, in a psychological approach called acceptance and commitment therapy (ACT), we talk about dropping the tug-of-war rope. Stop being pulled. Stop

The Empathetic Classroom

pulling. To do this, you need to know exactly what it is within you that is being tugged at. You need to step away from your current state and become an observer. Discovering this is a process of reflecting on your past. To dive in, the next time you feel a big mood shift or get feedback that your behavior suddenly changed, use these questions to identify what's at work and how to care for it:

- What am I feeling?
- What behavior seemed to bring this feeling on?
- Have I felt this way before? When, where, and what happened?
- What role might this part of me be trying to play?
- Is it a firefighter that is trying to protect me or a manager that is trying to help me adapt?
- How did this part believe it was helping me in my past?
- How can I care for this part of myself that might be wounded? Try doing a check-in with this part of yourself. Let it know you see it, and ask it what it needs. These parts often feel like a younger version of ourselves and often need attention, comfort, acceptance, and sometimes action.
- Can I offer gratitude (rather than feeling fear or shame) to the parts of me that are showing up to help me adapt or protect myself in a challenging situation?
- How might these parts be able to help me in ways other than how they are currently showing up? For example, an angry part may be able to use that energy to focus on a difficult task or do something physically challenging. A scared part might be able to use its inner wisdom to connect with others who are afraid. A judgmental part might be able to use its observational skills to notice a student's quiet strength.

Here's what Bill's inner dialogue might be after his interaction with Sammy, and after he answers the questions above:

I have a thing about lying. I feel angry when people lie. I also feel powerless when someone is lying to me, because it seems like they feel like they can't trust me with the truth. I would prefer the truth, even if I don't like it. I usually feel this way when anyone lies to me. It's not unique to this student. I even felt this way when I was a kid. I remember being lied to as a kid by an important person I thought I could trust. I think that was scary for me. I think my fear felt too

Chapter 2: Know Your Unique Triggers

vulnerable, so anger stepped in to protect me. With anger, I could push someone away rather than let them get close. I do appreciate that my anger tried to protect me, but I don't need it to do the same job anymore. I don't want to push Sammy or anyone away. I can handle lies differently as an adult now with more experience. I am no longer my vulnerable younger self.

Of course, we usually don't come to these realizations that quickly. Sometimes it requires extensive work with a trained professional. Sometimes our triggers are rooted in past trauma. And even when we are triggered by things that seemingly have no strong link to our past, knowing what these triggers are and how to soothe them is still important.

Noticing Your Patterns

I know I am triggered by repetitive sounds while I'm trying to speak or think. If someone is munching on a bag of potato chips beside me (my mom, especially!), I will feel my irritability start to boil. I know that if I am starting to feel sick, my patience will wane, and I will snap more quickly at a student or a friend. Sometimes triggers occur because someone reminds you of yourself at an earlier time in life, and you can't handle the sight of them doing things you haven't accepted about yourself. For example, adults who didn't "respect authority" as children may not know what to do with a child who challenges authority.

Coming to terms with your own triggers requires a seriously honest look in the mirror. It also requires knowing that changing your response to your triggers is not easy. When you know what your triggers are, you can slow down your interactions with others. Feel a sudden shift in mood? That's a good place to stop in your tracks. There is rarely a reason that any behavior needs an immediate response, aside from a safety concern. Take three deep breaths and notice what is happening inside of you. Tell yourself what you need to know about what's happening: *I'm not actually angry at this student. I'm angry because a behavior triggered an old insecurity.* To help you work through this thought process, you can use the Observation Point exercise on page 49.

Finding Your Footing

Once you know that a person, behavior, or sensory experience may be a trigger for you, you get to decide how you want to tell your system that there is no reason to question your security and your own sense of self power.

40   *The Empathetic Classroom*

There are several things you can do to care for yourself before and when you feel triggered. It's important to note that when you experience a trigger in the classroom, you may not have the immediate opportunity to fully give this triggered part of yourself the care it needs. Sometimes we must regulate even as we continue teaching or caring for our students. The suggestions in this section will help you do so, and they will be most helpful if you can adapt them to take into consideration what is happening and who or what created the trigger. You can then explore and build your understanding of what happened later when you have the space, time, and energy to do so.

- **Anticipate and prepare for triggering interactions.** Once you know your students and their families well enough, you can usually predict the likelihood of triggers. For example, I might save certain interactions for times of the day when I know my energy is better (I'm thinking of certain parent emails here). If I know a student's typical lack of preparedness for class will get to me, I will meet with them to find out how we can lighten their load to more realistic expectations—a win for both of us! If I know from past experience that certain situations or questions tend to lead a student to feel they need to lie, I'll find a new way to approach those scenarios.

- **Anchor yourself in an internal or external experience that returns you to a regulated state.** Anchors are sensory cues of safety. (You can read more about anchoring in chapter 9.) Each person has their own. It might be drinking water, holding a deep breath and then releasing it slowly, rubbing a smooth stone, changing posture, using mental imagery (nature works well for many people), placing your hand on your chest or belly, watering a plant, or focusing on a picture or quote in your classroom. Choose something that you can access at any time in your classroom, and make a habit of using it. When you think about your anchor, try to slow your breathing with a technique called box breathing: exhale to a count of four, hold for a count of four, inhale to a count of four, and hold for a count of four. This exercise helps your lungs send your brain the message that it is not actually under threat.

Chapter 2: Know Your Unique Triggers

- **Communicate if you can.** Your reaction to a trigger may result in students believing they are the threat. It is important to quickly de-escalate the situation if you can. When we are stunned by a behavior, it can be difficult to talk right away. However, if you *can* verbally relay something to your student fairly quickly, try to do so. They just witnessed something change in you, and they'll need some support so that they do not blame themselves. Focus on communicating something simple about your own experience rather than what they did. I might tell a student that I'm feeling a little off today or ask them to please pardon my briefness. Depending on the student, I might say—with as much of a warm smile as I can muster—that my heart is really pumping. The key is to let them know they are not the problem—even if their behavior at the moment is problematic. Escalating the situation will only cause the student's nervous system (and your own) to go on higher alert and make any communication even more challenging. And even if their behavior *was* problematic, it's best not to address it while you feel triggered unless there is a safety risk.
- **Take some space.** This is not always an option and can seem difficult to do in a busy classroom, but you and your students will benefit from some breathing room if the situation warrants or allows it. Do communicate first before taking space. You want to be clear and let them know you are not abandoning them. You are not leaving the classroom. For example, if I'm trying to help a student with their writing assignment and they suddenly scream at me and tear their paper up, this is a clear indication that a break is needed. First, give them the opportunity to get relief. Suggest getting some water, taking a walk, or changing tasks. Then, with a calm tone, let them know you will give them some space. (This is actually space for you too, but keep the focus on their needs while addressing your own.) *I'm going to take a walk around the classroom, and I'll come check in with you in ten minutes.* Then find that anchoring activity that grounds you. Maybe you feel calm when organizing your desk or watering a plant. Maybe just sitting in your chair and allowing yourself to stare at a wall for thirty seconds does the trick. Doodle. If you have younger students, you may need to encourage the whole class to join you

in whatever grounding activity you need. If you need to close your eyes and turn out all the lights for five minutes, there's a good chance everyone would benefit from it. Allow your students to see you engaging in and normalizing self-care.

- **Care for your triggered parts with self-talk.** You can use the questions provided earlier in the "Recovery" section on page 39. You can let these wounded parts know you see them. Gently ask why they are showing up and what they are trying to do to help you. Let them know you appreciate their attempts to help and that you've got this. You can even ask them to go hang out somewhere else for a while. Some people envision putting these parts of themselves in a container or a waiting room for a time. When you feel your calm, curious, compassionate perspective return, you can address the situation that first triggered you.

- **Repair.** If students have witnessed or experienced a triggered part of you, set aside time when you are feeling regulated to address your reaction. You do not need to share personal details about what part of you was triggered or why. Repairing offers more than an apology in that it provides an opportunity for growth in both parties. As shared by clinical psychologist Becky Kennedy—author of the highly regarded parenting book *Good Inside* (2022)—when adults model repair, they are showing children how to navigate from distress to safety and security. This allows the story of self-blame children tell themselves to change. She recommends naming what happened, taking responsibility, and then stating what you would do differently next time. *I know I snapped at you yesterday at the end of class. I could see that really scared you. I am sorry. That is not how I want to react. I'll work on doing better. Next time, I will take a moment before I respond.*

KEY POINTS

- Triggers are your body's way of alerting you to past or present threats.
- Students may familiarize themselves with your triggers and might try to activate them to communicate an internal need of their own.
- Your triggers are unique to you—they may be linked to one or many past experiences and may more easily be engaged depending on how you are

Chapter 2: Know Your Unique Triggers

feeling physically or emotionally. Use the Identifying My Triggers exercise on page 45 to explore your own triggers.

- Experiencing a trigger can result in your personality compartmentalizing, a process known as structural dissociation, to help you go on with normal functioning.
- These traumatized parts of the self that show up are attempting to protect you and help you adapt.
- You can heal wounded parts, vulnerable to being triggered, by reflecting on why they are there and identifying what role they play for you.
- You can care for all parts of yourself by offering gratitude to them for the role they have played to try to protect you and giving them opportunities to use their energy more effectively.
- You can notice your own trigger patterns and the insecurities to which they are connected using the Observation Point reflection activity on page 49. You can self-soothe your triggered state by regulating your nervous system: pause, breathe, and adjust your self-expectations.
- You can build rapport and predictability with students through mindful disclosure of some triggers.

For Teachers

IDENTIFYING MY TRIGGERS

Your triggers are unique to you. You can use this activity to begin the process of discovering what gets to you. Read through each behavior that you may encounter from a student in your classroom and rate what your immediate reaction tends to be using the 1 to 5 rating scale. This exercise requires you to be really honest with yourself. There might be a way you would like or hope to react in a given situation, and then there may be how you actually respond. Be gentle with yourself as you review this list. If you have not encountered a situation listed here, notice what your body tells you when you read it, and imagine how you might react.

Identifying My Triggers

When a Student . . .	My Immediate Reaction Is . . .				
	Compassionate: 1	Neutral: 2	Anxious: 3	Angered: 4	Rageful: 5
Acts impulsively all the time					
Acts overly cute and charming when they want something from me					
Always delays, stalls, or tantrums when it's time to switch tasks					
Always denies their actions even when I catch them red-handed					
Always seems to need my attention when I'm doing something else					

continued

Chapter 2: Know Your Unique Triggers **45**

When a Student . . .	My Immediate Reaction Is . . .				
	Compassionate: 1	Neutral: 2	Anxious: 3	Angered: 4	Rageful: 5
Argues with me					
Behaves well with everyone but me					
Blames me for their problems					
Breaks items deliberately					
Can't seem to learn from mistakes					
Chronically lies to me					
Displays sexually explicit behaviors					
Does exactly what I tell them not to do					
Doesn't make or sustain eye contact with me					
Is abusive to other children					
Is demanding of me					
Is extremely hyperactive					
Is noncompliant with simple rules					
Is sneaky					
Lacks hygiene					
Makes me feel afraid when around them					
Makes me feel exploited and manipulated					
Makes me feel like I'm walking on eggshells					

When a Student . . .	My Immediate Reaction Is . . .				
	Compassionate: 1	Neutral: 2	Anxious: 3	Angered: 4	Rageful: 5
Mopes around; seems depressed					
Needs my constant, close supervision					
Pokes me; grabs me; hangs on to me					
Puts forth minimal or no effort on assignments					
Refuses my help					
Seems to lack a conscience					
Self-harms					
Spaces out when I'm talking					
Takes no accountability for their actions					
Uses a "baby voice" around me					

Exercise adapted and reprinted in part with permission from Intermountain and ChildWise Institute. Copyright 2016 by Intermountain and ChildWise Institute.

After completing the exercise, look back at your ratings and highlight or note where you rated a behavior as a 3 or above. Take a moment and reflect on why these behaviors might be particularly triggering for you. Ask yourself:

- Do I notice any commonalities among situations that increase my sense of a trigger?
- How might these types of behaviors be connected to traumatized or wounded parts of myself?
- How do I react to each of my main triggers?
- Can I picture specific students who tend to set off these reactions in me?

continued

Chapter 2: Know Your Unique Triggers

- How often does this happen?
- What do students typically do after I react?
- How do I feel after their reaction? What do I often do next?

If you like, you can also spend some time revisiting or working through the questions in the "Recovery" section on page 38, focusing on the feelings and reactions you experience during and after student behavior that is triggering to you. You can use all of this information to better anticipate, manage, and regulate during triggering situations.

For Teachers
THE OBSERVATION POINT

You can start to notice your trigger patterns by becoming an observer of your own experiences. The Observation Point activity (Martinez, n.d.) can be done alone or in a safe group of your coworkers. Take a look at the figure below. Think back to a situation that occurred in which you didn't understand your own behaviors, thoughts, or feelings—possibly when you remember feeling triggered. I recommend starting at the top of the wheel with naming your sensory experience, and then slowly making your way around the wheel counterclockwise, answering the questions as you go. If you are doing this in a group, you are processing your experience aloud. This is a vulnerable exercise, so try to focus on allowing what comes up to be said rather than attempting to control or judge your answers.

Figure 2.2 The Observation Point

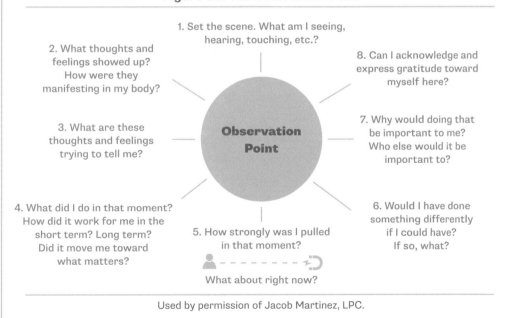

Used by permission of Jacob Martinez, LPC.

continued

Chapter 2: Know Your Unique Triggers   **49**

When you reach the question "How strongly was I pulled in that moment?", think about how attached you felt to your thoughts or feelings in the midst of that situation and how strong a pull they exerted on you. When we feel really attached to our thoughts or feelings, it can lead to a stronger emotional response or a more reactive behavior. It can feel like our emotions are in charge and telling us what to do.

For instance, I might have been really "pulled" in a moment in which I observed a student vaping, and my angry reaction was to yank it out of their hand. Often, when we look back on our immediate behavior or language in a moment, we might recognize that it seemed kind of extreme or rash. But when we step back, we can see that our thoughts or feelings are not commands. My anger was just what I was experiencing, not a set of directions for how to handle things. The next question on the wheel—"What about right now?"—is asking you to compare your feeling at the moment of the experience with what it looks like now that you've stepped away from it. How does it feel looking back? Would you respond the same way in this very moment?

If you are doing this in a group, one of the ground rules must be that everyone listens to the person doing their observation. When you conclude, you can share how it felt to reflect on this experience in this way. Be clear about what type of response from others would be helpful or if no response is preferred. Some groups that process emotional experiences request that all comments validate the emotions shared and acknowledge that what people choose to share is their truth. It is not a place to tell others how to do something differently.

If you are doing this alone, writing can support a different type of processing than just thinking about your responses. If you choose to journal, you can revisit your reflections the next time you encounter this trigger and notice what may have stayed the same and what might have changed.

This activity allows you to see the separate parts of the scene and slow the moment down. Being an observer allows your brain to connect a physical experience to your emotional experience. This activity also gives you the opportunity to both take accountability and provide yourself with internal emotional repair. Return to it whenever you need to revisit a stressful situation with compassion and clarity.

50   *The Empathetic Classroom*

3

BUILD A NEW RELATIONSHIP WITH EMOTIONS

*Kendra fiddled with the handle of her purse as she waited for her therapist to look up from her notes and begin the session. She could think of about a million other places she'd like to be right now. She wasn't necessarily here by her own choice—her school principal had recommended seeking help after students and parents shared that she had seemed "checked out" for the last few months. She was shocked that anyone seemed to notice or care. She felt as if she was living behind a veil where no one could see who she was or how she felt—and she was fine with that. She wanted to scream at the therapist sitting across from her, looking so perfect and relaxed in her big sweater with her cup of tea and slippers on.

"I'm looking forward to getting to know you better, Kendra," her therapist said, glancing up. "Looking over the history form I asked you to complete, I see you left many of the questions blank. That's okay. Let me ask a funny question: If I asked you to pick an emotion that you believe you experience frequently, what would it be?"

Kendra started to sweat. She suddenly felt as if she were sitting on that couch naked. How could she randomly pick an emotion on the spot?

"Most people tell me I'm grumpy," she said finally. "I guess that's the only emotion I have." Her therapist looked at her with an expression she wasn't used to—something like surprise.

"Other people tell you what your emotion is," her therapist said reflectively. "Do think that grumpy is accurate?"

> Kendra thought and thought. "Sometimes yes and sometimes no."
>
> "What other emotions might be bound up in the 'grumpiness' that other people see?"
>
> "I honestly don't know," Kendra said, with tears welling up in her eyes. "I don't think I feel anything."

"How are you feeling?" It's one of the most ubiquitous phrases in psychology, and beyond. Its banality, at times, has caused all of us to lose sight of how the answer to this question can provide genuine insight into ourselves and others.

I usually consider myself an emotionally aware person. I notice when sadness is creeping in at the edges. I'm not afraid to admit when I'm angry. I can name the body sensations that happen within me when I'm scared. As a teacher, though, I did not talk about emotions. I didn't discuss my own, and I didn't ask my students about theirs. Maybe it was because I thought everyone knew their emotions as intimately as I did. Maybe it was because talking about emotions seemed to conflict with the cognitive nature of the academic environment. Plus, I had no training in emotional work. Who was I to go poking around in my students' personal emotional landscapes?

Emotions as Data

An emotion is a label for a state of being in the mind. A chemical state in the brain accompanies emotion. When you feel happy, the chemicals of serotonin, dopamine, and endorphins are at work. When you feel sad, a chemical called monoamine oxidase A (MAO-A) is at war with your neurotransmitters so that your brain can't process happy chemicals. The chemical state of your brain affects your mood, your thoughts, and your behaviors.

When I am engaging in happy-chemical-enhancing activities such as hiking in the Bridger Mountains near my home in Montana, I notice that I feel lighter, my thoughts are gentle and reflective, and I suddenly feel motivated to connect with an old friend I haven't seen in a while when I return. Oh, the world looks good from the top of the mountain! That same day, while sitting in traffic on the drive back from my blissful rendezvous with nature, I feel my mood darken as I observe the black smoke rolling out of a pickup in front of me. My thoughts turn to the obligations of the day and how I may not be interesting enough for my old friend—they probably have more engaging activities they're up to anyway. I return home and scroll the news instead of reaching out. How quickly my outlook changed! One moment I was on top of the world—almost literally—and the next, I was down in the doomscrolling dumps. If I were to pull out my feeling wheel, I could probably map at least twenty emotional shifts that occurred in the span of a couple of hours.

Why might identifying our emotions accurately be important? From a logical point of view, our emotions are important data about ourselves. I know that if I do X, Y, and Z, my emotions will likely be more positive, or I will feel lighter and freer. If I do L, M, N, O, and P, my emotions will tend to be more negative, or I will feel heavier and more limited. I am careful here not to label emotions as "good" or "bad." Even those I am calling "challenging"—a category where we often place feelings such as sadness, anger, jealousy, fear, or resentment—do not make you a bad person, and should not be avoided, buried, or ignored. Our more challenging emotions are real and worthy of our attention. Of course, we don't want to become stuck in them. The body sensations that accompany these more challenging emotions may not be helpful for the body if we experience them at length. For instance, after long bouts of anger or sadness, we can feel exhausted and unmotivated. Existing in more challenging emotional states for a long time can also impact our thoughts and behaviors and, in turn, our self-esteem and relationships. Yet despite their seemingly menacing qualities, these emotions are here for a reason, and they deserve to be listened to with as much attention as we give to less challenging emotions such as happiness, joy, and excitement. To help you make this identification and attention to feelings more of a habit, try the Emotional Mapping exercise on page 61.

The power in becoming more aware of what may be contributing to specific emotional states is that you can then make more informed decisions about how you engage with or view certain activities, places, ideas, and people that seem to correlate with mood shifts. A case in point: One time, my husband was brave to point out that I seemed a little irritable after large social get-togethers. As my husband is well aware, there is risk involved in providing observations about the emotional experience of another. He's learned to be gentle and selective in his feedback. While I was initially in denial about his observation, I soon realized there was something important there. A part of me wanted to like big buzzing groups of humans, so I put in a lot of effort during large events. Another part of me was most comfortable

Chapter 3: Build a New Relationship with Emotions   **53**

with one-on-one social interactions, yet *wanted* to be capable of more. So I'd push myself through countless gatherings, come home thoroughly exhausted, and turn into a cooked carrot on the couch. And who doesn't want to be in a relationship with a cooked carrot?!

From this insight, I learned that when I force myself to do something without awareness of my emotions, I can do harm to my body and to my most important relationships. Now when I am tempted to say yes to that large social gathering, I check in with myself first. How many have I been to this week? How long do I plan to be there? Why am I going? What was I planning to do afterward, and how much energy does it require? This way, my emotional awareness does not need to lead to disengagement from challenging experiences, but it does allow me to be a more active—and healthy—participant.

This type of thinking in psychology is known as psychological flexibility. When we practice flexibility instead of rigidity, we are present with our emotions and thoughts while not ignoring important data from the past. We understand how our beliefs about ourselves impact our perspective and decisions. We have an awareness of what matters to us, and our actions reflect this. We also realize that our thoughts are not us—they are products of many factors, and we can step back to look at them from a safe distance. Finally, we're willing to accept an experience for what it is.

When I am practicing being flexible, I probably won't make the same decision each time. I will take into account my current mood, my physical needs, and my values. Sometimes I will choose to socialize in a big new group, because having relationships in my life is important and I want to get to know new people from time to time—it keeps life interesting and new people will keep me growing. I also know that if I choose to do this, I will be done for the day afterward, and I don't make any other big plans— toaster waffles for dinner! I may even give my loved ones a heads-up about my plan and let them know that I'm hoping to just relax for the evening. Knowing that big groups are a lot of work for me, I can also build in some self-acceptance of the fact that I may not feel grounded during the whole event, and I may later regret something I said or did. I will have to work with these realities and give myself extra gratitude for taking the risk of doing something difficult.

Emotions Are a Shared Experience

The best people to serve as external emotional processors for children are their primary caregivers. In a secure version of this relationship, a child bonds with their caregivers, is encouraged by them to go out in the world and explore, has emotional experiences out in the world, and returns home to make sense of these emotional experiences with their primary caregivers. However, some children do not have primary caregivers who are prepared or even present for this role. This means that a lot of individuals grow up without an experience of safely processing emotions with others. Maybe you can identify with this experience. In some cases, emotions are not a priority in a family because providing food, clothing, and shelter demands so much energy. In some families, there can be danger in recognizing a challenging feeling because there isn't understanding of how to process and manage that feeling. This is where we find stories about children "being seen and not heard" or being told to "pull yourself together" or "wipe those tears off your face" when upset. Even if you grew up in a household where there were attempts at emotional language, there may have been a mismatch between words and actions. I often hear clients say, "My parents said they loved me, but they would punish me for making a mistake. It was confusing." Many adults face the work of learning how to discover safety in emotional processing within their self and with others.

The absence of true emotional support from caring adults makes relationships as a child—and later, as an adult—challenging. It can be difficult to know when and how to trust other people throughout life if emotional language is absent from communication growing up. If left to process their emotions alone, many people stay unaware of the close ties among thoughts, emotions, and behaviors and may repeat unhelpful or unhealthy patterns. For example, they might continue to seek the same dysfunctional friendships and partnerships, they might have beliefs about themselves that deter them from trying new things, or they might deny that they even have certain feelings because the thought of facing them is too overwhelming to consider.

While teachers aren't caregivers in the same way as parents or other adults in the home, there's no question that you, too, are a critical figure in children's development, emotionally and otherwise. So what's your role in this process? First off, remember that classrooms filled with peers can be sensitive and vulnerable environments in which to discuss private emotional experiences. There are lots of feelings going on, but naming them

Chapter 3: Build a New Relationship with Emotions   **55**

out loud is one of the highest risks your students could engage in during the school day. Social dynamics in peer groups often function through complex exchanges, with cost and benefit analysis occurring constantly, invisibly, and right beneath your nose.

If you notice a student having a strong emotional expression in class, naming it aloud in the moment could lead to embarrassment, anger, or denial, and likely will—at least for the moment—negatively impact the student's trust in you. It's essential to have an awareness of your students' general emotional maturity, as well as the collective mood of the class on a given day. Do they quickly empathize with each other and support students who are feeling down? Or is there a sense of fear in the room when any sign of emotion appears? If you observe silence, downcast eyes, whispering, or students looking at each other for permission, it's likely best not to push it in that moment.

Instead, first, provide the student with an out. *Would you like to get some water? Take a walk?* Giving them space and relief from the pressure of the classroom setting and their peers is essential for them to find their feet again. You're also assessing safety. If you have information that suggests their emotional expression is out of the ordinary, or this student has a history of harming themself or others, call in backup—a school counselor or a trained administrator. Next, use this transition as an opportunity to switch gears with the entire class. Often, a sudden and noticeable emotional experience by one person can set off a domino effect. Practice psychological flexibility and be willing to temporarily let go of your plan and give every-one a chance to shift physically or mentally to release tension.

When you have an opportunity to connect with this student privately, either during a break or after class, it's okay to let them know you noticed them. If you have a sense of what their emotion might have been, it's alright to say it and check for accuracy. Heads-up, though—some emotion words may be triggering for students. If being sad or angry in their home elicits challenging or unsafe interactions with caregivers, even your suggestion that they were feeling sad or angry in the classroom might result in denial or shutdown. Use your intuition and speak the language of your student.

Hey, I wanted to check in with you. I noticed you seemed upset during class. Is that what you were feeling?

Key words here are "noticed" and "seemed." They help your student hear that you aren't telling them what their emotions are. Rather, you're guessing

The Empathetic Classroom

based on your observations, which still allows you to be wrong. If the student says you are wrong—*I wasn't upset, I just wasn't feeling well!*—don't dig in and explain to them why you thought they seemed upset. They get to determine the meaning here. To let them know they've been heard, use *their* language to further engage.

You weren't feeling well. I'm glad you told me.

Students may not have extensive experience understanding where physical sensations and emotions begin and end. Feeling crappy might lead to increased irritability, but being able to say *My body aches, and that's making me feel irritable* is a fairly mature emotional skill. Building emotional awareness is largely about listening to the body, so if a student describes emotions as a physical sensation, go there with them. Letting them know that you appreciate their sharing intimate feelings with you is an approachable way to say, *Yes, I can handle all your big emotions. I won't abandon you.*

Putting Together the Emotion Puzzle

The next step is to support your student in putting the pieces together and making sense of their emotional experience. Now that you've started to explore your own relationship to emotions through the mapping activity (page 61), you can use this awareness as a foundation for your work with students. Strong physical or emotional states can feel unsettling and confusing, especially for young people with still-developing brains, and connecting the dots can provide a way to build understanding in students that, in turn, supports a growing comfort with their emotional experiences.

Some students will be happy to talk more with you about what is happening for them. Others might give you cues that they're not in a good place internally to do the work in that moment. Either way, follow the student's lead. You can begin with something as simple as *Would you like to tell me more about what isn't feeling good?* Again, this is an opportunity for your student to see that you respect the boundaries they set. If they say no, remind the student that you are there for them and that you'll check in again with them later. If they seem open to a bit more processing with you now, put yourself in their shoes and wonder aloud to build understanding, rather than playing the investigator. For example:

Student: *My head kind of hurts.*
Me: *Can you show me where?*
Student: *Inside. Like my brain.*

Chapter 3: Build a New Relationship with Emotions   **57**

Me: *That sounds painful. Do you remember when it started?*
Student: *After our math test this morning.*
Me: *Hmm, was the test stressful for you?*
Student: *I studied the wrong chapter until midnight last night. I was so mad at myself!*
Me: *That sounds frustrating. And exhausting. I wonder what might help your brain feel better right now?*
Student: *Nothing.*
Me: *Yeah, maybe nothing will help right now. That's okay. I have one idea though, and you can let me know what you think, okay?*

Here, you can see me doing some light emotional guesswork, feeling for the gentle push and pull of this dance. I'm not here to fix things but to provide avenues for change. The thing about change is that it is often most difficult to do when we need it most. So while I'm not leaving the student to do the work all alone, in the end, the change will have to be self-led if it's to make a meaningful difference. In this example, my attempt to brainstorm with this student is met with a boundary. In response, I agree with the student's perspective that nothing may help. It's true, sometimes nothing helps. But I don't completely back away here. I stay with them and offer a little rescue tube should they want it. I float it out to them with an idea on it. Because that's all it is—an idea, not necessarily a solution. They might try it, and their bad head feeling still might not go away. I can't offer any guarantees. But I can show students what I might do if I have a similarly uncomfortable feeling myself.

During this check-in, I am both listening and tucking away important information about this student—they cared about doing well on their test, they had gotten the wrong information about which chapter it was on, they are short on sleep today, they didn't feel comfortable telling me that they didn't know the material during the test! All this emotion-related data can help me reorient my teaching and my communication with my students. I want my classroom to be a place where students feel safe telling me when something is up for them, but for some reason, on this day, this student did not. And that matters.

Getting close to your students' emotions and seeing them through their eyes is humbling work that exposes truths about not only your students but also you as their teacher. If someone feels truly safe sharing with you, you will get a wide range of their emotional spectrum—the highest of highs and

The Empathetic Classroom

the lowest of lows. Some of these might be about things you have done, or how students perceive your feelings about them. It might seem natural to go on the defensive and explain your true intentions. This will not go well for anyone.

Whether students are aware of it or not, their emotions are trying to communicate something important to you as their teacher. *I am angry; see me. I am sad; comfort me. I am happy; celebrate with me.* Gaining comfort with your own emotional patterns will increase your confidence in holding and caring for all kinds of emotions with your students. If we can stand as a lighthouse for our students—letting them know we are there to help with navigation whether the seas inside of them are stormy or calm, and that we are solid and constant no matter what they bring to us—we support them in doing the tough work that is needed for emotional development. Emotionally developed students will be more prepared to thrive in the tasks of learning and healthy risk-taking. And in turn, you will build a deeper and more satisfying connection with your students and your work.

KEY POINTS

- Emotions occur alongside chemical states in the brain that affect overall mood and can motivate behaviors.
- Accurate emotional identification is important for understanding the correlation between feelings and your actions. If you understand yourself better, you can make more informed decisions about how to engage with the world. The Emotional Mapping activity (page 61) can support this process.
- Harmful or unhealthy behaviors and thought patterns can occur if emotional language was absent from primary relationships, such as with parents or caregivers.
- Students may not feel safe emotionally processing with you if this kind of behavior has not been modeled in their home.
- Strong emotions will occur in your classrooms. It is best not to call attention to the emotion on the spot but instead to provide students an out.
- Check in with students privately after emotional experiences.
- Use language like "I noticed . . ." or "It seems . . . ." Do not try to tell students what they are or should be feeling.

Chapter 3: Build a New Relationship with Emotions   **59**

- If students are open to it, help them make sense of their emotional experience. Help them connect the dots among feelings, thoughts, and behaviors.
- It's important not to try to "fix" or eliminate a student's emotions. Instead, provide opportunities for processing or for shifts in emotions.

For Teachers

EMOTIONAL MAPPING

Each person's emotional experience is as unique as their finger-prints. Knowing how, why, and when specific emotions show up for you prepares you to acknowledge, accept, and care for them. Creating an emotional map can help you start to identify connections between events, thoughts, feelings, and behaviors. Of course, these are all chickens and eggs in their order of occurrence. Sometimes a certain emotion precedes a thought. Other times a thought pops into your mind, and then you feel something. There is no right or wrong here, and you can focus on what is relevant to you.

Begin by keeping a log for one week connecting thoughts, feelings, behavior, and the context in which they arise. You can document these digitally, but I recommend a small notebook that you carry with you so you can jot a quick note in the moment. And you do not need to log *all* of your thoughts, emotions, and behaviors. Rather, choose a strong emotion or a common thought that tends to feel challenging or uncomfortable to you. If you like, you can use the feeling wheel on page 31 to locate an emotion.

If you are unsure of what emotion you're feeling, record what you notice happening in your body. For example, *difficulty speaking, shaking*. Or look at a common behavior that has caused challenges in your life. Any of these routes can lead to increased emotional understanding. Here's an example:

Date: *January 9, 2024*
Thought: *I am so unlovable.*
Feeling: *Sad, annoyed*
Behavior: *Scrolling social media*
Context (Time, Place, Activity): *7 p.m., home, eating dinner alone*

When you record the experience, there is no need to analyze it right away. What's important is that you document as accurately as you can what you were feeling (emotion or body sensation) just after it happened.

continued

Chapter 3: Build a New Relationship with Emotions   **61**

Sometimes, if we wait until too long after something has happened, our assessment of it can change. And remember, you might be experiencing more than one feeling at once, so try to record all the emotions that happened in this moment.

You might ask, *What if I can't name a feeling?* First, know that difficulty identifying feelings is not uncommon. You might feel something like tension but struggle to sort out if it's because you are angry or annoyed or sad—or all three at once! When an emotion causes a physical sensation, this is called *somatization*. For instance, you might feel like your heart is broken or that you have "butterflies" in your stomach. When an emotion occurs, your body prepares for whatever event that feeling might be warning you about. Research shows that it is common to attribute specific feelings to specific areas of the body and that humans share many of these bodily emotional experiences (Nummenmaa et al. 2014). Familiarizing yourself with what your physical sensations mean can help you better understand what emotions are linked to them and why the sensations might be happening. You can use the chart below to start connecting physical experiences to emotions.

Emotion	Common Sensations
Sadness	• Sensations focused in the chest and head • Decreased feeling in arms, legs, and feet • Achiness throughout body • Pain • Low energy • Difficulty sleeping or eating
Anger	• Sensations focused in the upper half of the body and arms, and somewhat in legs and feet • Muscle tension • Increased breathing and heart rate • Headache • Clenched jaw

62   *The Empathetic Classroom*

Emotion	Common Sensations
Anxiety	• Increased activation above the pelvis, excluding arms • Decreased feeling in arms, legs, and feet • Dry mouth • Increased heart rate • Difficulty breathing • Numbness in hands and feet • Sweating • Upset stomach
Shame	• Sensations focused in the torso and head • Decreased feeling in legs, arms, and feet • Feeling weight in the stomach • Feeling hot • Increased heart rate • Difficulty with maintaining posture
Disgust	• Sensations focused in the upper half of the body and arms • Nausea • Decreased heart rate • Gagging sensation • Covering sensory areas (eyes, nose, mouth) • Change of facial expression (scrunched nose, eyes, mouth) • Moving away from someone or something causing the feeling
Happiness	• Sensations throughout the body • Increased energy • Increased body temperature • Increased heart rate and breathing

After you have a week's worth of data, get out a new sheet of paper. Look at your log and find one emotion that seems to pop up frequently. For example, you could start with sadness or hurt. Write this feeling at the top of the page.

I want you to get to know this emotion well, so find a cozy spot—maybe on the couch with your favorite blanket, if it calls to you. This part of the exercise is going to help you create a visual for the emotion, as if it were a living, breathing being. One of the goals here is to become friends with your emotions, rather than enemies, and this is an opportunity to get to know

continued

Chapter 3: Build a New Relationship with Emotions **63**

this emotion better. Now, answer the following questions about your chosen emotion:

1. When I think about feeling this way, where do I notice it in my body?
2. What shape, color, or texture does the feeling have?
3. What adjective describes it?
4. Is it familiar to me? How long has it been there? Has it changed over time?
5. How do I feel toward the emotion?
6. Do I feel close to it, or do I try to distance myself from it?
7. Do I picture any images (real or not) associated with it?
8. What words or phrases are attached to it? Did someone say these words to me? Who?
9. What did this emotion mean in my home growing up?
10. How did people in my childhood react when this feeling appeared? How do people in my life react today?
11. What person in my life do I think of as most closely associated with this feeling?
12. What do I usually feel right before this feeling arises? During? Right after? Long after?
13. If I look at the feeling wheel, can I trace the emotion to the center of the wheel, to a core feeling? (For example: Scared is the core emotion of embarrassed. So you might say, *I first feel scared, then I feel frozen. Afterward I feel embarrassed, and then annoyed.*)
14. In my log, what patterns or themes do I notice being associated with this feeling?
15. What do I do when this feeling happens?
16. What do I think my behaviors are trying to do for this feeling?
17. What do I want to communicate to others when I show them this feeling?
18. What do I hope they will do, think, or say?
19. How is my hoped-for reaction from others linked to my past? Did I ever get my hoped-for reaction from my primary caregivers? Did I always get it?

64 *The Empathetic Classroom*

20. What story do I tell myself when I feel this way? (To help you answer this, look at your log and refer to the thoughts you've documented being associated with this feeling.)
21. What do I know about this feeling as an adult that I did not know as a child?

After completing this reflection, review your answers. Consider how your past narrative about an emotion might be affecting your ability to acknowledge, accept, and care for your emotion today. When you adopt a new narrative about an emotion, the emotion doesn't disappear, but you are letting it change how it appears in your mind. Maybe you have always viewed an emotion such as sadness as scary, heavy, or dangerous. But there's no emotional rulebook that says what an emotion should be or feel like. You could adopt a new view of sadness—perhaps as something that is fluid, like water.

The final part of this exercise is to give yourself a new mental image of the emotion—starting with a literal image. Maybe you envision this fluid feeling of sadness as a bright pink ocean wave. Using art supplies of your choosing, paint or draw what your feeling looks like as you know it right now, with all the wisdom you just collected by reflecting on your answers to the questions. Try not to overthink it. Let your intuition guide the colors and shapes you make. When you're finished, put this art somewhere you'll be able to see it for a while. As you look at it over time, see what you notice that you didn't initially. Recognize how your relationship to the emotion might be changing as you get to know it anew.

Chapter 3: Build a New Relationship with Emotions   **65**

4

VALIDATE THE EMOTION, UNDERSTAND THE BEHAVIOR

*When Principal Meyers of St. John's Upper Elementary opened her email that morning, she didn't expect to see Julie's name within a message marked "Urgent." It was from another student's parent. Principal Meyers's eyebrows shot up as she scanned the contents of the long message. She learned that Julie had assumed the identity of another classmate by stealing that girl's phone from her locker during class and sending private photos to several classmates. Many of these images were clearly not meant to be shared, including photos from what appeared to be a sleepover. Screenshots were attached. The parent said they would not be pressing charges, but they wanted to see immediate action taken.

At the staff meeting that morning, Meyers gave her group a condensed version of the parent's message. The response from the room was swift. Everyone wanted to voice their thoughts and express hopes for disciplinary action. Ideas rolled in. Suspension was thrown out there, as were mandatory community service and an apology to the whole class. Even typically quiet teachers and staff members wanted a piece of the action. Some even wanted to share stories of when something similar happened to them.

It was the most energized staff meeting the school had experienced in months. Overall, the resounding feeling in the room was how disappointed everyone was in Julie, an excellent student with no previous history of poor behavior. In fact, she was a week away from being given the school's annual Star Student award. What everyone agreed before the meeting adjourned was that all phones would be banned for the week. It seemed simple enough, and at least it would put any further retaliation or copycat episodes on pause.

As educators, much of our focus is on student behavior and performance. This is likely because our training has encouraged us to focus on the tangible—if we can measure student performance, we can identify and address needs. This mindset leads to the belief that if we manage student behavior, we can positively affect performance. Not wholly untrue—but not the whole picture either.

The Behavior Train

At times it can seem like—as a teacher or a group of teachers—we jump on the "behavior train" together and our perspective of students is focused only on their outward actions. When that happens, it can feel difficult to be the first to jump off that train. Think about what is talked about during your staff meetings. At mine, student behavior was often a dominant theme. *So-and-so constantly talks during class, they misuse privileges, they never turn work in* ... the list goes on and on. This establishes a culture that says focusing on behavior is the solution to correcting the behavior.

None of my college education courses adequately prepared me for the behavior I experienced in my classrooms. I remember joining in the grumblings at staff meetings with my list of behavior woes. Mostly, I didn't know what else to do. At least hearing that I wasn't alone felt like some solace. But rarely did it resolve the problem. And it was often the same handful of students who showed up on staff radar as everyone nodded in agreement about how "difficult" they were.

Many of us try to stop behavior in ways that we observed or experienced when we were students ourselves. My teachers growing up were fans of "put your heads down" or extensive lectures on what happens if certain behavior persists. I'll certainly never forget my sixth grade teacher's threat to bring a jar of blood to school to demonstrate the dangers of playground fights. The intention of these approaches is generally to scare students enough to stop the behavior. Have you ever known motivating through fear to work long term? I haven't. What I have seen is peers who further distance themselves from a "problematic" classmate, or teachers who give up on their class midyear, or behavior that gets significantly worse—or all of the above.

Chapter 4: Validate the Emotion, Understand the Behavior

Why We Avoid Feelings

What is missing in this conversation about behavior is the question "What is the feeling?" Behaviors are always accompanied, and often initiated, by feelings. Anger leads to the punch. Jealousy comes with the hurtful comment. Feelings are as real as any behavior; they just aren't as visible. But it's scary territory to start talking about feelings. And some feelings seem more challenging to talk about and respond to than others. We might side with Julie if she's sad because her mother was recently diagnosed with cancer, but it might be more difficult to understand what is happening inside Julie if she's expressing anger rooted in years of neglect. Sadness is often a more socially acceptable emotion than anger, fear, irritability, or jealousy (to name a few).

Feelings also aren't as easy to identify as behavior. We can all observe as a child throws a toy at another child. We can agree that one child just threw a toy at the other. Easy. And in schools, behaviors have consequences. So we observe the thrown toy, we record it, and then we determine the appropriate consequence. *No more toys for you until you learn not to throw them.* Picture your adult self and something you do that you wish you didn't. *No more phone for you until you learn to moderate your usage!* How's that going for you?

When we *do* gather the courage to talk about the emotions that accompany student behavior, I think we fear that by recognizing the humanity in another person, we would somehow be excusing the behavior. Think of the worst student behavior you have ever encountered. It is hard to imagine excusing that behavior, isn't it? But here's the thing: You can validate someone's emotional experience without validating their behavior. Some behaviors should *not* be encouraged, excused, or validated. However, the emotion that is behind that behavior can be recognized and validated. We've all experienced anger, frustration, sadness, confusion, and irritability, whether or not we've had the exact experience of those emotions fueling a certain type of behavior. Even if it initially feels like you cannot understand why someone behaves as they do, you can work to identify with their emotional experience. This connection then allows you to get closer to understanding the origin of their behavior.

Shifting the Focus

Imagine a different type of staff meeting, one where the administrators and staff have all received training on emotions and their link to behaviors.

The Empathetic Classroom

"I'm concerned about Julie. She's had a sudden change in behavior. Has anyone else had concerns?" Several people nod. "Does anyone have any ideas about what might be causing this?"

The music teacher raises her hand. "I know she's been having a tough time with her mom being away from home for work. She's been having to watch her little brother every day after school lately." Another teacher chimes in, "That sounds frustrating and lonely. I imagine Julie is sad about her mom being gone, and probably angry at her too for being given more responsibility. Julie's always taken on more responsibility than most kids her age already."

The principal rubs her chin. "I plan to check in with Julie after this meeting to see how she's feeling and find out if our perspective is accurate. We may have to reach out to her mom and provide Julie some options for de-stressing during the school day since she's not getting that opportunity at home."

If Julie were to listen in on this conversation, she would feel cared about by her teachers, rather than feeling shame for not behaving appropriately. All behavior has a reason. Only through emotional identification, and then validation, can we start to address the true root of the behavior. So, once we've accurately identified and validated the emotion, what do we do about the behavior?

The Goals of Behavior

In evaluating and responding to behaviors, it's immensely helpful to remember that behavior is an action that often has a message attached to it—something a person wants to communicate but may not know how to put it into words. The Goals of Behavior charts (Koltz and Franklin 2012) that follow in figure 4.1 can help you spot a behavior at work and connect the action to what a student's (often unconscious) hopes or goals might be. These charts are helpful when it is difficult to understand what a child's behavior is trying to communicate and how best to respond to it. You'll start by observing their behavior and identifying your own emotional reaction to it. The charts can then point you to the child's underlying belief about themself that is motivating the behavior, and the goal of their behavior. It might be contact, power, protection, withdrawal, or challenge. Once you can more clearly see their goal, you can help them meet it in more meaningful and productive ways. In addition, the Empty Chair activity for students on page 80 can help you guide students through role rehearsal as a way of moving toward different and encouraged behaviors.

Chapter 4: Validate the Emotion, Understand the Behavior

Figure 4.1 Goals of Behavior

When students express their needs through behavior, it can often be a cause of concern, irritation, surprise, exhaustion, or even disappointment for their teachers. When a teacher implicitly or explicitly expresses their feelings or thoughts about the behavior to the student, it can lead to the student feeling more shame or hopelessness, or it may spark in them a desire to work even harder to be understood. Put together, this creates an unproductive push-and-pull dynamic. To stop this pattern of reactivity between you and your students, it's essential to first understand the belief that a student holds about themself and that is motivating their behavior, then evaluate how you can show up differently for them to allow for more effective communication of needs.

When observing behavior you'd like to discourage, find the chart that most closely matches that behavior and then progress through the rows to understand the behavior's likely goal and how you can respond by encouraging new behaviors.

Discouraged behaviors: Undue attention-seeking (keeping others busy or making bids to get special services); whining; complaining; demanding

If the adult feels . . .	Annoyed; guilty; irritated; worried
The adult tends to react by . . .	Reminding; coaxing; doing things for the child that they are capable of doing for themself
And if the child's response is . . .	Stopping the behavior temporarily and then starting another discouraged behavior
The belief behind the child's behavior may be . . .	"I belong only when I'm being noticed. I'm only important when I'm keeping you occupied."
The goal of the child's behavior is . . .	Contact

Behaviors to encourage: Contributing; cooperating; collaborating

Discouraged behaviors: Rebellion; winning power struggles (to be the boss)

If the adult feels . . .	Angry; provoked; challenged; threatened; defeated
The adult tends to react by . . .	Fighting; giving in; wanting to be right; engaging in power struggles
And if the child's response is . . .	Intensifying the behavior; defiance; compliance; feeling they have "won" when adults are upset
The belief behind the child's behavior may be . . .	"I only belong when I'm the boss. I'm proving that no one can boss me."
The goal of the child's behavior is . . .	Power

Behaviors to encourage: Independence; individuating; leadership

---

Discouraged behaviors: Revenge; retaliation (to get even)

If the adult feels . . .	Hurt; disappointed; disbelief; disgusted
The adult tends to react by . . .	Retaliating; removing privileges and freedoms; taking behavior personally
And if the child's response is . . .	Retaliating; hurting others, self, or property; escalating the behavior
The belief behind the child's behavior may be . . .	"I don't believe I belong, so I'll hurt others as I feel hurt. I can't be liked or loved."
The goal of the child's behavior is . . .	Protection

Behaviors to encourage: Assertiveness; expressiveness; advocating for self

continued

Chapter 4: Validate the Emotion, Understand the Behavior

Discouraged behaviors: Assumed inadequacy; unusual avoidance ("I give up—leave me alone")

If the adult feels . . .	Despair; hopeless; helpless; inadequate
The adult tends to react by . . .	Giving up; doing things for the child; over-helping; showing discouragement
And if the child's response is . . .	Retreating further; passivity; no improvement; no response
The belief behind the child's behavior may be . . .	"I don't believe I can belong, so I'll convince others not to expect anything from me. I am helpless."
The goal of the child's behavior is . . .	Withdrawal

Behaviors to encourage: Centering; renewal; recharging; taking time for self-care; relaxing

Discouraged behaviors: Thrill-seeking; risk-taking; substance use; risky sexual behaviors; stealing

If the adult feels . . .	Fearful; concerned for safety; nervous
The adult tends to react by . . .	Controlling activities; lecturing about safety; restricting environment
And if the child's response is . . .	Breaking rules; taking more reckless risks
The belief behind the child's behavior may be . . .	"I'm important and belong only when I'm living on the edge and/or winning."
The goal of the child's behavior is . . .	Challenge

Behaviors to encourage: Skill-building; healthy risk-taking; seeking adventure or new experiences

Adapted and used by permission of Rebecca L. Koltz, Ph.D., LCPC, NCC, and Katey T. Franklin, Ph.D., LSC, LCPC.

The Empathetic Classroom

Take a look at each chart and identify the one focused most closely on the observed behavior. In Julie's case, if I were Principal Meyers, I might see a couple that could be a good fit. Stealing a phone and sending hurtful messages could be considered rebellious. Or it could fit into risk-taking behavior. But I think the closest behavioral fit seems to be revenge or retaliation.

As I move down the rows of that chart, I can see if my feelings (or the feelings of parents or other adults) match this type of behavior. Ah yes, there it is—disappointment was the prevailing feeling of everyone at the staff meeting. This row is key—in fact, sometimes, if I am unsure what the discouraged behavior is, I will instead start with noticing what I am feeling and go from there.

Next, I check for the adult reaction. I see this too is a good fit in Julie's case; everyone at the meeting wanted to find some way to "retaliate" for Julie's behavior—even if this is not what they intended. And they were certainly taking her situation personally, as shown by their sharing of their own stories.

Next, I consider how Julie might respond if she observed these reactions from her teachers. The next row tells me that a child's response in this case may be to hurt themselves, others, or property. I also see that sometimes the behavior escalates. And indeed, I can imagine a student like Julie being hard on herself if she knew her teachers were disappointed in her—even to the point where she might harm herself.

As I continue moving down the chart, I think I'm coming to understand the belief that exists under Julie's behavior: *I don't believe I belong, so I'll hurt others as I feel hurt. I can't be liked or loved.* Interesting. When Principal Meyers reflects on what she observed before Julie sent the messages, she begins to see the whole scene much more clearly. Julie spends most of her free time caring for younger family members, which likely means she is not able to have friends over. Julie also seemed aware that a birthday party recently occurred to which she was not invited. Julie's family struggles to make ends meet, so she often wears the same outfits each week. And Julie spends most of her time during breaks in a corner, nose in a book—a behavior Meyers had found endearing.

Looking at the second-to-last row, you'll find the goal of the behavior: protection. Imagine how differently we might view Julie's behavior if we understood that she is hoping for protection. As her counselor, I would want

Chapter 4: Validate the Emotion, Understand the Behavior

to know what she is working to protect. As her teacher, this might not be so easily accessible. When Principal Meyers meets with Julie one-on-one, she learns that, during the birthday party, several classmates made fun of Julie's little brother's appearance and a classmate reported this back to Julie. Julie, believing she is the sole protector of her brother, was willing to do anything to make sure no one hurt him—including put her own reputation at risk.

After identifying what she believes to be Julie's emotions and the goals of her behaviors, Principal Meyers's job is three-fold: validate Julie's feelings, discourage further ineffective behavior, and encourage effective behavior—behavior that meets Julie's need for protection without causing harm to others. Often when children do hurtful things, it is because that *seems* like an effective option. And in some ways, it is—people listen and react to big behaviors, after all. But what students aren't always aware of is that the behavior is not a great long-term solution to the problem they are working to solve. It is your job as the adult to help them see this and offer realistic alternatives.

In the final row, you'll find specific behaviors to encourage. In Julie's situation, Principal Meyers can encourage assertiveness, expressiveness, and self-advocacy. If Julie is generally a quiet person at school, some role rehearsal and coaching might be needed to support her in trying on these new behaviors. The Empty Chair activity on page 80 is one way to put this into practice. In my counseling office, I often encourage quiet kids who feel like they don't have a voice to try out over-the-top versions of using their voice. For instance, I'll have them pretend I'm the person bullying them. They can yell at me and say whatever comes to mind, and even make strange noises that well up in them! Of course, I don't expect or want them to leave my office and go yell at people. But what usually happens is they get to experience feeling something different in their body. Something they may have needed to feel for a long time. They often say that instead of feeling sad about themselves, they feel invigorated.

Guidelines for Behavioral Intervention

Consistency and compassion in our response to student emotions and behavior are essential to supporting young people in discovering lifelong skills for functional, healthy human relationships. Play therapist Garry Landreth suggests a method called limit setting (2002). He uses the acronym ACT:

The Empathetic Classroom

A: Acknowledge the feeling.

C: Communicate the limit.

T: Target the alternative.

In this method, the adult avoids using words like *no*, *don't*, and *stop*—all words that can be ineffective to a dysregulated child. Saying *no* also invites a power struggle that can often lead to increased dysregulation. When we tell a child *no* or *don't*, these words are usually directed at the child themself, and as a result, they feel personal. Instead, try using a version of the phrase "this is not for that." This wording is directed at the behavior rather than the person.

For example, suppose I am working with my eight-year-old student Kylie. Kylie seems angry because at recess another teacher asked her not to make paper dolls to represent kids she's mad at. In this situation I might say something like this:

A: *Hey, I see you're angry because you want to make the dolls and you were told not to. I know there are some kids who have been mean to you. That must hurt.*

C: *Those dolls are not an okay way to respond to their meanness, though.*

T: *Instead, let's visit with counselor Henley about some ways you can feel better. Why don't you start by telling me about some of the things that happened that have you feeling angry?*

When engaging a student in a behavioral intervention, you want to create an environment that promotes their sense of dignity, provides clarity, and supports alternative ways of expressing needs. When I've worked with students on emotional and behavioral concerns, I often observe that they initially exhibit shame. My goal for our work together is not to avoid what happened but to address it while also helping students find a path out of shame so they can see themselves more clearly and learn from what happened. This has ongoing benefits. In my experience, when students become accustomed to adults who know how to kindly hold them accountable, they learn to ask for behavioral support rather than waiting for an adult to notice that they need it.

Here's a step-by-step guide for handling challenging behaviors in the classroom:

1. Acknowledge the emotion first: *I see you're frustrated right now. That was a really challenging assignment.*

Chapter 4: Validate the Emotion, Understand the Behavior   **75**

2. Reflect internally on what you believe the student might be trying to make happen with their behavior: *I see them seeking contact.*

3. Then, directly address the behavior with a limit: *Pencils are for writing, not throwing.* (Notice here that the directive is not "Don't throw pencils.")

4. Next, look for a safe, reasonable alternative to address the emotional need immediately: *I would like you to take a stretch break in the back of the room and get some water.* Or, *You are welcome to make a paper airplane, and we can throw it when everyone is finished.*

5. When the student is in a more emotionally regulated state, address the issue with the behavior. Most students will already know that their behavior was inappropriate. For example: *Can we talk about what happened today during your math assignment? Do you know why I was not okay with throwing something? What could you do instead when you're frustrated?*

6. Not all behaviors require consequences; sometimes students will respond to limit setting alone. However, if a behavior persists and a student is not responding to limits, you may need to provide a reasonable, age-appropriate consequence and then encourage new behavior. A consequence should not act as a threat: *If you do this, this is what happens to you!* Consequences naturally happen to all people, young and old. The goal of giving a child a consequence is not to scare them out of a behavior but to help them see a connection between ineffective behavior and its outcome.

   Also keep in mind that secure, caring relationships with adults are environments in which young people can safely test limits. So first consider if a consequence is warranted or if the student seems to have already grasped a "lesson" through their own reflection or your explanation of why their behavior was problematic. Next, if there *is* a consequence, make the process of explaining and enacting it as collaborative as possible, and avoid issuing a swift reprimand without context. And remember that if your student is dysregulated and seems overwhelmed, it's most productive to wait to discuss consequences until they are not in this state. When we are dysregulated, we can't listen or process well; hearing a consequence will only further ignite strong emotions.

For younger students, approximately up to age ten, you can create this collaboration by offering choice: *If you choose to throw things, then you are choosing to lose free time today. If you choose to take a break, then you are choosing to have free time today. Which do you choose?* This choice puts a certain amount of power in your students' hands, which is important for maintaining their self-esteem in situations where it feels like their actions are at odds with your expectations. For students older than ten, you can include them in the process by discussing why their behaviors might not be effective in the long term (or maybe even the short term) and supporting them in exploring what might help them avoid doing it again. For example, if fifteen-year-old Grayson seems to have difficulty keeping their cell phone put away in class, my first reaction might be to take it away. But after talking with Grayson and having them consider why their behavior may create problems for them down the road and for our classroom currently—not being as connected and present with others, missing important details—we decide they can try giving me the phone on days when it feels particularly challenging to keep it in their bag. Through our discussion, we also identify that they take their phone out more often when they are feeling bored, so we brainstorm other ideas to help them be more focused even when the content isn't super exciting to them.

7. Then, encourage new behavior. Use the Goals of Behavior charts on page 70 to identify what goal seemed to be at work for this student when you observed their behavior. Review the second-to-last row in the chart to find this goal. If the child's behavior indicates they may be seeking contact, how can you provide opportunities for them to contribute, cooperate, or collaborate? A student who throws a pencil when frustrated is likely not the only student feeling some stress about an assignment. Are there other students who could identify with this feeling and who have found methods to work through it? You could provide space and time to allow this student to contribute their own ideas, as well as learn from others through a collaborative group brainstorm on the

Chapter 4: Validate the Emotion, Understand the Behavior

topic. You might also allow for optional group work or mentorship opportunities in an area of the student's strengths in which they can support others. Work with the student to find more appropriate and effective ways of meeting their goal.

8. Finally, circle back and check on emotions regularly. This doesn't necessarily mean asking students how they are feeling. You can observe them engaging with a task that is typically stressful for them and notice whether they identify and use any adaptive coping mechanisms on their own—and, if not, if there are ways you can provide further support without doing it for them. For students who you know have difficulty with emotional regulation, provide opportunities for easy outs. Encourage and allow breaks *before* a break is urgently needed. When emotional dysregulation is frequent, point students and families toward trained mental health professionals.

KEY POINTS

- Traditional educational approaches emphasize correcting behavior.
- Students often experience shame about "inappropriate behaviors" and don't always understand why they are behaving as they are.
- Behaviors are attempts to communicate strong feelings and unmet needs.
- Trying to "stop" behaviors through tactics of fear, restriction, or pressure does not address the underlying needs the behaviors are seeking and can actually increase the occurrence of the behaviors.
- You can validate an emotion without validating the behavior that accompanies it.
- Many cultures and societies tend to encourage validating emotions such as sadness and fear over more uncomfortable and challenging emotions such as anger, disgust, and jealousy.
- All emotions are real to the person experiencing them and are worth validating, even if you don't understand why the person is feeling a given emotion.
- By identifying and validating emotions, you engage with the "root" of the behavior rather than staying at the surface.

78   *The Empathetic Classroom*

- You can use the Goals of Behavior charts to understand what a behavior might be communicating and to know what new behaviors to encourage. You can then directly address the behavior using the ACT Method: **A**cknowledge the feeling, **C**ommunicate the limit, and **T**arget the alternative. If needed, provide relevant consequences and redirection.
- Chronic behaviors are often rooted in deep and complicated insecurities. It's important to accept that you may not be the person who can heal these wounds.

For Students

THE EMPTY CHAIR

A good way to do role rehearsal safely in an academic setting is to have students speak to an empty chair, a technique from a type of therapy called gestalt. Prepare the student by having them imagine something they'd like to communicate to someone but are having a difficult time with. Set up the space so that there's a spot for a student to sit across from an empty chair. Explain that they're going to pretend the empty chair facing them is the person they're having a hard time talking to.

- Let the student know that in the first round of this practice, they can say what they really want to say, how they want to say it. (This is rehearsal for you too, as you get to practice not expressing judgment for their true thoughts.) Maybe they're extra loud or really quiet. Maybe they say something they might regret if they *actually* said it to the person. But it's okay here. In this round, the work is to release the strong emotional reaction they've been holding on to.

- In round two, guide the student in communicating what they think they might say if the person were really sitting in front of them. Before they begin, ask them to take some slow breaths. You may offer some guidance here on tone, volume, or helpful word choice. The ultimate goal is for their communication to be successful, so feedback may be needed.

- In round three, have the student say their piece again, this time adding more self-regulation, including awareness of their breath as they're speaking. I ask them to start with a slow breath, take their time, and try to be as relaxed as possible while maintaining the power in their words. This is certainly where we all struggle the most. It may help to suggest that they sit with their shoulders back, hold their head high, and do anything else they can with their body to help them feel strong and confident.

- Now check in with the student about their readiness to communicate to this person. They might find that getting their feelings out in this activity has been enough, or they may also be ready to take the next step and actually speak to the person. If the latter is true, you may offer additional guidance or support. You might offer to hold the meeting in your space if the student prefers that. You may also want to prepare them for responses they may get once they say what they need to. Honest feedback, even when done with care, can prompt defensive or strong responses, and you'll want to support the student so they're ready for a variety of reactions.
- If you wish, bringing in a school counselor during this exercise can help further support your student and you.
- Finish the rehearsal with authentic words of encouragement for the student's efforts. Speaking your truth is hard work!

Chapter 4: Validate the Emotion, Understand the Behavior   **81**

5

YOUR CLASSROOM AS A REFUGE

At Bella Vista Elementary School in Oakland, California, fourth and fifth grade teacher Melissa Barry-Hansen has learned in her thirty-plus years of teaching that the physicality of her classroom is essential to creating a community. Her school is home to students who are from primarily low-income households, students whose families include refugees, students with special needs, and students from single-parent households. From the stories they share with her, Melissa knows her students have lived through a lot in their ten years on Earth.

Entering her classroom brings her students a feeling both of excitement and of being grounded. Her shelves are lined with books and bins with little labels like "watercolor pens," "greeting cards," and "colored sticky notes." Plants line the windows. Rugs and a reading nook take up a third of the space. Evidence of *who* belongs here is everywhere. She features her students' artwork throughout the room. A hallway-long history timeline tells a story of where her students have been, what they are curious about, things they find funny or strange. Throughout the year, students post notecards with facts and drawings when an idea strikes them. Melissa doesn't limit what they put on the timeline—sports events, the day the Blue Angels flew over the classroom, the histories of the places they came from, that time her license plate was stolen. In this communal record, there is a shared ownership of their current place in time. The place feels alive.

"I tell my students if they want something to take home, they can ask me for it, and they can have it. If you like a book so much you want to keep it forever, just ask. I don't have an attachment to anything." As a result, she has students who ask her if they can have art supplies

> to use at home, and even some who tell her when their shoes don't fit anymore. It's a place where shame has a difficult time manifesting, and this is important to Melissa.

In all our hat-wearing as teachers, it can be easy to lose sight of the physical reality of our teaching environments and what these spaces mean to our students. In the busyness of a school morning, rarely do we stop and think about how each student comes from an environment that is completely different from our classroom and that, no matter how good our intentions, we tend to expect them to automatically adjust to *our* environment. We might do this even when we know how different their home lives are. We may have met their parents or caregivers, and knowing them has provided us another piece of the puzzle. We may have noticed what items they do or do not own. What condition their clothes are in. Their early or late arrival to school.

Also important to keep in mind is that, unlike you, your students are not here by choice. Can you notice the difference in yourself when you are required to attend an event compared to when you choose to attend? I know that my mood can become mildly depressed when I feel I must do something. Add early start times, developing bodies and minds, and demands at home, and your students may enter your cheery world with the mindset of a hibernating bear.

You might not be used to thinking of your classrooms as a reception area as well as a learning one. You have likely internalized that your room must be a hardcore, multipurpose learning zone with desks, carpets, and cubbies. And learning must *always* be occurring. At all moments. Or else your principal might stop in and catch you not doing your job! I would like to invite you to look at your space with new eyes. Imagine designing your classroom with your students' well-being—and your own—in mind.

The Psychology of Your Classroom

In psychology, the idea that a place has influence on us is called environmental psychology. A therapist might use a nature-based or ecotherapy approach with a client who has returned from military service and has been experiencing post-traumatic stress disorder (PTSD) or with a mother recovering from childbirth. They might suggest the client select an outdoor place where they can spend some time alone and some time together.

Chapter 5: Your Classroom as a Refuge

For example, forty-six-year-old Ryan—who is experiencing anxiety and panic attacks after witnessing a shooting—chooses a massive old oak to sit under and lean his back against. His therapist checks in about why he chose this spot. Ryan closes his eyes. "I feel protected by the tree," he says. "It's quiet right here too. I can't hear the road as much. I also like that this one is in the corner of the park, where I can look out and keep watch." The therapist supports Ryan in noticing the metaphors that nature can offer for healing. In this context, nature is a partner in the therapeutic relationship and supports the client in discovering insights through their interaction with it.

Most of us, our students included, spend most of the day in indoor spaces where experiences of nature can be much harder to come by. Fortunately, these indoor spaces can provide opportunities for enhancing our quality of life too. I am always surprised by how much my counseling office space and decor matter to clients. I often hear, "Oh, I am so glad you have a window and a tree!" Or "I like looking at your forest picture while I talk." My therapy room communicates something about who I am without me having to say it. I always conclude a meeting with a potential new client by saying, "Before you decide whether you'd like to work with me, I want you to go home and reflect on how you felt talking to me and how you felt in this space. Did you feel safe?"

What Does Your Space Say?

A key difference between a place outside your classroom and the space inside your classroom is simple: You are in it! You are the greeter who welcomes someone in and offers them a role within your classroom's community. Can you recall what it feels like to be welcomed into a space? I think of my last visit to the dentist. Dentists must have it worse than educators when it comes to a customer's expected mood upon arrival. This dentist's office has me excited to arrive before my appointment because they have figured out how to receive people well! When I walk into the lobby, someone immediately notices me and greets me by name. They invite me to have a chocolate, coffee, or a glass of wine (gasp!). I sit in a comfortable chair and listen to relaxing music. They have discovered that by making it about more than just the teeth cleaning, people will get their teeth cleaned *and* enjoy the experience. Did they spend a bit more to get me there? Yes. Did it take a moment to provide this care? Yes. Did I get my teeth cleaned, and was I more relaxed during the process? Yep and yep.

We have our goals for the day as educators, our demands from policies, administrators, and parents. And we have our hopes for offering our students a future filled with options and opportunity. If we want students to truly be receptive to the learning experience we are offering, we need to put all these goals and hopes on pause. We first need to provide a secure place for our students to take learning risks—a place where they trust that their needs will be taken care of. A place where someone will notice if they don't return.

Learning is about letting go of or building onto previous ideas to accept new ones. It requires trying something new. Risk-taking doesn't happen if we don't feel safe. We need to be able to let down our guard. This can be difficult to achieve when walking onto the very grounds of a school dredges up fears for so many students and teachers. School is a place that represents a lot of expectation and pressure to perform and behave a certain way. Even being themselves at school can be a risk if students' ways of being don't align with the school, their teacher, or their peers' desired ways for them to be. This is true for educators too—there is great risk in showing up to teach. Your livelihood depends on it, so it makes sense that it could activate survival mechanisms within you. The stakes are high. The loss on the line is one's sense of self, or even life. There is no grade level unaffected by and unaware of the risk of school shootings or bomb threats or other forms of violence. We enter "secure" zones each day with safety policies, cameras, detectors, and locked doors, and yet, it can be difficult to be able to trust that everything is going to be okay.

In a given day, both you and your students may encounter danger cues without even realizing it—the sound of unknown activity from the hallway, a fan kicking on, a smell from a locker, a person, a look, the absence of someone, a door opening or closing. There are so many little ways our body tells us something is wrong. Your classroom space can counteract these cues by offering elements that are soft, safe, protective, and familiar for when students or you are feeling unsure, overwhelmed, or distressed. At the same time, your space should offer opportunities to step just outside of safety to invite experiences of freedom, creativity, challenge, and energy. You don't want to invite only comfort—this might put everyone to sleep! Still, as educators, we have an opportunity to make our classrooms into environments

Chapter 5: Your Classroom as a Refuge

that provide for many of our students' basic security needs. We can even take one more step beyond this to make the classroom a place of feeling held, a place you enjoy spending your day in too.

What Makes a Great Learning Place?

In a significant study out of the United Kingdom (Barrett et al. 2015), researchers visited 153 rural and urban classrooms to better understand how learning environment impacts learning outcome. They observed how children used the spaces; collected environmental measurements like light, sound, carbon dioxide levels, and temperature; checked out the quality of the furniture; noted what was on the walls; and surveyed the teachers to better understand their experience of the classroom. The researchers collected data on student performance and composed a picture of students' progress from the beginning of the school year to the end in each classroom environment.

After distinguishing the effects of the environment from other factors that might impact learning (such as the teaching and learning styles, the curriculum, the school culture, or students' backgrounds), the results showed that classroom environment can cause a variation of up to 16 percent in student performance. In other words, same student + different classroom environment = different outcome. This is likely not surprising to you, because you've surely noticed an environment's effects on you before—the hot room that made you sleepy, the windowless room that made you feel depressed, the room with lots of bright colors that made your eyes bug out.

In this study, the researchers were able to identify the specific components of great learning environments: naturalness, individuality, and stimulation.

To assess **naturalness**, you can ask:

- How does my classroom space provide connection to the natural world?

For **individuality**:

- How does it provide options for expression and choice?

And for **stimulation**:

- How does it invite my students and me to engage with it?

To think more about these ideas and explore them with your students, you can use the Re-Envisioning Our Spaces activity on page 92. Of course, as an educator, you are often stuck with the classroom you are given, and you may not feel like you have a lot of choice when it comes to literally transforming your space to create an ideal learning environment. The standard for school design has long been about accommodating a certain number of desks in classrooms, rather than preparing to meet a variety of human needs daily. And rarely is improved classroom furniture or decor a line item on school budgets. Thankfully, creating safe and inviting spaces can happen with little or no additional monetary input. What feels like reception is unique to everyone, but we know that certain things send a message that we are *wanted*.

Here are some ideas to play with for making your space a refuge for you and your students.

Stand by the door and greet each student by name and with eye contact as they enter your room. This lets them know they are seen. The moment of awareness gives you time to take note of any cues the student might give you (whether consciously or unconsciously) about how they are doing.

Create entrance and exit rituals. Rituals increase feelings of belonging and instill a sense of identity. These consistent entrance and exit rituals can also help your students feel connected with the space of your classroom. For example, Montana teacher Buck Turcotte brings his traditional indigenous rituals into his classroom. At the end of each week, he lights sage, and he and his students participate in a smudging ceremony to ground them before going home. One example of a classroom entrance ritual is to have students draw from a jar of self-care prompts. (See the Self-Care Jar activity on page 95 for specific ideas.) You might have to practice a ritual with students several times before it becomes habit and feels natural.

Consider your lighting. Sensitivity to light can increase feelings of fatigue or irritability in some people. Even those who are not photosensitive can experience shifts in mood related to lighting. Natural light has been found to be most conducive to supporting productivity and alertness. If your classroom windows are covered by anything, do what you can to get them uncovered. If window light is not an option, you could use lamps with

Chapter 5: Your Classroom as a Refuge

full-spectrum daylight bulbs. Ask your students in a confidential survey what they think of the light in your room. They will have opinions—many!—and then you get to decide what to do with that data. If overhead lighting is needed for work, take the opportunity to turn down the light at times when students are just listening or observing.

Bring in natural elements. Often, school can feel very distant from reality for many students. Whether you're in an urban or rural area, grounding students in a natural environment can increase serotonin levels and lower cortisol, which in turn decreases rates of anxiety and depression. Take cues from the environment where your school is situated. Have plants in the room and teach students their names and how to care for them. Visit a plant store and ask if they'd be willing to donate plants for your classroom or if they'll allow you to take some cuttings. (You may be surprised by how many shop owners will respond positively and be excited to donate.) Provide a basket of smooth stones for students to hold or rub when they are feeling stressed. Hang favorite photographs or paintings of natural places. Students will connect with you when you share places that are inspiring to you, even if you've never been there. If you're feeling brave, find a simple way to incorporate water into your space, such as a basic fountain (which makes a great DIY project!) or a reflection pool in a small basin (including a water plant, if you like). Notice if your anxiety rises here at the thought of water in your room and try to deepen your understanding of your hesitancy. Even simply turning on a water sound on your laptop or another device during study time is a great way to help students connect to their aquatic roots.

Revisit your feelings about food in the classroom. This is an age-old battle. Every educator is different—plus, your school might have a policy on this. Yet it's guaranteed that the topic of food will come to the surface in your classroom at some point because the human brain needs calories. And unmet hunger needs lead to poor learning outcomes. Of course, this doesn't mean each student can pull out a feast with all the fixings whenever they feel like it. On day one, students need to know your expectations about food in the classroom—for example, trash goes in the garbage can, students need to seek permission to snack at certain times, where students can get a snack if they need one, what food allergies everyone should be aware of, and so on. But when these expectations are known and met, talking about and modeling eating with students is a source of untapped potential. Food is foundational to your students' cultural identities and offers opportunities to celebrate together. It is also rife with larger cultural messages about body image and dieting. Even for teachers, it can feel difficult to take care of bodily needs. I remember my early days of teaching and feeling as if I needed to sneak my bite of chocolate between lessons. You can support your students' learning and growth when you teach them to listen to their bodies. (If you have concerns about students who may have disordered eating, reach out to parents or caregivers, school health providers, and school counselors.)

Provide choice. What do your students have choice over when they enter your room? It shouldn't be everything. Age-appropriate choices support a sense of autonomy, but too many choices can create an environment of chaos. The type of choice is important as well. For example, I do not advise allowing choice in seating unless your students are fourteen or older, in part because the process of seat selection can bring up deep insecurities for students. Remember that choices do not need to be high stakes. You might ask students to choose an animal that represents how they are feeling that day, or post a poll on the board where students can vote on what type of music is featured during Friday's morning ritual.

Provide "pockets" throughout the room. A pocket is a small place within the larger space of the classroom that gives students options for experiencing something other than their typical chair and desk. Corners are obvious spots for these because they are out of high-traffic areas and allow for students to be surrounded on two sides. Pockets offer variation in perspective (such as by allowing students to sit lower or higher than their regular chairs) and changes in texture and mood. Stable, low dividers, such as bookshelves, plants, or small tables, can create a sense of separation that is sometimes needed for different types of thinking (such as reflection or brainstorming) or behavior (such as regulating or connecting). Consider how these spaces can meet the needs of all bodies and abilities.

Make your classroom fun for you too. Your personality should come through to your students via your space as well as your demeanor. Love coffee? Keep a jar of your favorite beans on your desk and invite your high school students to write "smelling notes." In Phoenix, Arizona, teacher Eric Álvarez runs his middle school civics class like a business meeting—each

Chapter 5: Your Classroom as a Refuge   **89**

student comes in and finds their role for the day. Someone has a gavel to keep things moving while other students read minutes and take notes. Eric says he can feel the energy in the room when students get a chance to play a role. One of my own favorite math teachers loved baseball, so he told baseball jokes all through his lessons. They were bad, and we all knew it, but it made him a real human to us and helped us feel like we could relax while learning. If even a small percentage of classroom time is spent on building rapport with students, it is almost guaranteed they will care a bit more about what you have to say when it is time for you to teach.

> *If the financial realities of creating your classroom environment are less than ideal, which is the case for many educators, consider taking advantage of grants for schools. In Oakland, Melissa purchases items for her classroom using grants through DonorsChoose, a nonprofit organization founded by former teacher Charles Best in 2000 to connect teachers' requests for their classrooms with willing donors. It is free. Teachers need to teach at a US public school or public charter school to qualify. It takes about twenty minutes to apply. To date, over 88 percent of public schools nationally have posted projects on the website, and over a billion dollars have been donated to schools. Find more information at donorschoose.org.*

KEY POINTS

- Students may not come from physically or emotionally secure homes.
- Classrooms are places of risk-taking for you and your students. You can help make this risk-taking feel safe for everyone.
- Invite your students to contribute to the safety cues of their classroom space through the Re-Envisioning Our Spaces activity (page 92).
- Ready your classroom to be a place that inspires calm, focus, and passion.

- Start each day anew with familiar rituals that remind students that they belong.
- Provide opportunities for self-care with a jar of prompts.
- Meet sensory needs when and where you can.
- Connect students to the natural world within your classroom.
- Promote age-appropriate autonomy, since students do not have a choice in coming to your classroom.

For Students and Teachers

RE-ENVISIONING OUR SPACES

Students are often excited by the idea of contributing to something that has a real impact on their world. This activity invites students to create their ideal space. By collaborating with your students to reimagine spaces, you can consider alternative perspectives on the shared living environment of your classroom. Even if the ideas are completely wild, you will learn something about your students' cues of safety. This activity also supports students in beginning to consider and recognize their own cues of safety, which is important for increasing their sense of agency.

Begin by brainstorming with your students in response to the following questions. Write their responses for all to see.

- Describe how you feel when you are relaxed.
- What kinds of things or places help you feel relaxed?
- Do certain colors help you feel more relaxed? What are they?
- Describe how you feel when you are awake and full of energy.
- What kinds of things or places help you feel awake and full of energy?
- Do certain colors help you feel more awake? What are they?
- Describe how you feel when you feel protected and safe.
- What kinds of things or places help you feel protected and safe?

Explain to students that they are going to design a space for themselves that meets three requirements: It needs to provide for relaxation, it needs to allow for feeling awake and energetic, and it needs to offer protection and safety. Ask students to look around the classroom as it is currently and see if they can identify any of those elements in the room. This could be as simple as a wall display, a reading corner, or a window. If you are feeling brave, you could ask students what their favorite and least favorite parts of the room are. Remind students that what feels relaxing, energizing, and safe may be unique to each person.

92   *The Empathetic Classroom*

Depending on the grade level and time available, you could make this a drawing exercise, or you could use shoeboxes to allow students to design in three-dimensional space. Also depending on the grade level, you can make the guidelines as specific or as flexible as you like. You may want students to use measurements, for example, or to incorporate elements of something you are currently studying. If you are using shoeboxes, you may recommend using found objects rather than purchasing items. Students in most grade levels will really get into the idea of creating a miniature space and will find this imaginative activity both engaging and calming. I recommend joining students in creating a space so that they can see your investment in the project as well. Plus, students usually love to see what their teacher's imagination looks like . . . so have some fun with it yourself!

Explain that students should imagine living in the space and should consider what they need in a day—though this one space doesn't have to do everything. (For example, they wouldn't have to include a bathroom.) The space also does not have to be a classroom. Even though you may use this activity to gather ideas for making your classroom more of a refuge for your students, the goal here is not to put many limits on what type of a space students design. It can be indoors, outdoors, or a bit of both. It can be real or imaginary.

When students are finished with their spaces, offer them the opportunity to share their designs and ideas with the class. Conclude with the following questions:

- What were some of the challenges you encountered while designing this space?
- Where did you get ideas? What inspired you?
- What is your favorite part of your space?
- Is there something you would change or add now that you have seen the spaces other people designed?
- Why might it be helpful to live, learn, work, and play in spaces that are relaxing, energizing, or safe?
- Where in the real world do you feel this way?
- What might be one way we could improve our shared classroom space to make it more like this?

continued

Chapter 5: Your Classroom as a Refuge   **93**

As you listen to your students share ideas, take note of what you learn about individuals in the class. Consider:

- Who needs more feelings of protection?
- Who craves more energy?
- Who wants more opportunities to relax?
- In what realistic ways could you better accommodate your students?

For Students

SELF-CARE JAR

Support your students in feeling they belong in their classroom by creating beginning- or end-of-day rituals that can provide students with a sense of purpose, routine, and grounding. Repeated acts of self-care, even if simple, can help you and your students slow down and transition your minds to a new place or action. Think about how your own morning routine, such as making tea or brushing your teeth, can feel essential to feeling at peace about what is to come in your day.

A self-care jar can become a simple yet powerful ritual in your classroom. Place slips of paper with self-care prompts in a jar. You can use the following sample ideas or create your own. (These prompts are available for download at freespirit.com/empathetic.) Have students draw a slip each day and spend the first few minutes of class considering these ways of showing and practicing self-care.

Choose one item you own that needs cleaning today and make it extra clean.	Do one thing during your free time today that you don't normally do.	Do something kind and out of the ordinary for one person today.	Take five deep breaths each time you wash your hands today.	Write yourself a note about something you appreciate about you and put it in your desk, locker, or bag today.
Talk to someone you don't usually talk to today.	Each time you look at the clock today, say to yourself, "I am worth it."	Each time you stand up today, reach up to the sky and stretch.	Notice how many colors are in your lunch today.	Listen to your favorite song today.

continued

Chapter 5: Your Classroom as a Refuge **95**

Try eating your lunch or a snack as slowly as possible today.	Find one way to make your desk area feel better today.	Think of an animal you like and take on a trait of theirs for the day.	Try to sit with good posture for today.	Give your brain a break from self-judgment today by telling yourself, "I'm okay just as I am."
Spend a little quality time with someone you trust or care about today. That person may be you!	Name one thing you're curious about and learn something about it today.	Think of a color you currently like and use it in some way today.	Name one thing you liked doing as a younger kid and do it today.	Find one moment to dance today . . . secretly or not.
Pick one emotion you enjoy feeling and do something to feel it today.	Pick one thing you normally do and do it extra carefully today.	Take time today to smell something really good, such as soap, a favorite food, or the outdoors.	Write your name extra decoratively today.	Create a miniature piece of art today.
Find a photo you love and put it in your desk, locker, or bag today.	Find a way to thank your hands or feet today for all they do.	Take a deep breath and smile each time you walk through a door today.	Compliment someone on something specific today.	Pick a word that makes you feel good and picture it if you feel down today.
Think about someone you look up to each time you start something today.	Find and feel five different textures today (without touching someone else). What was your favorite? How did it make you feel?	Share something with someone today . . . a happy thought, a smile, a favorite item, or another positive thing.	Each time you look in a mirror today, remember one thing you've done that you're proud of.	When you finish a task today, try to find a way to let your whole body relax—each and every muscle. Close your eyes for at least a minute.

96   *The Empathetic Classroom*

6

FORM A SECURE ATTACHMENT

At Glenn L. Downs Social Sciences Academy in Phoenix, Arizona, Eric Álvarez—educator and winner of a 2022 Esperanza Latino Teacher Award—knows that by allowing students to see who he is, he's inviting them to open up about who they are. He's aware of the performative nature of teaching, so when his students talk about him as the "teacher with corny jokes," he embraces it.

For instance, he's all about making and celebrating mistakes, and he wants students to have fun with this too. His students keep a tally for each time he makes a mistake. He jokes about how he's going to try to make two mistakes since it's Tuesday. He'll make a show of tearing a page out of his notebook and ripping it up. His students feel free to do the same when they, say, want to rewrite an introduction. Dramatic? Sure. Effective at getting his kids comfortable with mistakes? You bet.

Eric will be the first to admit that sometimes he too misses the mark. One year, he had a group of eighth graders who were highly motivated and engaged in all projects he threw their way. One student, though—we'll call him "Johnny"—seemed to fit nearly all the labels teachers might use for a "difficult" student. He seemed withdrawn, always misbehaving. He was a student, Eric later noticed, who seemed to "allow adults to define who he was." In the frenetic energy of the school year, Johnny initially went largely unnoticed by Eric. Eric didn't even think to invite him to the engineering competition because he didn't think Johnny would be interested.

Then one day, a couple of Johnny's classmates approached Eric after class.

"Hey, Mr. A," they began. "We've noticed that Johnny could really use your help right now. If you could just show him some attention and care, that would really make a difference."

Eric remembers feeling stunned and a little defensive. He had noticed Johnny, hadn't he? He cared about all his students, didn't he? Once he had a moment to reflect, though, he could see the ways he too had participated in pigeonholing his student. He knew he needed to do something different, to *be* different.

This moment flipped a switch for Eric. He began identifying specific roles in the group that could help Johnny start to feel a sense of confidence. He was more conscious of showing support for him. He also worked to change the narrative in his own head. Soon, Johnny started to show up differently in his classes. Other teachers noticed too: Johnny was participating and seemed interested in life. Eric felt deep gratitude for the students who had been brave enough to give him feedback. He could now see that it was coming from a place of love.

Connection Is Survival

Your relationship with your students is the foundation of all your efforts in the classroom. There is nothing more important than this connection. A student who loves science can encounter a teacher they don't click with and suddenly arrive home reporting they "hate science." Missed opportunities for connection in the classroom lead to missed learning opportunities. If we only place emphasis on content, there's a good chance that many students will tune out what we have to say.

Teaching, like many of the caring professions, has a slightly blurrier line between the personal and the professional than many other careers. And for good reason: true care requires bringing aspects of ourselves into our work. Many of us appreciate a highly skilled doctor who also knows how to smile, asks how we are doing, and hands us a tissue if we tear up. We are especially grateful to the child care provider who sits on the floor to comfort a toddler who has melted into a puddle of tears at the sight of their parent leaving.

You may *intend* to show up in "super professional mode." Maybe you have the best-laid plans to wear your nicest button-up shirt for school (and by "nicest," I mean the one with the wild print you know your students will love), for example. And this may end up being the same day that shirt will endure a mission in the rain, a glop of grape jelly, several stickers, and frank comments on how oddly it fits. You are working with young, creative humans! There is no way to completely separate Professional You from Personal You. If you try, your students will sense it—and call you on it.

So in this blurred space, who are you? In short, you are an attachment figure. In the counseling world, attachment work is a foundational approach that considers how our first attachments with primary caregivers have affected our relationships with ourselves and the rest of the world going forward. The idea seems extreme, doesn't it? The idea that your first inter-actions with a parent or caregiver could have set in motion the fact that you repeatedly dated the same type of person in college? Or that your difficulty with calling people back might have to do with how often you were left with a thirteen-year-old babysitter while your parents worked?

Yet our very idea of *relationship* is established well before we are aware of its concept. Babies must form attachments to survive. Their first relation-ship is so strong because it is based on their primal needs for food, comfort, and care. Babies innately know that they need to cry to draw attention to themselves and that they can stop crying and start displaying happier expressions when their needs are met. But what about babies who don't get attention when they cry, or babies who get constant attention? How do these responses impact their sense of security?

The Strange History of Attachment in Psychology

In the 1970s, Mary Ainsworth's research sought to understand the nature of the relationship between an infant and their primary caregiver. In an exper-iment called the Strange Situation, Ainsworth observed a parent and their baby (generally twelve to eighteen months old) in a room with toys. Then a stranger enters the room and interacts with the parent, and the parent leaves while the child is distracted. The stranger hangs out with the infant. Eventually, the parent comes back and rejoins their child. Pretty simple. But from this situation, clear patterns emerged (Ainsworth and Bell 1970).

Some infants were unable to explore freely and play even when their parent was in the room. Some infants didn't seem to care whether their parent was there. Some babies were instantly comfortable with a stranger.

And some little ones cried when they realized their parents had gone but quickly returned to play as soon as they returned.

What did Ainsworth learn from all of this? One discovery was that some of the babies had what she called "avoidant" attachment with their primary caregivers. These babies did not explore the room much, had little interaction with their caregivers—often avoiding or ignoring them—and did not respond when their caregivers returned. Other research with these same babies indicated a history of unmet basic attachment needs by the caregivers, resulting in the children learning to maintain some emotional distance to avoid rejection and distress.

Another group of babies were described as having "anxious" attachment. These babies clung to their caregivers, cried when they left, and continued to cry and hold onto them when they returned. They also struggled to play. Based on other data she'd collected, Ainsworth believed this response from babies arose when caregivers were unpredictable. The babies with anxious attachment had learned to require constant attention in an attempt to maintain control of the situation and keep their caregivers available.

Other babies, she observed, had what she called a "secure" attachment with their primary caregivers. These babies showed an uninhibited ability to play. They explored freely when their caregivers were present, they expressed concern about their caregivers when they were absent, and they were comforted and able to resume play when the caregivers returned. A securely attached child had learned that their caregiver was dependable, someone who offered consistent comfort when needed.

Attachment theory, like all theoretical angles, has its flaws and limitations. It too has found its place in the great nature-nurture debate. One argument is that there is much about a child's personality and character that cannot be shaped by their primary caregivers, no matter a caregiver's intentions (Harris 1998). The environment and people outside the home also play their part in the traits a child develops. A child's unique genetic and physiological make-up can lead them to respond to caregiver's interactions in unexpected ways. For example, a child who is on the autism spectrum may not mirror their primary caregiver's expressions. And real-life attachment is nuanced and more complicated than dividing individuals into categories makes it seem. We all express elements of each attachment style. Nevertheless, knowing some basic principles of attachment theory can illuminate aspects of our interactions and relationships with students.

The Empathetic Classroom

Attachment Goes to School

First point of interest: your students bring their attachment styles to school with them. You know that kid who plays with your zipper pull five inches from your face while you're trying to monitor the playground on recess duty? Maybe some anxious attachment tendencies. Or that other kid who doesn't seem to hear you and turns their back to you? Likely some avoidance going on there. Kids who present with secure attachment styles tend to be engaged in friendships and seem comfortable being alone. They're often willing to try new things, even if they're a bit nervous, as long as they have your support. When they mess up, they seem to recover fairly easily.

Notice and consider how each of these types of traits is regarded at your school and in your classroom. Are there ways in which you give positive praise to certain attachment styles or negative or critical feedback to others?

Next, reflect on your own attachment style. You can use the Identifying My Attachment Tendencies at School activity on page 110 to begin exploring how your attachment style shows up in the classroom.

Finally, consider that when you pair your students' attachment styles with your own, each combination will result in a unique snowflake of a relationship. When I started teaching, I was unaware of my own attachment style. I had some anxious attachment in my make-up. I remember when I had a student who also had anxious attachment and would seek my approval for everything she did. She had a million questions, was always fearful of doing something wrong, and read my every facial expression. I was new, unaware of attachment dynamics, and eager to ease her anxiety. So I did everything she wanted. I thought this is what I was supposed to do as a teacher. Answer questions. Help. Comfort.

However, by responding to her anxiety with my own anxiety, I was unintentionally signaling that I was not able to handle her worries. I was saying that her anxiety was too big for me, so I had to fix it. In a way, I was giving in to her anxiety and going along with her on that ride. This also gave her the control she believed would make life easier—subconsciously, she was thinking, *If this adult cannot handle my big emotions, I need to take control and* **make** *her care for me.* And while I'm all for individual control to a certain extent, children feel most secure when they know a safe adult is in control. They can learn and play more freely and joyfully if they don't have to worry about what is going to happen next. I was not letting this student

Chapter 6: Form a Secure Attachment   **101**

take healthy risks in the learning environment. I was not telling her, *It's okay, I've got this.*

This experience can be visualized through a concept known as the Circle of Security (Cooper, Hoffman, and Powell, Circle of Security International 2018), shown in figure 6.1. This infographic was developed for teachers and is part of the Circle of Security Classroom Approach, a professional learning series to bring attachment to the classroom. You can find further resources on the topic of attachment in the classroom at circleofsecurityinternational.com/cosc-approach-an-overview.

Here, you are a "secure base" for your students as they go out and explore the world through learning. They need your support and encouragement to engage in this brave act. There are times when they might

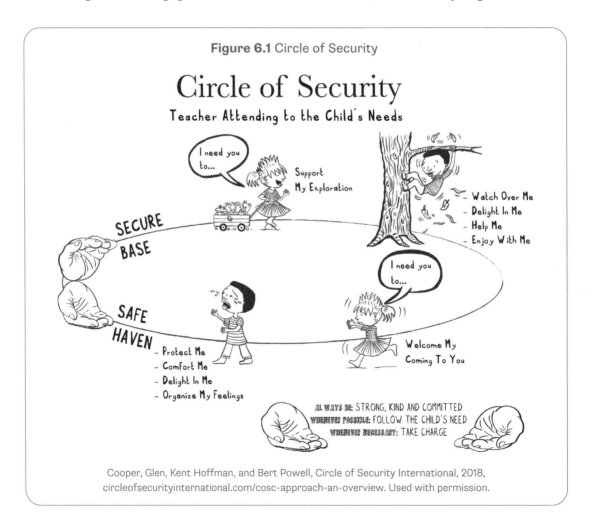

Figure 6.1 Circle of Security

Cooper, Glen, Kent Hoffman, and Bert Powell, Circle of Security International, 2018, circleofsecurityinternational.com/cosc-approach-an-overview. Used with permission.

The Empathetic Classroom

encounter trouble. Then you may offer encouragement, reminders, guidance, and sometimes help. You are excited about their journey of growth, and you show approval of who they are and delight in them through the ups and downs. If, at some point, they choose to come back to you with a need—for emotional support, protection, comfort, or more encouragement—you can welcome them back into a "safe haven" before encouraging their return to their journey.

Knowing Your Students

To build a secure relationship with students, you need to know who they are. This means taking time to prioritize this process. When I reflect on my first few years of teaching, I wish someone would have told me to pause and look up. I wish they would have told me it was okay to get to know my students as individuals. That doing this would make our learning more effective. As a counselor, I am expected to ask the big and little questions, to get to the hidden gems that exist in each one of us. Counselors are trained in deep listening, reflective statements, noticing patterns, pointing out areas for possible improvement or greater insight, and asking different types of questions. While it is not your work as an educator to dive into the psyche of your students, there *is* a sweet spot between these two worlds: building true insight into the hearts and minds of your students.

Arizona teacher Eric Álvarez does this by spending time between classes wandering the hallways—noticing what students are reading, asking what music they're listening to or what sports teams' gear they're wearing. "People want to talk about the things they love," he says. "I can get excited with them, and then we're excited together."

He emphasizes how it's not important to already know everything about the things your students are interested in. In fact, getting names of things wrong or sounding "old" can be part of the goofiness that leads to more connection. He finds that the energy he puts into connecting with his students finds its way back into his classroom and teaching feels easier.

At Bella Vista Elementary in Oakland, California, Melissa Barry-Hansen opens the school year by asking each student to write an autobiography. Understanding that this puts her students in a potentially vulnerable position, she goes first. She creates a web on the whiteboard to tell her students about herself. On the parts of the web closest to the center, she provides some general details about herself: where she went to school, what

Chapter 6: Form a Secure Attachment   **103**

languages she speaks, who she lives with. From each of these branches, she goes into more detail. Her students learn that she has a son with a disability. She was divorced before she met her current husband. She shares that her father drank a lot and was once sent to jail.

"I share these different things so [they see] that whatever they have in their lives, it is not going to shock me. It lets them know that I'm vulnerable, that I've made mistakes, that I've had things I've had to deal with in my life, and then they can feel more comfortable sharing the truth about things in their life," she says. She reminds her students that a big part of this project is about building their community of people, one that will follow them into middle school and high school. Students can keep their stories private, but they also learn that sharing them can be an opportunity to let their classmates get to know them.

"I tell them, 'When someone tells you a secret, that is like a gift that someone gives you. You need to be honorable and respectful with that.'"

A more formal way to get to know students is with an Insight Survey like the one on page 112. The information from a survey like this will give you your first peek into the amazing minds and personalities of your students. It also says to them, *I see you; I am listening to you; I respect you.*

I was always surprised by what students were willing to share with me on day one. What this tells me is that our students know themselves, and they want us to know them too. "What do I need to know about you?" will usually dredge up some vulnerable information. I've had students tell me that they are adopted, or that an older brother died by suicide, or that a parent has alcohol use disorder. (Again, you may want to follow up with a student individually if they share any information that needs further clarity or warrants concern.) Like us, students carry rich and complex identities, some visible and some not. It's our responsibility to accept the whole child as they are—and to continually grow in awareness of our own assumptions or biases.

As a teacher, I might do a variation on this survey several times throughout the year to continue connecting more deeply with my students. It is an opportunity for a quiet student to say something loud, and a chance for the talkative students to tell you something that even they can't voice out loud. Writing provides a slower and more focused space to let big thoughts or emotions come to the surface.

The Empathetic Classroom

In some school cultures, you may find that the approach of the Insight Survey isn't a good fit. You know your school and students best. Longtime educator Stephen Davenport found that discussion of feelings at one school he taught at was almost considered a kind of narcissism within the culture of the students. Rather than avoid emotional interactions altogether, teachers at this school went about getting to know their students deeply and forming attachments through more subtle and implicit paths. For example, when they noticed one student seemed to be having a rough day, they spent a little extra time reading aloud—an activity they knew this student liked. They also got out art supplies and asked students to paint during a math lesson, an academic area this student felt competent in. Stephen also discovered one route to getting to know his students by mistake: His weekly free writes resulted in students writing about what was on their minds, rather than what they thought they should write about. He treasured his students' writing dearly, and his students could see this.

Traits of a Secure Teacher

Your students need to form secure attachments with you and their other teachers to survive and thrive in the educational environment. Here are some key traits of secure teachers and classrooms that I've found can transfer effectively from general relationship psychology into the unique space of classrooms. You can harness these traits to model and establish this healthy attachment with your students.

- **Be consistent when you can, and be honest when you can't.** Your students need to know what they can expect from you. Early in your relationship, you can let them in on who you are and what matters to you. If you sometimes feel off or not like yourself, that's okay (and natural)—just give students a heads-up. For example, if you are generally a talkative person and suddenly you're not saying much, your students are going to notice. Rather than creating a situation in which they assume the silence is about something they have done, you can provide some age- and context-appropriate information—*I've been feeling a little down lately.* Frequent communication when you are feeling or behaving in ways that aren't consistent with your norm can help reestablish a sense of security for your students.

- **Allow for dialogue.** Conflicting opinions will occur between you and your students. If your students don't believe you are listening to them and capable of adjusting based on their needs even when the two of you aren't seeing eye-to-eye, they will start to cut off connection for fear of being unfairly treated or even harmed.

- **Have a structure—and know when to bend it.** Research shows that structured classrooms (and homes) are beneficial to all types of learners and attachment styles. Predictability can seem boring, but it allows students to know where the boundaries are. And, in turn, it allows them to explore and practice creativity within them. If you receive meaningful feedback that a classroom structure is not working well, be open to making changes, but clearly communicate these before implementing them. It's okay to let students in on your thought process about why you are making a change.

- **Be aware of what you say and do.** Students are highly perceptive about what the adults around them are doing. If you say something negative about another teacher or react poorly to a student's mistake, students will notice. If a teacher is unkind to any living being (including spiders and small rodents!), some students will assume they may also do this to them. Your actions will always be interpreted by students through the lens of how the actions impact your relationship with them.

- **Be willing to repair.** All teachers make mistakes. If you say or do something you know has broken the sense of trust and security with your students, you will need to address it—maybe more than once. Be willing to go the extra mile to regain trust with your students. This will show them that they can repair trust as well. When you repair, take time to sit down with a student or your entire class and address the mistake with intentionality. Be clear about what you believe you did that may have affected others, and apologize for it. Offer students the opportunity to discuss it with you more—right now if they're ready, or later if they need time to gather their thoughts. Try to avoid justifying your mistake or making light of it. It may take time, but most students will regain trust in you (and build a stronger trust going forward) if they know they can rely on you to own up to something.

Secure Attachment Versus Emotional Detachment

One of the challenges of creating a secure attachment is to avoid slipping into becoming overly emotionally attached to our students. Secure attachment and emotional detachment coexist alongside one another in healthy adult/child relationships. This might sound confusing after the last few pages encouraging attachment. However, for both mental health professionals and teachers to do their jobs effectively, we have to develop a certain level of *emotional detachment*. This means that you can—and must—separate your own emotions from those of your students. For some of us, this is not easy at first. But when a child expresses a strong emotional reaction or behavior, it is important to manage your own emotional response. If your student is crying, for instance, you may feel like crying as well. But in most cases, this will be overwhelming for them. It also moves their focus from their own experience to wondering what to do about *your* feelings. When students come to you for support, the emotional focus should stay on them.

When you have a healthy and appropriate level of emotional detachment, you don't get stuck in expectations about how your students "should" react to you. You can say or express what you need to, but you detach from the outcome. Just because I am upset about who lost the game last night does not mean my students should also be upset. If they want to laugh about how upset I am, they are free to have that reaction, and I can try not to take it personally. When you model this type of detachment, students learn that you can handle your own emotions as well as theirs. Being emotionally detached does not mean you are lifeless or cold. It means you are able to separate your own emotional experience from that of your students, and you are able to be present with them no matter how they are showing up.

Chapter 6: Form a Secure Attachment   **107**

KEY POINTS

- One way of understanding human relationships is through attachment theory.
- Primary attachments are the ones we experience at birth.
- Babies must form attachments with caregivers to survive.
- If caregivers are neglectful, absent, abusive, or unregulated, babies learn behaviors to avoid caregivers. They grow up to exhibit avoidant attachment characteristics.
- If caregivers are unpredictable in their care, babies learn to show signs of distress or anxiety to gain attention. They grow up to exhibit anxious attachment characteristics.
- Caregivers who are present, predictable, and capable of meeting physical and emotional needs allow babies to take risks and explore the world, knowing that when they need help, their caregiver will respond. These children grow up to exhibit secure attachment tendencies.
- The Circle of Security infographic demonstrates a cycle of security and healthy risk you can engage in with your students.
- Your own attachment tendencies paired with those of each of your students will create unique relationship dynamics.
- You can observe the signs and characteristics of attachment styles in your students and yourself.
- Using an Insight Survey (page 112), students can slow down and reflect on what they want to share with you. Having students share in writing also allows for you to keep the information confidential.
- The information students provide in an Insight Survey can alert you to their current concerns, challenges, or hopes.
- It is important for you to meet with students whose Insight Survey responses warrant further discussion to ensure that you understand what they wanted to convey. If a student indicates any signs or risks of physical or psychological abuse or neglect, reach out to the appropriate support professionals at your school and/or agencies listed in your state's mandatory reporting policies. You should always report, even if you only have a suspicion.
- As an attachment figure, you can practice secure attachment tendencies to support internal and external security in your students, including

The Empathetic Classroom

consistency, structure, direct and open communication, self-awareness, and flexibility.

- You can be an attachment figure and also bring a balanced level of emotional detachment. You can support your students in their emotional experiences without joining in their emotions with them or expecting them to join with yours.

Chapter 6: Form a Secure Attachment

For Teachers

IDENTIFYING MY ATTACHMENT TENDENCIES AT SCHOOL

Like your students, you bring your own attachment styles into the classroom each day. And you're not necessarily all one type of attachment or another. Most people have some of each style in their interactions but usually tend to lean more heavily toward one. This activity asks you to reflect on how your own attachment tendencies show up in the classroom. Being aware of how your attachment looks can allow you to begin to bring more intentionality into your relationships at school (and beyond).

Make note of any items that resonate as a way you interact with your students.

- I tend to ignore a student when I don't like something they did.
- I don't want to know too much about my students.
- I try to shut down any high emotions in my classroom as soon as they start.
- I try to avoid conflict in my classroom.
- I easily feel dysregulated at school.
- I don't want my students to know anything about my personal life.
- I dislike it when a student seems clingy or needy.
- My students tend to avoid talking to me about anything other than school.

- I feel like I am friends with my students.
- I excessively compliment or praise students.
- I try to avoid giving my students direct critical feedback.
- I worry that my students won't like me.
- I don't think I'm a very good person or teacher.
- I feel the need to share a lot about my life with my students.

110   *The Empathetic Classroom*

- I like to help my students fix their problems.
- I have difficulty saying no or setting boundaries.
- I feel good when my students feel good. Similarly, I feel bad when they feel bad.

- I am willing to take feedback from my students.
- I acknowledge my mistakes to my students.
- I can say no to students and parents and set boundaries with them.
- I can let students and parents know what I need from them.
- I appreciate my work with my students, but my self-worth extends to more than my job.
- I feel an emotional connection to my students.
- I trust my students, until there is clear reason to draw boundaries. Even then, I offer opportunities for them to regain my trust.
- I think about and do things other than school stuff in my free time.
- I can take care of my own emotional state even when my students are not regulated.

Look at which things you chose. Do you have some in each section? Do most of your answers fall into one section? The first section is what avoidant attachment teaching might look like, the second represents anxious attachment teaching, and the third section describes secure attachment teaching. First, know this: If your responses fall largely into the avoidant or anxious categories, you are not a bad person. The traits you might show in either of those sections can likely be attributed to a time in your life when you were very young and not able to conceptualize what was happening in relationships around you. These traits showed up to help you survive.

And you aren't permanently fixed in your attachment style. For example, being in a secure relationship can teach a person with anxious attachment styles about ways to provide security for another. Sometimes, certain relationships or times in life will bring out more anxious or avoidant traits within us. What you can do right now is bring awareness, interest, and curiosity to these experiences and traits and start trying on new ways of interacting with your students that will benefit them as well as you.

Chapter 6: Form a Secure Attachment **111**

For Students

INSIGHT SURVEY

Present students with a set of questions you feel will help you get to know them better. The list below is just a starting point—feel free to customize these in whatever ways make sense for your group. All-important is the foundation of trust that is being built between you and your students. Therefore, students need to know that they only have to respond to the questions they want to answer. They should also know that you will keep the information they share confidential.

- What do I need to know about you?
- How will I know if you're having a bad day?
- What seems to help when you are having a bad day?
- What could make the school day or year better for you?
- What parts of school feel easy?
- What parts feel challenging?
- What is your favorite memory from school? Least favorite?
- Is there anything you want to know about me?
- If you could pick a color to describe you, what would it be and why?

When you have the results of your survey, the next essential step is to integrate this data into your work with your students. That might mean referring to their answers when you experience a challenging situation with a student. I recommend following up on any responses that warrant it, including any indication of strong emotions or lack of emotions; explicit or implied trauma or abuse; or responses that you're confused by or would like to know more about. If a response is outside of your scope of responsibility as a teacher, refer to your school's mental health professionals.

7

SUPPORT THE CHANGE PROCESS

I was known as "the quiet kid" growing up. As my teacher, you would have seen me in my yellow cat-print sweatsuit, staring off into space in some deep daydream that had nothing to do with what you were saying. It's not that I wouldn't follow your rules—I just wouldn't always hear them. And it's not that I didn't have thoughts (though I feared my peers and teachers believed I didn't)—it was that I didn't feel the need to share them. And sometimes I didn't even know how.

As an adult, I love feeling free to verbalize without fear. No longer having *only* internal thoughts has given me exposure to new experiences, people, and feelings. Speaking has empowered me to shape my own world. As a teacher, I always felt a natural connection to my quiet students. It seemed like I understood who they were and also who they could become. Since I had gone through a decades-long change process related to my quietness, I knew there was so much on the other side of this process that was worth the effort.

One of my students, ten-year-old "Gabe," would never say a word during class, but from reading his writing I knew he had a rich inner world that I wished for him to be able to share with others. When our class began production on a play, I took a leap and cast him in a role that seemed primed to let his inner light beam out. He trusted me and worked hard to combat the part of him saying that this was too scary and that he should stop. In rehearsal, his classmates cheered for him and praised his talent. At recess, kids suddenly wanted to play with him, and in class, they asked for his help. I thought this was success. Gabe had undergone change and was reaping the benefits.

All was golden until the day before the performance. During rehearsal, he didn't speak when it was his line. He looked terrified and struggled to hold back tears. When I met with him after class, he said he wasn't ready and didn't want to perform the next day. At the time, I did not think to validate his feelings, but instead tried encouragement. *I know you can do it. I know you have it in you.* He got through the performance the next day, but it was not the joyful experience I had anticipated for him. His lines came out robotically, and he was quiet the rest of the day. After that, he generally avoided me. Looking back, I believe he sensed I might try to do something else to change him. I don't blame him.

Creatures of Habit

Being with our students for thousands of hours each year provides us with copious time to become familiar with their patterns and habits. Maybe too familiar. We know whose hand will pop up with a question before we're done explaining, who will not remember their homework, who won't be thrilled about speaking in front of the class, who will have to go to the bathroom as soon as you say "math."

Some students have developed behavior and thought patterns that are conducive to surviving in your learning environment and some have not. Both have arrived at their patterns for reasons that are mostly beyond their awareness at this moment in their life. Maybe when they're older they'll look back and be able to connect some dots and see more clearly why they were the way they were. But seeing why our own patterns develop requires a few things:

1. The desire to see the patterns themselves
2. The ability to step outside ourselves and view ourselves objectively
3. The hope for something better
4. The motivation and tools to change

I think my ten-year-old self would say, *Nope, I like my stubbornness. It's all mine. You can't make me eat that!* When life suggests that change might be a strategic move, even as adults we can feel our inner child balk. *But I don't want to change!* For all the reasons listed above and more, changing

The Empathetic Classroom

ourselves is hard and downright uncomfortable. Plus, we became who we are to meet the world in a way that made sense to us with the information we had at the time. Until what we do no longer makes sense to us or doesn't work anymore, we see no reason to change.

Teachers Have Healing Fantasies Too

As adults who are no longer at the same developmental stage as our students, watching the events of their lives can be predictable and painful. We don't want our students to suffer needlessly, and we think we know how to prevent it. *If only they would stop _____, then they would be able to _____.* In psychology this is known as a *healing fantasy* (Gibson 2015). Often, people develop these fantasies for themselves to cope with the pain left by emotionally unavailable attachment figures. *If only I were better looking, then I would be loved. If only I felt better, then I would socialize more.* These fantasies develop because our brain tells us that if we just do something in a realm we think we can have an effect on, we'll get what we hope for. It's our brain's attempt at being proactive and hopeful.

If you can identify one of your own healing fantasies, you'll see why this is often unattainable, no matter how hard you try. We might update our wardrobe, go to the gym, drink stinky green juice, and still not feel any more lovable. And just as we do for ourselves, we develop these healing fantasies for our students because we want to help them. It practically seems written into the job description.

You may have tried to conjure your healing fantasies for your students into reality. If so, you probably have already learned that the outcome tends to be similar to what occurs with our adult healing fantasies—just as I did when I tried to rush the change process in my quiet student Gabe.

Change Must Come from Within

Change is only meaningful and lasting when we come to the decision on our own. As teachers, we may have a lot of life experience and an educated perspective on where our students are developmentally. But this does not make us experts on their inner experience. Our experience *does* provide us with an idea of what our students might be going through. And having knowledge about child development can help us provide informed opportunities for change from which students might benefit. Yet the work of change

Chapter 7: Support the Change Process

remains solely their own. Why we finally decide to make some changes in our life is often mysterious. It may not make any sense to onlookers (or sometimes even ourselves). So even if students do engage in *your* healing fantasy and suddenly show they have changed, it is likely only an outward change made to gain approval from you, rather than inward change motivated by their own needs and desires.

This doesn't mean we need to throw our hopes about student change out the window. It just means we need to be aware of why we desire change for someone else. Having hopes for our students to become less fearful, more engaged, or more resilient is engaging in the belief of healing and growth for humanity. Noticing and figuring out how those hopes translate into interactions with your students is where *you* can do some work.

Whether we come to change by choice, force, resignation, or happenstance, all humans experience change in their lives at some point. As educators, we can support and model the experience of behavior change for students without taking over their change process and making it our own.

Stages of Change

It is difficult (or impossible) to predict when people are ready to make a change. But the fact that change can happen in stages is something psychologists have studied. Researchers James Prochaska and Carlo DiClemente (1983) observed people who were trying to quit smoking and found that they followed similar patterns. Prochaska and DiClemente were able to categorize these patterns into five distinct stages of change: precontemplation, contemplation, preparation, action, and maintenance. The insights from this relevant research are beneficial to work in both psychology and education, reminding us that change is often not a single choice or an easy one.

Precontemplation: Look for Open Doors

One way you can invite change as an option for your students is to watch for moments when they open doors to working with you. You may notice that the way your student is going about something is unsustainable and you think a change might benefit them. You know that if you just tell them to do it differently, it won't result in lasting change. So you wait for an open door. This is a moment that occurs when your student indicates they might be precontemplating change—beginning to think about trying something

116   *The Empathetic Classroom*

different. That's an open door. You can now enter and consider their "what-ifs" with them. Let's say you have a student who waits until the day something is due to begin working on it, especially essays. This behavior seems to cause stress for them, you, and their parents. *Change would be so nice,* you notice yourself thinking. Then a door opens.

You: *I see you threw your essay in the garbage.*
Student: *I can't come up with any ideas that I like.*
You: *Yeah, that's frustrating. I have a hard time with that too. I wonder what could help.*
Student: *Probably nothing.*
You: *Yeah, maybe not.*

Through this open door, you can see that your student doesn't enjoy feeling incapable, and they are also letting you know that they're not ready to engage in change talk. You validate their feelings and let them know you're on their side. When they're ready to really think about change, you'll be there to support them in processing ideas. Another open door presents itself the next time an essay is due. You see this student staying inside over recess, staring at a blank page. Now it looks like they are contemplating change.

You: *What's on your mind?*
Student: *Everything else I'd rather be doing.*
You: *So, you have a lot on your mind, and yet, here you are, trying to work on your essay.*
Student: *I can't get another zero in the grade book. But I still don't know what to do. If I could just come up with a good idea, I could finish this.*
You: *Yeah, I hear you. What would it feel like to come up with a good idea and finish this essay?*
Student: *Like, amazing. I could retire early.*
You: *That good, huh?! What's getting in the way of doing that today?*
Student: *Only about a million things.*
You: *Okay, give me your top three. I'm listening.*

Contemplation: Follow Their Lead

When students are in the contemplation stage of change, you are still not jumping on that horse and riding off into the sunset. Remember, change is slow, and you don't set the pace. What you *can* do is provide opportunities to transition to the next stage of change. In this thinking-about-change moment for your student, you are following their lead and presenting questions that nudge them to discover what change might offer and how they might get there. You can wonder out loud about what your student might be feeling or thinking, then allow them to decide if that's accurate. Be prepared for the door to slam shut on you again if you start wondering too hard—students will sense you trying to move them faster than they're ready for. So don't fear asking questions about the heart of the matter, but notice when they're telling you to back away. Let's say that in a few weeks, after this student has continued to struggle with getting those essays in, another door opens. One morning they show up at your classroom before you do. They've even brought you your favorite hot beverage! Hmm, something's up.

> **Student:** *I was wondering if we could work together this morning.*
> **You:** *I think I have some time, if you don't mind me working a bit beside you?*
> **Student:** *That's fine. It's no big deal really.*
> **You:** *What might make our time together most useful for you?*
> **Student:** *I don't know.*
> **You:** *Would it be helpful for me to give you some ideas?*
> **Student:** *Sure. If you want.*

Preparation: Be the Support Crew

In the conversation above, it's easy to feel the student's hesitancy about trying something new. The student feigns disinterest because they don't want to seem *too* motivated or get you *too* excited. Okay, you're with them. You're still asking for consent to engage in the change process. *Do you want help? Do you want ideas for how to change?* This stage of change is called preparation. It is the final step before action. In this stage, the possibility of changing finally feels real and almost tangible to the student. This is where your role is that of supporter. It might even be a good time to talk about some of the anticipated challenges of change. In this student's case, it may seem difficult to identify the challenges that could arise if they did start to get their essays written on time. It seems like that could only bring parades and puppy kisses! But as you well know, even generally positive changes cause shifts in our life and affect other parts of it. Maybe the student will have less time for hanging out with friends. Maybe they'll have to face receiving feedback from a teacher on what they *do* turn in. Maybe they'll start to be known as the type of student they don't think they'd want to be associated with. Maybe

The Empathetic Classroom

their parents will think they're ready for more responsibility. It's okay to prepare students for life changes, even if they may seem trivial to you.

Action: Be Their Biggest Fan

The action stage of change is what we all get excited about. *Yay, you're doing it!* The student is getting their essays in, not just once, but repeatedly. They're asking for support regularly and even asked their parents for a tutor. The tutor caught something you didn't and referred the student for an ADHD evaluation. Once diagnosed, they are provided even more supports, and you have specific, tailored strategies you can use with them. You notice this student's confidence begin to grow, and it almost looks as if you can completely step away and let them glide. *Almost.*

Maintenance: Look Out for Old Patterns

As soon as the student is in the action stage, be ready to support them in the maintenance stage. In any life change, relapse is to be expected. You can prepare yourself and your students for that likelihood. Relapses can bring up old feelings and old beliefs and narratives about the self. Even though the student has climbed the mountain once, that doesn't mean the mountain can't suddenly reappear.

> **You:** *Hey, I noticed your essay isn't in yet, and it was due this morning. I wanted to check that everything's okay.*
> **Student:** *I'm great. I was playing video games with a friend last night, and we lost track of time.*
> **You:** *I understand. That happens sometimes. I wonder if you'd be up to join me at lunch today to work on it.*
> **Student:** *I guess I could do that.*

If you continue to see the old pattern of not turning in essays creeping back for this student, it might be time to create a plan with them and their caregivers to navigate the pressures that contribute to its return. Keep in mind, though—this plan doesn't mean eliminating all potential pitfalls that might cause the student to return to old behaviors.

In this case, for example, it wouldn't mean restricting friend time or video games. The plan needs to be realistic to the student and offer them a clear benefit. For this student, you might discuss using something they already feel confident with, such as their phone, to set up a calendar with all

Chapter 7: Support the Change Process

major due dates and a reminder two days ahead of each. You'd walk through this process once together so the student can do it on their own later. You might also collaborate with the student and their parents to establish good times to set aside each evening for relaxing and for focus. Here, you would want to emphasize to this student that both rest and focus are important—and notice, I didn't say "focus" always means homework. Sometimes, focus might mean reading for fun or building something with LEGO bricks. This shifts the conversation from "get your homework done" to "let's set you up to be able to feel challenged." The maintenance stage is also a time to remind students and their families how far they have come, and that this progress was largely accomplished because of their own hard work. Be specific. For this student, you could highlight their consistent communication with you, their vulnerability in seeking help, and their willingness to try new things. You might even remind them of how challenging it was to come up with an idea at first, and how now they have a lot of interesting ideas. I doubt that students will ever get tired of hearing you tell them how great they are.

We feel pressures from all sides as educators. There is no end to the requests from parents, administrators, and even fellow teachers to correct something that doesn't seem functional. It takes a lot of effort to keep our sense of self and maintain steady ground. Parents often will view you as the catalyst for their student's change process and send you notes about the things they'd like you to work on with them. I can't tell you how many times I've had parents of children with messy backpacks and lockers ask me to get their student organized. And how quickly any system I put in place resulted in no tidier of a child. I am not a cleaning fairy!

When it comes to change and kids, "pick your battle" always applies. And we don't have to go to battle. We can do the work of noticing cues that suggest students might be ready for change, looking for those open doors to offer specific types of support, and then being ready to give space. To help you and your students explore and prepare for the process of change, try the Visualizing Change activity on page 122.

KEY POINTS

- You may desire new behavior patterns from your students. This is normal.
- Sometimes we use "healing fantasies" to wish change on our students (or on ourselves).

- These "fantasies" often convince us that if we do something different, we can have a better, more fulfilling life experience.
- Telling students to change their behavior rarely results in lasting behavior change.
- You can look for opportunities to support students in the change process.
- There are stages of change you can identify: precontemplation, contemplation, preparation, action, and maintenance. Students in each stage require a different kind of support.
- Maintaining a new behavior change requires realistic expectations and opportunities to make mistakes.
- You can explore your own change process or that of your students with the Visualizing Change activity on page 122.

Chapter 7: Support the Change Process

For Teachers and Students

VISUALIZING CHANGE

This is an exercise you can use for yourself or with your students when you want to better visualize a change. Sometimes "seeing" something provides needed clarity! With students especially, this exercise is useful to support the idea of goal-setting, which can be helpful to learning. If you are using this in a group setting, either with other adults or with students, provide reminders that this is an exercise meant to be for each participant's own benefit, and that sharing is optional.

Using a full sheet of paper, create a scene with a wide river running through the middle of the paper, with land on either side. On one side of the riverbanks, write down something you want to achieve. It can be a very specific idea (*I want to learn to play the bassoon*) or more general (*I'd like to be kinder to myself*). On the other riverbank, describe where you are at right now (*I listen to bassoon music and loooove it,* or *I always think I'm worthless*). This side might include words, phrases, feelings, pictures, or anything else you want to document.

Now, between the banks, create stepping stones across the river that detail small steps needed to get from one side to the other (*talk to band teacher, talk to mom, check into rental costs, get a music book, talk to Benny who plays bassoon,* or *make a list of kind things people have told me, brainstorm three things I like about myself or my life, write a few nice notes to myself on my bathroom mirror, draw a picture of me feeling loved and powerful, identify one way to challenge my negative thinking, meditate*).

Now draw some alligator heads that pop up randomly in your river. These are the obstacles that might get in your way. What are they? Name them. (For our self-kindness goal, the person might name people who get in the way of being kind to themself, write a memory that contributes to feeling worthless, or simply list "depression.") Reflect on the mindset you

122   *The Empathetic Classroom*

might want to cultivate as you anticipate the challenges that lie ahead in your pursuit of something new.

If it is helpful to you, display your river somewhere that will remind you to check in on how it's going. Over time, you might discover new stepping stones you'll want to include or new obstacles you're noticing as you work to achieve your goal. You might even notice that something that initially felt like an obstacle can be transformed into a stepping stone. (For instance, maybe you see a way to develop a new mindset on depression. Rather than depression being in the way of change, perhaps you recognize that it is one experience on your path to change and not only a "problem.")

Adapted from Katey T. Franklin, PhD, LSC, LCPC, 2022.

Chapter 7: Support the Change Process   **123**

8

YOU CAN PLAY

"Maddie" was nine and had been diagnosed with ADHD when she came with her parents to my office for therapy. I was a new counselor, and I was excited to interact with children in a new way. During the intake session, her parents reported that she seemed sad and disinterested in things she once liked. No hikes, no ice cream, no fun. It seemed like any invitation to join in a family activity quickly turned into an argument. They missed her and wanted her to enjoy her childhood.

For better or for worse, I initially fell back on what I knew and took a very teacherly approach with her by preparing lesson-style sessions. I would come to our sessions prepared with a topic from my ADHD workbook—friendship, conflict resolution, impulse management—and we would talk about her experiences. We would practice the skill and reflect on how it went. It all felt very, well, orderly.

Like most nine-year-olds, Maddie was super smart and could spot the interventions a mile away. After a few weeks, I could tell she was bored with therapy and was not experiencing any benefit. She would sigh as soon as I started the skill work. I didn't blame her. I was yet another adult who seemed to be telling her what she should change about herself so that she would be happy. I was talking too much.

Play Is Communication

Child psychologist Robin Walker suggests that "to help a child, you have to 'speak the language of youth' and find ways that aren't lecture or punishments" (2011). Play is the language of young humans. Even we older humans communicate through play. If you've ever found yourself searching for the words to describe a feeling or experience, you have experienced the limits of relying only on regions of your brain associated with speech. For young humans, whose speech and language skills are in development, play becomes even more critical to expressing and processing experiences in the world. As educators, we can invite play into our classrooms to enhance learning and care for our students' well-being and our own. Play supports the brain's limbic system's ability for emotional processing. It moves our body in ways that feel good and releases endorphins. Play also naturally regulates our nervous system, and playing with others allows us to feel the important effects of co-regulation.

Do you remember the last time you truly played as an adult and how hard you laughed? How good it felt to feel those happy tears in the corners of your eyes? And how well you slept that night when you plopped into bed exhausted? We now know how vital play is to the development and long-term health of the human brain and how, by playing more, we live more fulfilling lives.

Many parents—along with other adults new to using play as communication in therapy or their classrooms—will wonder if there is any actual therapy or education happening when a child and therapist engage in play or when students and their teacher play together. I had my own skepticism early in my mental health education. Observing a therapist playing with a young child, I didn't see any of the hallmark signs of progression you might observe in talk therapy. No ah-ha moments—*I hadn't thought of it like that*—no recognition of emotions, no verbal processing. Play's unpredictable nature can be scary for adults to both encourage and participate in.

I experienced this myself. Despite having read the theoretical foundations of therapeutic play work and watching experts in action, early in my career as a counselor I still struggled to believe that simply playing truly did anything for clients—as you can see from my work with Maddie. My mind said, *Kids play all the time, how is this any different?* What my mind was revealing to me was that I didn't see the actual value in play, despite being a great lover of play myself.

Play therapy, within the clinical setting, is a specific type of therapy that began in late 1920s with Anna Freud (yes, Sigmund's daughter) and has been well-researched since the 1940s. Much of this research has focused on the use of play therapy for children in hospital settings, supporting those who

Chapter 8: You Can Play **125**

have experienced trauma, and providing exploration into emotional and behavioral concerns (Lin and Bratton 2015). Play in a therapeutic setting is different from free play among peers in that there is a desired outcome attached to the play. In many cases, the goal is relief of symptoms. Among the many benefits of play therapy, it has been shown to decrease anxious and depressive symptoms, increase self-esteem (Baggerly 2004), and develop emotional management and coping skills (Jones and Landreth 2002). Imagine the benefits for a child if they were able to engage in play around going to the doctor or hospital before beginning chemotherapy treatment or undergoing surgery. Practicing with toy stethoscopes or lab coats, and even going through the routines they might need at the hospital, can make the new environment more familiar.

A play therapy office is very different from a traditional talk therapy office for adults. Here are a few things you might notice as an observer:

- The play therapist's room is set up to invite activity, creativity, curiosity, and comfort.
- Foremost, a play therapist's space encourages free expression. The variety of objects, materials, and furniture in the room allows for the child to be as realistic or imaginative as they desire. In a therapy room, a child may use a dragon figurine to represent a parent, or destroy a picture they drew of their house, or hit their therapist with a foam sword.
- Many play therapy offices have child-sized versions of furniture you may find in a home, such as a kitchen with a washbasin and a table with chairs. There might also be a sand tray and many options for figurines to place in the tray, art supplies, dress-up clothes, games, books, and more.

Depending on the age of your students, some of these elements may sound similar to your classroom. But there are, of course, many key differences between a therapy space and a school classroom. Completely free expression at school could be problematic for several reasons—for instance, just imagine twenty-five seven-year-olds with foam swords! Plus, in most classrooms there is a lot going on at once, and for many children, a low-distraction environment is required for releasing more deeply felt experiences. In therapy, the focus is on one child at a time, and the child's needs can be given the full attention they require from a trained professional.

The Empathetic Classroom

And, critically, the private and confidential nature of the therapy space is often an essential cue for vulnerable processing.

Though you are not in the role of therapist, many features of play *can* be encouraged in your classroom. You can provide your students with opportunities to try on new perspectives and chances to take healthy risks and experience consequences in a safe environment. By welcoming play into your classroom, you are also providing students opportunities to observe others at play, which can give them insight into themselves. For example, seeing another student resolve a conflict in a way the observer has never thought of suddenly creates new connections in the brain.

Play During the School Day

As teachers, we might feel uncertain about how play fits into our day-to-day schedule and how we should or should not involve ourselves in that play. We are already so exhausted from all the classroom management and grading that it can seem downright hard to play. And typically, schools in the United States haven't made it any easier. They have squeezed play into the schedule of the school day in a very structured way. Play happens during designated recess periods and physical education. Some schools have found ways to bring it to other subject areas, but the common theme tends to be: "How can we design it so that we don't have chaos? We don't want students to start to think chaos is okay at school." I get it! The idea of turning a classroom into a bouncy castle is concerning. We fear a lack of structure because it could mean that we lose control of the situation. As with all things, there's a middle ground here, and there is room for vital, life-giving play.

You can be playful even in the ways you teach. Yes, you can have structure, expectations, and boundaries—and still show up playfully. *Playful* here doesn't necessarily mean silly. That's not everyone's thing. You can be serious *and* playful. Think back to what *playful* meant to you as a child. It *may* have included silliness, but maybe not. Playful people are curious, they are explorers, they are experimental. They ask questions they don't know the answers to. They linger on interesting details. They're not afraid of trying on new identities. In fact, if you use special voices for characters as you read stories to your students, you are already engaging in play.

Now take it a step further. What makes your heart beat a little faster or invigorates you? What do you want to show students about your playful side? To connect with this part of yourself, try the Explore Your Playful Side

Chapter 8: You Can Play   **127**

activity on page 134. And when you put your ideas into action, watch how your students respond after you turn up the volume on your computer to share a song you loved in the '90s. Notice the comments you get when you wear funky earrings. Try dancing into your math lesson for a change. Be your nerdy Star Wars self. Students will howl with laughter, squirm uncomfortably, and give you the eye—but you know what? They are also learning to see the real you and to see themselves in you.

Play Isn't Always Fun

When introducing play to your students, it's also important to be aware that the mere suggestion of play can produce anxiety for some—just as it does in many of the adults I see. If a child is from a home where lack of structure is indicative of danger, then spontaneous play might bring up unconscious fears. They may not even notice this, but you can. As you suggest play or as you are playful yourself, be aware of students' reactions, and don't assume everyone is having fun. Feel free to encourage, but be willing and prepared to allow for an "out." The point of play is to support nervous system regulation, not to throw it into chaos. Play is only fun when students have the choice to engage and the choice of how to engage.

Ideas for Playful Teaching

If play feels challenging or out of character for you, here are some ideas for tapping into play during the school day:

- Change how and where you sit or teach. Join your students at a desk or table. Invite a student to step into your role for five minutes.
- Change one thing about how you normally dress and see if students notice.
- Display a cartoon image with no words. (Remember *The Far Side?*) Ask everyone to come up with text to go beneath it.
- Spice up a dry lesson with a karaoke moment. Pick a song that ties to a word or concept from the lesson. They'll never see it coming!
- Hide-and-seek never gets old. Hide slips of paper with vocabulary or symbols around the room. Everyone has two minutes to find one and define it.

The Empathetic Classroom

- Keep a collection of something quirky. I know a school counselor who collected students' pencil nubs in a jar. Students would try to get their pencils as small as possible (much to the delight of their writing teachers, of course) and then proudly deliver them to him.
- Do an overly dramatic awards ceremony where everyone's a winner for some academic accomplishment that week. *Best use of an adverb goes to . . .*
- Make up a song using only noises—no words. You can play the conductor and point to a student to make a noise that's easy for them to repeat. They keep that noise going while you point to the next person to add a new noise. You do this until everyone in the room is making a noise in the collective "song." You can even use an imaginary conductor's baton to indicate when to get louder or softer. Then point to each person to stop their noise one at a time until there's only one sound left, and the song ends. (Be prepared for students to dissolve into laughter along the way!)
- Have students choose a character from a movie or book who represents how they feel at a specific stage of learning something new and ask them to tell you more.
- Play the Gifting Improv Game (on page 136) with students.

I became more playful in my later years of teaching because I realized I needed play to survive. The world had become increasingly serious, and my self-prescribed play was a way to defend against contributing to this version of students' future. Depression and anxiety were high in my middle school classrooms. It seemed as if what I was teaching was pointless. I began opening class by reading a script about an imaginary world. I invited students to move silently during my reading as if they were the main character. In response, they would crawl under tables and peek into dark caves. They'd shiver in the cold and hug themselves to warm up. They'd see colors pulsing in the sky. This reading often lasted just five minutes, and the story would end in a restful way, conveniently depositing students back at their school desks, and we would then transition together into the lesson for the day. After I began this practice, I noticed their moods were up, as were their participation and focus. Mine too! Students trusted me enough to go with me during serious learning time because they knew I would engage them in play as well. I had their backs.

Chapter 8: You Can Play

A Different Approach to Connection

While working with my client Maddie, I revisited my training and decided to take a risk: letting her take the lead. I released the reins a bit. I pledged to go with her where she wanted to go in session. I would not have a rigid plan—despite fierce resistance from the teacher part of me! Maddie wanted to draw, so we started with her picking a topic, and then we both drew something from that topic. *Okay, today will be cats with purses.* At the end of each session, she wanted to show her mom the drawings and have her pick a winner. This started to give me insight into what it might be like to be Maddie's friend. Most activities became competitive. I could feel how it might seem challenging to her peers to always have to compete during play. I stayed with Maddie here, though, and didn't try to change her.

One day Maddie said she wanted to draw a farm. I asked if I could draw with her instead of separately, and she accepted. We put the notebook between us and talked through some ideas for the farm. Our hands bumped into each other as we concentrated on the farmhouse and the gardens. We asked each other permission to draw something new on the farm. This went on over many sessions—Maddie came in each week and sat down across from me on the floor and started on the farm. But suddenly, we started collaborating rather than competing! Though I didn't realize it at first, she began to work through her own feelings and experiences through the characters on the farm, whom she imagined in rich detail.

She identified with the oldest son on this imaginary farm, Randy, who went missing as a child. Unbeknownst to his parents, Randy had run away. They thought he was dead, but he was really living in a corner of the yard behind a hedge, watching his family's life pass by for years. From his removed hiding place, Randy saw all the barbecues, apple picking, and birthdays.

Maddie—not feeling accepted for her behaviors after years of teachers and classmates telling her she was not behaving or was not following directions—felt she did not belong. She showed me that she felt so much shame about this lack of fitting in that she wished she could be invisible to others. If only she could watch life from the bushes, like Randy!

Maddie and I drew this farm for over fifty weeks. It was the same farm each time, with some new activity occurring on it. As an adult, drawing the same thing for weeks on end sparked in me the strong desire to suggest something different. But as a clinician, I knew my role was to let this play out in full for my client, no matter how long it took.

After a few months, Maddie decided Randy would be found while the family was hunting for eggs on Easter. "Symbolic," she said with a twinkle in her eye. In the next week's farm drawing, Randy was welcomed home with a colorful celebration, and the flower beds spelled out *RANDY* in purple lavender (purple was his favorite color).

While all this was afoot, Maddie's parents met with me every few weeks and reported that she seemed to be interested in life again. School hadn't changed, yet she seemed to recover from the pressures of the day on her own. She didn't seem as sad or angry anymore, and she was "fun to be with," they said. She wanted to go climbing after school and bake giant cookies with her parents. She was polite most of the time, they said, eyes wide with disbelief.

Of course, I can't take full credit for the change here, as there are a lot of factors that lead to increased self-esteem. But I *was* able to observe and support a child who needed an adult to see her for who she was and not try to change her. Through playing together, I was able to understand the world through Maddie's lens. And by playing alongside her as an adult, I was able to represent a different kind of adult for her.

Thinking about Maddie helps me remember my own child self. Once upon a time, I could effortlessly transition from school to my tree-fort world, where there were maps to be drawn, berries to be gathered, and warring neighbors to fortify against. I could stretch out, belly-down, on the floor of my living room, roll smooth indigo cat-eyes between my fingers, and get into a game of marbles with my brother. I would crave being picked up in my dad's strong arms and "thrown out the window!" (Don't worry, no harm done.) You used to do these things too—remember? And any adult who took time to be kind and playful with us was like a bright star in our world, giving us light, guidance, and hope for our futures.

You can be this sort of adult too—while still being true to yourself! Reflect on how you communicate with your students. Do you find yourself talking *at* them, and trying to tell them how to do things—as I did in my early work with Maddie? Does your mind focus on the goal and seek the seem- ingly most direct route to get there? I know there were times as a teacher when I just wanted to usher students through a concept, believing that was comprehension. Naturally, you won't always have the time or bandwidth for the type of repetitive play through art that I got to experience when counseling Maddie. What you can do, though, is try some of the following ideas:

- Watch your students in their free time and notice how they play. Are there ways you can bring that play into the world of the classroom? If you catch students creating a mystery on the playground, why not bring your best detective act to science class?
- Give yourself permission to feel inspired. You need time and practice in letting your mind roam for this to happen. (Yep—that means putting your phone down during your own free time!) Be brave when inspiration strikes. If you suddenly decide it would be fun to act out a scene from a book you're reading as a class, see where your students stand on the idea. Don't force anyone to participate, but see if you have any takers. You might be surprised who really gets into it.
- If play in your teaching is new to you, set a low bar for yourself. This is not the Olympics of play! What if you plan to make just one math lesson just a little more creative this week? Teaching multiplication by dancing to music may take quite a bit of time and planning on your part, so keep your plans simple as you begin, and realize it may take a few tries to blend learning and play.
- As students get older, they still enjoy play, but it looks different, and they may be more resistant to certain types of play. But here's a secret: The more authentically *you're* committed to play, the more likely it is that they will be too. I used to hold a *Macbeth* banquet every year with my seventh graders, during which they not only acted but also served a medieval feast to their classmates and played instruments if they could. Even the kids who were "too cool for school" got into speaking with Scottish brogues and personalizing their coat of arms. It was very merry! Because I took it seriously, they did too, and each year the next group of students looked forward to memorizing pages of Shakespeare for their own ghoulish feast.

If we want to teach children to navigate the wild world ahead of them, we need to make sure that they are hearing us. We can learn to stop relying solely on the language of adults. This might require some work as our adult

132   *The Empathetic Classroom*

selves rediscover our child selves. We have responsibility in adulthood that children shouldn't have, so it makes sense that being both professional and playful is not always written into our being. Just as I learned with Maddie, we must challenge our own discomfort and immerse ourselves in how children see the world. By making play a part of your classroom, your students will learn in ways you can't put into words.

KEY POINTS

- Children may have difficulty expressing certain thoughts or feelings verbally because of their stage of development.
- Play is the language of children.
- Play therapy is a form of psychotherapy that encourages free expression.
- Through play, children explore new ideas, practice ways of being, express emotions, resolve conflicts, take risks, experience consequences, and observe how other children behave.
- Imaginative play engages the whole brain, improves mood and focus, and regulates the nervous system.
- What is playful is unique to you.
- Revisit your past to reconnect with what could be playful for you.
- You can be playful in how you teach.
- Play can be stressful sometimes. You can allow students options to adapt.

For Teachers

EXPLORE YOUR PLAYFUL SIDE

This activity invites you to get in touch with your child self and rediscover what used to be fun for you. First, find a quiet (or as quiet as possible) place where you can close your eyes and let your mind wander. Begin with three slow breaths, letting the air gently flow in and out of you. Settling in, see if in your memory you can locate a time and place when you felt happy or peaceful. If you struggle with this, try instead to identify when you remember feeling calm. Maybe it was while playing outside or taking a bubble bath. Visualize this moment and notice if any details come to mind. The smell of the soap, the feeling of the earth below you, the sound of a chickadee. Take some time to just watch or feel your child self enjoying the little things. Notice how totally immersed this young version of you is in what you are doing—almost as if time has stopped. Let your child self know that you see them and that you are here for them. Come back to the room you are in with three more slow breaths.

The second part of this exercise is an action. I would like you to check in with your child self and ask them if there is anything they would like to do for fun. It can be challenging initially, but try to distinguish between what Adult You might want to do (like take a nap!) versus what Child You would like to do. Maybe they would like to visit a toy store, build a fairy house, or go to a museum. It doesn't need to be big, grand, or expensive. Remember, children delight in the little things. Plan to give your child self an hour of your time to do something that feels nurturing to this part of you. If you can, do it alone. This gives you a chance to focus on whatever you might need, want, or feel during the experience. Maybe at the end of your time alone you notice you want a root beer float. It wasn't part of your plan, but it's Child You saying "please"—so go for it! Finding your playful side is about engaging with your ability to be flexible and present.

When you have finished your time with your child self, you may want to reflect on the experience by noticing or journaling about what it was like. Or maybe you want to share about it with a loved one.

- What feelings came up?
- Did any memories surface?
- What did you like about it?
- What might have felt uncomfortable?
- How did Adult You show up during your time with Child You?

Finally, try to offer yourself gratitude for taking care of your playful side.

For Students

GIFTING IMPROV GAME

This game will take fifteen to twenty minutes, depending on your group's size (and the level of detail they go into). Gather alongside students so everyone can see each other and you, either in a circle or at their desks. If you can, allow for an arm's length of space between each two people. Explain the game with the directions that follow and demonstrate the gameplay with a volunteer student so everyone gets how it works before the group begins. There is minimal talking involved, which may help some of your quieter students feel relatively comfortable participating. However, if you do anticipate that this activity will be nerve-wracking to some in the group, give them a minute or so ahead of time to brainstorm what they want their "gift" to be. If a student seems hesitant to participate—and you know your students best—you can also pair them up with a friend so they can work together to imagine and act out their gift. (Besides, if they decide to gift someone a pony wearing ice skates, it's preferable to have two wranglers!)

Directions: One person begins by holding an imaginary object. While they can only see it in their mind, they should really express its weight, size, movement, smell, texture, and so on by pretending to interact with it. For example, let's say that I'm imagining I have a wheel of smelly cheese—the really good kind. I would pantomime this without words, grunting as I roll the wheel into the room or circle for dramatic effect and sniffing it while making exaggerated expressions. Maybe I'd even cut into and sample it.

As the beginning participant, after acting out the object, I then gift it to the person next to me, telling them that it is something clearly different from what I acted out—the more ridiculous the better! *I hope you enjoy my . . . tiny pig wearing rain boots.* Because what I am saying is very different from what I just acted out, this usually is quite funny to students. The recipient of my gift should now act out handling the item they have

136   *The Empathetic Classroom*

been gifted, in whatever way they wish to do so. When they have fully acted out receiving and handling the gift (some kids will get into this more than others), they find a new person to gift the item to and change it into something else with their own words: *I would like to give you this . . . blanket made of belly-button lint.* This person now acts out handling the blanket of belly-button lint. Do this until everyone in the room has been given a "gift."

Of course, the delight in this game is coming up with something ridiculous to gift the next person! Facial expressions are encouraged.

Modification: If you are playing this game with younger elementary students, you may need to sit in a circle and have the two students who are giving and receiving a gift stand up when it is their turn so that the focus is clearly on who's performing. You may also want to provide more basic examples, such as a "an elephant" or "a balloon," rather than the more abstract ideas that might appeal to older groups.

End of game reflection: Students tend to revel in reflecting on highlights of a dramatic game such as this. If you have time, you can check in with any of the following questions:

- How did you feel playing this game?
- What was it like for you when you were given your gift?
- What part of the game was most challenging for you?
- What did you see someone else do that you may not have thought of?

Chapter 8: You Can Play

9

TRAUMA AWARENESS

Montana Teacher of the Year nominee Jacob "Buck" Turcotte grew up on the Sioux and Assiniboine reservation in northeastern Montana. Buck's middle school students would describe him as a teacher who has a welcome sense of humor and who doesn't sugarcoat things. He's not afraid to say, "I'm the boss," and, in the next moment, let a kid who needs a good angry rant go at it. Most students already know him when they start the school year because they and their families interact with him all summer long at local powwows where he serves meals out of his food truck. He's also at the sweat lodges and sun dance ceremonies that are part of his Assiniboine culture. Students know Mr. Turcotte as a whole and interesting person.

Growing up, Buck was all too familiar with hearing the stories of his classmates and then his students when he became a teacher in the town of Poplar, Montana. Rape, drug and alcohol use, physical abuse, and poverty were part of the fabric of everyday life, even amidst the beauty and the comfort he found in his community and traditional ways. One story he never envisioned as part of his life was the death of his son.

Buck's son, William, loved wrestling and traveled around the state and country to compete. He was about to start college in the spring and hoped to take his sport to the collegiate level. One November day, Buck and his wife, Angie, found William unresponsive in his room. He had started to experiment with fentanyl a few weeks prior and had unexpectedly taken a lethal dose. Buck, Angie, and their family were devastated.

> Buck took a week and a half off from teaching, but then decided to come back even as his principal encouraged him to take more time. He remembers the difficulty of getting out of bed, of feeding himself, of moving. He remembers crying in front of his students—who responded with hugs and kind words.

No matter our age, most of us have experienced a significant traumatic experience that changed life as we knew it. Some of us, unfortunately, have many. The death or illness of a friend or family member. The separation and divorce of parents. The death of a beloved family pet. Experiencing harm to your own body. While some traumas are personal, like Buck's, others are experienced collectively. One that I have seen in my office for several years now is trauma resulting from the COVID-19 pandemic. During the pandemic, students were fearful of losing family members or becoming ill themselves. They were disconnected from valuable social interactions and lost opportunities for learning. Many families were under significant financial, physical, and emotional strain. The result of this traumatic experience has been lasting, and its effects are seen in fears of social missteps, increased anxiety and depression, and general aversion to any form of risk. Just as I have witnessed in clients with other forms of trauma, children often say they feel a sense of emptiness or numbness when reflecting on their life during the pandemic, as if it wasn't real.

For a long time, there was this commonly held idea that trauma only happens to some people. Or that it consists only of certain types of events that most people would consider outside the norms of human experience. Trauma was abuse, car accidents, witnessing a murder. It even took a while for medical professionals to recognize that soldiers coming out of war were traumatized. However, we now know all too well that trauma to the human mind can occur on seemingly ordinary days and can happen to anyone. Going to school can be a source of trauma for students or teachers. And it doesn't have to be one event; it can be a steady drip that becomes an ocean. Trauma, as it is understood now, is not the event itself but what happens inside of you during and after the experience. You have likely met trauma in your life, and your students may have too.

Trauma, simply put, is an overwhelming emotional or physiological response to a distressing event. It represents more stress than our brain thinks it can handle. It may look like shock, denial, anger, numbness, or

Chapter 9: Trauma Awareness   **139**

other indicators of emotional overcapacity. Trauma can include witnessing horrific events that threaten one's life or the lives of others, or events that leave a lasting impact, such as bullying, death of a pet, or a break-up. We now know that trauma can be transgenerational, with symptoms passed from one family member to the next. Sometimes the effects of trauma are so acute that they render a person ineffective in managing the requirements of daily life. Other times, we learn coping skills that allow us to continue functioning—but in those cases, the trauma may still live under the surface and reemerge in unexpected ways.

The Neurological Impact of Trauma

So, what should we as teachers know about what is happening inside the human brain when trauma is a factor? A good place to start is an understanding of what extreme and sudden distress does to the human brain. With regard to trauma, the brain can be considered in three parts: the brainstem (evolutionarily, the oldest part of the human brain), the limbic system (the emotional processor of the brain), and the prefrontal cortex (the part of the brain that helps you organize, plan, and reason). When a threatening event occurs, a part of the limbic system called the amygdala sets off like a fire alarm, warning the rest of the brain that something is up. Because the brain is all about efficiency, it immediately reacts by shutting down the prefrontal cortex (no time to think!) and engages the brainstem, which is certain that the way to survive a threat is to fight it, run from it, or freeze and prepare to die.

In other words, when a human (or any animal, really) is under threat, there isn't a lot of emotional processing going on (limbic system), nor plans being made to navigate the way out of it (prefrontal cortex). The person under threat is acting on basic animal instinct. That is why many people in shock may be unable to speak, or may run faster than they've ever been known to before, or may display seemingly superhuman strength by lifting a car off the train tracks. Humans under threat often become highly physical, as the emotional and intellectual parts of their brains are quite literally turned off.

What happens to people who experience this type of traumatic event is that the amygdala remembers quite well what was happening in the moment, because—being the smart thing that it is—the brain doesn't want to experience that trauma ever again! So, in a way, it records the sensory

The Empathetic Classroom

experiences of the event: the sounds, sights, smells, tastes, and feelings of it. These sensory memories become triggers for the amygdala to go on alert again. And in fact, brain scans by Yale University and the Icahn School of Medicine show that when a person has post-traumatic stress disorder (PTSD), the memory of the traumatic event is being processed as if it is happening in the present, not as a memory, which in turn causes repeated re-traumatization (Perl et al. 2023). As combat veterans report, the seemingly benign sound of a car door slamming can be registered as a threat and send them right back into the moment when they experienced an IED exploding near them. Triggers exist everywhere because they can be so unassuming—a time of day, a type of light, the smell of a certain food, the quality of someone's voice. In the context of a classroom, asking a student to hurry up, displaying a look of disdain, specifying where a student sits, or even your gender could be a trigger for students.

What Trauma Can Look Like in Your Students

Imagine a nine-year-old student named Benji. He seemed like a typical kid. From June to August, he was the king of his neighborhood. His parents saw him twice a day—tousle-haired at breakfast before he flew down the hill on his bike and then bounding in the door five minutes before dinner. With five bucks in his pocket (and plans to make more with his lucrative putty sales business), he'd hit up the convenience store for an ice cream bar, followed by hanging with his buddies at the park, where they'd fill their day with dares and pranks. His best trick of late was to launch frogs over a fence at unsuspecting swimmers at the neighborhood pool. At night, he feigned sleep until midnight when he'd get online to play games with his friends. He was like a different person. He liked himself in the summer.

But come late August, Benji would not get out of bed. At this time of year, his parents were all too used to his complaints of headaches and tummy aches. They had taken him to the doctor several times, concerned they were missing something, but each time the doctor would say Benji seemed just fine. It wasn't until they took Benji to see a counselor that his symptoms started to make sense. In play therapy, Benji's narratives were about "bad" kids and "good" kids. After meeting with Benji over several months, his counselor learned that "bad" kids did not follow the rules and they did not do well at school.

Chapter 9: Trauma Awareness

Looking through school reports provided by his parents, his counselor saw a distinct pattern: Benji was a regular in detention; he was asked to move seats in class, to stop talking, to "quit annoying" others. Several meetings had taken place with all of Benji's teachers present to address his "problematic behavior." Year after year, every report card was almost exclusively a report on Benji's behavior and how it was never good enough. Even his favorite teacher, Benji shared, had subtly showed her disapproval of his hyperactivity. His counselor could easily see how Benji would believe he was never good enough to belong, at least at school.

Kids—like Benji—can be especially "good" at coping with trauma—in part because they sometimes don't realize that the trauma they have experienced isn't normal. Their traumatized selves will show up to school and blend into their environment. Sometimes their behaviors lead educators to think they are being lazy, disorganized, disobedient, or attention-seeking. Developmentally, they may seem noticeably younger or older than their peers. Socially, they might seem detached from others, or willing to be friends with anyone. All of these behaviors can be signs of unprocessed or untreated trauma.

Trauma can impact your students' development, particularly depending on *when* in their development the trauma occurred or is occurring. So remember that there can be a difference between a student's chronological age and their developmental age. Cognitive, physical, social, and emotional developmental milestones can be delayed or completely missed because of the massive toll any amount of trauma has on the human body. In my practice, it is not uncommon to work with adults who are learning basic social skills at age forty that were missed during their adolescence when they were emotionally abused by a parent. In my classrooms, I have encountered teenagers who were easily swept up into a tantrum that would typically be exhibited by a five-year-old—and then, an hour later, they were joking with their friends again. Noticing this type of difference in how your students' behaviors are exhibited can allow you to respond in ways that meet the needs of your students' developmental ages.

The Empathetic Classroom

Why Traumatized Students Have Difficulty Learning

"Gracie" was a ten-year-old student of mine who was afraid to do anything. It seemed that the entire world was a risk not worth taking. Even in instances when I expected her to be free and have fun, such as while playing a board game, she shut down. Partway into the year, during a parent-teacher conference, her mother let it slip that her father would yell at her when she did something wrong. A light bulb turned on for me, and I understood Gracie's reactions quite differently. I now imagined myself being yelled at each time I made a misstep. I pictured feeling afraid about every attempt at something new, not knowing what might cause my parent's anger. I imagined I would rather do nothing and avoid feeling shame or the risk of abandonment. And now I could see Gracie's view of me, her teacher, asking her to take risks and try something new. To her, taking risks entailed the potential for making a mistake, and therefore being yelled at. This equated to repeating the trauma experience for her. Because her brain was trying to protect her in any situation that felt like the one at home, it dictated that her emotional and logical processing abilities had to shut down when they faced a trigger, even if it was not the actual trauma. And while she knew I was not her father, her brain had not yet made sense of the experience enough to know she could trust me.

Stephen Porges has dedicated his life's work to understanding what occurs inside us when we experience trauma of any size. He's a well-known neuroscientist and psychologist credited with the 1994 development of polyvagal theory, which is—relatively speaking—a new kid on the block in the psychology world. This theory recognizes how the autonomic nervous system (ANS) plays a role in our behavior and mental health. Porges's work suggests that behavior is not a choice but a biological reaction. In other words, while I might think Gracie is choosing to disengage from classroom activities, she likely is not choosing at all. Similarly, in Benji's case, it may have appeared to his teachers that he was choosing not to follow rules. But polyvagal theory suggests that, in fact, his nervous system was doing the choosing for him. This protective reaction is a child's survival instincts kicking in as they perceive a risk that they feel might threaten their very existence, even if this is far from the truth. When our nervous system is

Chapter 9: Trauma Awareness

regulated, on the other hand, we can behave in ways that are aligned with our reasoning, planning, and reflecting capabilities (Porges 2022).

And yet the learning environment is all about risk-taking. To learn, we must leap into the unknown, try something new, risk being wrong. Think about learning and risk with a wider lens than the classroom. Often, to learn something new, we must let go of an old belief or old knowledge. This is dangerous because there could be real consequences. We never have any guarantee that new knowledge will be useful. Our old beliefs were formed for a reason (even if it's not always a good one), and they likely provided us with a sense of security. The act of learning something new can be difficult and uncomfortable.

If we apply this idea of learning risk to early humans, a person who has a tried-and-true method for making a weapon for hunting may be skeptical of the guy who's showing off his fancy new bow and arrow. Trying a new method *might* be a great success, but if it doesn't work or is a waste of time, the consequences could be life threatening. After all, wasted time hunting means no food, and that's a real threat. Our brains are still wired to anticipate major consequences when letting go of old ideas or trying new things. New things could be dangerous because, by definition, they represent the unknown.

Challenging our automatic reactions is no easy feat. Success in the learning environment requires a student to have a fully engaged prefrontal cortex so they can understand that the risks in our classrooms are not (usually) actual threats. When the prefrontal cortex is smoothly humming along, the limbic system can process emotional and sensory experiences. The prefrontal cortex can also tell the amygdala's alarm system to turn off. The brainstem does not have to tell the student's nervous system to get ready for fight, flight, or freeze when learning something new.

In any given classroom, there will be some students who are easily thrown into threat mode. What that means for you as a teacher is that you may have interesting, purposeful, exciting content to share with your students, but because of their trauma history, they may not be able to receive and retain it. Often, students who fall behind because of trauma-induced behaviors are "treated" in the school system for defiance, poor attendance, or learning deficits. Some educational mindsets believe more time with the subject matter will make a difference or a certain punishment will motivate the student. But this is a backward approach to responding to trauma-induced issues.

The Empathetic Classroom

The Nervous System's Role in Healing

This brings us to what may be the most important questions: What can we do about this? How can we help ourselves and our students? First, it's key to acknowledge that many students with trauma slip past us. That's why it's important that we learn how to accommodate the unseen trauma in our classrooms. Being a trauma-informed educator includes the assumption that you will be working with trauma at all times, which will make you a better teacher for everyone.

Polyvagal theory suggests that we prepare for interactions with traumatized individuals by regulating our own nervous system, because when our students are with a person who has a regulated nervous system, it can increase their ability to regulate (Feldman 2007). The research on co-regulation is founded on the study of interactions between infants and their parents, starting in the womb. During pregnancy, biological rhythms between mother and child become synchronized. This type of bond for-mation occurs in other mammals too. Think about it as one person (or dog or sheep) showing, or modeling, the path to regulation for another. Our survival depends on it.

What about when we are experiencing our own trauma? Can we still support others in their regulation? After his son's death, Buck Turcotte found that there was no way to avoid talking about it in his classroom. Students saw it on his face and heard it in his voice. He still tears up at times when he walks by the poster he put outside his classroom, showing his son geared up for wrestling. He knew that the way to bring his own sense of regulation was to talk about his son. So when students want to know what happened, Buck tells the story of a kid who is like his students. This puts Buck in a vulnerable position, but he knows it's worth it. He prefers to be open with his students. "Allowing students to see me at my worst allows them to feel comfortable being at their worst."

Often when we are in distress, it's like someone has put a blindfold on us; we cannot see our way out of the distress. Even if we know a spider is not going to hurt us, every part of our being might be telling us otherwise. But when a parent places a crying baby on their chest, or a caregiver holds the hand of distressed patient, they communicate through their physical state that they can handle the distressed person's needs. When the receiver of this action encounters a regulated nervous state in someone else, this can send their own nervous system the message that it is okay. Similarly, when we cue

Chapter 9: Trauma Awareness

to our students "I've got this"—just as Buck did when showing his students how to continue to live while grieving—we help them know that they've got this too.

The nervous system controls a lot: heart rate, blood pressure, body temperature, breathing, digestion, bladder, and even our ability to speak. Think about the time you were asked to give a talk and suddenly the words didn't flow or the time you suddenly needed a bathroom when a flight was taking off. That was your nervous system at work, assessing for safety. We can learn to listen to its unique cues to help us navigate in and out of safe, uncertain, and dangerous situations.

In polyvagal theory, Porges describes our ability to sort out what is safe and what is dangerous as *neuroception*. This system awareness covers inside, outside, and between. *Inside* is noticing what is happening in your body—breathing, heart rate, sweat. *Outside* is noticing your surroundings—checking where the door is, noticing the speed of a car, watching a person move toward you. *Between* is when your nervous system engages with other people, individually or in groups. All this noticing happens in the background, and we often move among nervous system states without realizing it.

Our neuroception is what encourages us to connect—to ask someone on a date or give a hug to a friend. It may also lead us to avoid—to put off calling someone back or pretend we didn't see someone we knew at the grocery store. Increasing our understanding of our own neuroception in the classroom helps us see how our biology might be making decisions for us at times. Certain noises, smells, textures, or colors might indicate danger to us. People can send danger signals too. What causes a shift out of safety can be very subtle, such as the sound of the cooling system turning on, or a specific student moving out of our eyesight, or a certain adult entering the classroom. You can use the Noticing Cues activity on page 155 to begin tuning into your own cues.

The States of the Nervous System

Polyvagal theory also suggests that our nervous system has three states: dorsal vagal, sympathetic, and ventral vagal. The dorsal vagal state is our system of shutdown, and when it's in charge we feel numb, depressed, and disconnected. It's a branch of the parasympathetic nervous system. The sympathetic state is our system of action, and when we're in this state we are typically anxious, chaotic, and angry. The ventral vagal state is our system

The Empathetic Classroom

of connection, helping us be present, flexible, and able. Like the dorsal vagal state, it is a branch of the parasympathetic nervous system. It helps us feel like socializing.

Deb Dana, who is a major contributor to polyvagal work, uses the image of a ladder with her clients to show how the nervous system operates (2021). When we are calm, we are at the top of the ladder in a ventral state. As soon as we sense danger, we may drop lower on the ladder into an anxious sympathetic state. Finally, if we sense extreme danger, we drop even further into dorsal vagal state of freeze. The idea is that to return from a dorsal state to a calm and regulated one, we must pass through the experience of the sympathetic state again. Dana recommends also using your own words or images to identify which state you are in at a given moment. She uses weather as another way to differentiate the experience between states: sunny (ventral), stormy (sympathetic), and foggy (dorsal).

With a polyvagal lens, it's easier to see how the same situation—say, losing your keys—can elicit a different response depending on where you are on the ladder of your nervous system states, ranging from "No big deal" to "Everything is wrong!" The state of your nervous system or that of your students plays a role in every single one of your interactions and contributes to the inner narratives you create about yourself and each other. It isn't uncommon for a student to believe they are disliked by a teacher or peer based on that person's reactions, when, many times, it is the teacher or peer's own nervous system that is sending signals of danger that may have nothing to do with the student.

A Day in the Life

Let's imagine how your nervous system might look on a typical school day. You start your day at home by making coffee and catching up on social media. Looking at pictures of loved ones puts you in a happy ventral state. You write a few comments and like some posts. You're at the top of the ladder. You see that cousin Ed posted something about how unfair it is that teachers get their summers off, but you're able to shrug it off.

When you arrive at school you see several students waiting outside your door to talk to you about last night's homework. Realizing you're no longer in relaxation mode, your nervous system shifts into a more mobilized sympathetic state. You're not necessarily anxious, but you're no longer at home. When you begin working with students on their questions, you

Chapter 9: Trauma Awareness   **147**

realize that their anxiety is starting to increase your own. You're starting to move down the ladder.

It's a full day, and you have a stack of grading to catch up on since you decided not to take it home last night. Normally, during recess breaks, you roam the halls catching up with fellow teachers or wander outside to watch your students play. Today, though, your head is buried in papers. You notice your irritation increase toward yourself for not doing these sooner and toward your students for not following the homework directions you repeated to them several times. The beginning of a headache comes on. Cousin Ed's post comes to mind again, and you start to envision how you might uninvite him from the upcoming family game night.

At noon, you're starving and looking forward to heading to the lounge and enjoying your leftover green bean casserole from last night. Right as you exit your classroom, you see a certain parent making a beeline toward you, and they don't look happy. You've seen this look before. This is a parent you've bumped heads with in the past, and you don't want to do it today. But rather than move toward them or away, you suddenly feel stuck in indecision. As they walk up to you and start talking, your brain struggles to hear anything other than *you've done something wrong*.

You have moved down the ladder again into an immobilized dorsal state. You stay here for a moment, until you work up the courage to ask the parent if they'd like to have a seat in your classroom. The offer is a risk, and you feel your fight or flight instincts kicking in, meaning you've moved back up to a sympathetic state. This offer catches the parent off guard, and you notice them relax a bit. They suddenly notice the casserole in your hands and realize you were off to lunch. Taking their own risk, they suggest meeting at the end of the school day so you can have a break for lunch. You notice your regulation increasing as you move further up the ladder—so much so that you feel downright amicable toward this parent and even ask them how their new business is going.

What Nervous System Changes Tell Us

While we might prefer to exist in a regulated ventral state most of the time, our other states can serve an important purpose too. Sometimes we might need to dip into a dorsal state and disconnect from our surroundings for a moment to protect ourselves. Or we might need to cue our sympathetic system's anxiety to give us a burst of energy to do something difficult. It can

The Empathetic Classroom

help to remember that anxious or sad feelings are not "bad" or problematic emotions—they are our nervous system alerting us to something that *feels* threatening. By the same token, avoiding all things that might cause anxiety or sadness, rather than facing them head on, often only perpetuates our fears. In addition, "blended" nervous system states are required for both play (ventral and sympathetic) and rest (ventral and dorsal). It's only when we become stuck in a dorsal or sympathetic state for an extended period of time, or constantly cycle between the two, that we experience symptoms associated with a clinical diagnosis of depression or anxiety.

With practice, you can learn to discern when your nervous system is activated and which system it might be operating in by noticing how you feel in your body. Did your heart rate speed up? Did you start to sweat? Are your breaths shallow? Do you feel like you might faint—or explode? How's your stomach? In a knot? These might be signs that your body is in a sympathetic state. Even your senses are often heightened when your nervous system is in the sympathetic state and on high alert. Noises, light, touch, or smells might seem more troubling than usual. If, on the other hand, you are in a deep dorsal state, sensory experiences might seem dulled. Clinicians hear people who are experiencing depression talk about how colors appear less bright.

Nervous system changes can also manifest in your emotions. To spot sympathetic activation, be on the lookout for increased irritability, extra energy, anxiety, anger, or higher reactivity. To spot dorsal activation, be on the lookout for feelings of hopelessness, tiredness, sadness, numbness, or dissociation, which is a feeling of disconnection from your own body or mind. You know you are in ventral vagal when your emotions include calmness, clarity, curiosity, confidence, and compassion.

You can regulate your nervous system by letting it know you are safe. One way of doing this is through anchoring. Deb Dana suggests identifying people or things that help you feel "anchored" when you get dysregulated (2021). When a ship anchors, it is able to still move about somewhat freely without drifting out to sea, where it will get lost. Anchoring is about finding the just-right balance of freedom and safety. To do this, make a list of people, things, sensory experiences, places, or actions that bring you a sense of calm (though not tiredness) and clarity. Choose one that has a strong sensory element and is easy for you to quickly access or imagine. Maybe it is being tucked away in a favorite corner under a blanket as a kid, or listening to the sound of rain on your roof, or touching a bracelet that a friend made for

Chapter 9: Trauma Awareness   **149**

you. Any time you start to notice anxious or depressive feelings taking over, imagine, look at, or feel your anchor. You may have to return to your anchor many times in a day.

For me as a teacher, anchoring was as simple as having a hot cup of anything. Observing my nervous system at the start of the school day, I noticed I was often anxious, even though I knew my students and felt prepared. My biological reaction didn't make logical sense. I started making a habit out of having a handmade mug and a hot drink ready to go at the start of each day. I also know I feel safe around water—spending time by a creek is one of my most grounding activities—and even the visual of the tiny body of water in my cup brings me calm. When I felt dysregulated, I could press the warm mug to my belly and feel safe. My heart rate slowed, and I could feel my breath again. Some teachers regulate by reading aloud to their class to start the day or moving to a place in their room that feels safer (maybe this is not the front of the room). You might regulate through adjusting conditions to support optimal body temperature, such as lowering the room temperature to increase alertness or wearing a warm jacket to increase feelings of safety. If you have a visual of a location that grounds you, frame a photo of it on your desk or put a photo of it on your wall. Notice what happens when you allow your body to be the compass for your classroom behaviors. You can also guide students in a similar process using the activity Getting to Know My Nervous System on page 157.

Sometimes we are so accustomed to operating in a state of anxiety that we fear losing the drive that comes with anxiety if we regulate. Often, our anxiety can be so integral to our experience that we don't even notice it. We might just feel like we are buzzing or jittery. We might fear that we won't get as much done or that we won't seem as engaged or excited. So, we avoid regulating even when we know it might be good for us. Feeling calm shouldn't mean the absence of engagement, productivity, or excitement; it is the absence of a dysregulated physical state. It is thought and action without fear.

What to Do When Students Perceive Threats

Part of being a trauma-informed teacher is noticing when your students become triggered, as well as identifying—when you can—what caused a triggered reaction. Here are some signs that a student might be sensing danger and is in a sympathetic state:

The Empathetic Classroom

- Changes in posture: becoming physically small, hunching, turning away, looking deflated; or getting big, disregarding others' physical boundaries, looking ready to fight
- Sudden reactions: throwing items, yelling, shaking, crying, self-harm (be especially on the lookout for students who are "accident-prone" with items like staplers, scissors, or any sharp or hot objects, as some self-harm can easily go unnoticed and is also a sign of needing professional support)
- Irritability or angry outbursts
- Face or other skin suddenly flushing or sweating
- Repetitive, tic-like, or impulsive behaviors: hair pulling or twisting, nail tearing, skin picking, rocking, scratching, excessive rubbing on skin, changes in blinking patterns, shaking
- Running away
- Damaging objects

These are indications that a student may already be shut down and in a dorsal state:

- Poor grades
- Difficulty concentrating
- Excessive tiredness
- Lack of facial expression
- Difficulty verbalizing; becoming mute
- Increased absences
- Substance use
- Low motivation
- Withdrawal
- Changes in personal care or hygiene
- Dramatic weight gain or loss
- Freezing or shutting down at comments or questions

When you notice a reaction that indicates a student feels under threat, check in with them about their reaction. *I noticed you were shaking today when Sam was presenting the news report. I'm wondering if hearing about the war was scary for you? What was on your mind?*

Not all reactions are based in trauma, but if you notice fear or blankness in a student, that can be a sign that their prefrontal cortex is not functioning well. If a student seems shut down, approach them with warmth and provide

Chapter 9: Trauma Awareness

a sense of security. *I can see you're shutting down again, and I wonder if you might like to try wearing earplugs during work time?* By contrast, responding with anger, distrust, or even exhaustion reinforces the message to students that they are under threat from all sides. To make myself "smaller" and less threatening, I may kneel next to a distressed student and lower and soften my voice. I might then offer an opportunity to change environments temporarily to provide relief. Introducing a different and safe element can work to de-escalate the level of threat in your student's brain and begin to reengage their prefrontal cortex.

In addition, working with a student who is in threat mode calls for avoiding talking extensively and offering endless choices. When the brain experiences a trauma response, it cannot process language. So we are not helping students by talking at them in these situations. I find that many of my young clients who have experienced trauma need space and closeness at the same time. Their body language may be telling me to distance myself from them, and I respect that, yet I also know that it is a conditioned response. It is how they have learned to protect themselves. When I first started counseling, I gave clients the distance I thought they were asking for. Often, after doing this, I observed increased anger or further shutting down. Now I have learned to stay present with them rather than avoiding them or moving away. I let them know I am with them, and that we will work through it together. I might find a lower position such as on the floor, set down anything I am holding, relax my facial expression and shoulders, and find my own regulation through slow, quiet breaths. Security comes when they trust that you know what you are doing and that you will take the lead.

Your goal when working with a student who is experiencing threat is to support them in engaging their ventral vagal or regulated response and to help them find ways to feel anchored. You are also seeking a balance between addressing this student's nervous system needs while respecting the space and the nervous systems of the students around them. Here are some ideas to start.

Do breathwork. Remind the student to take a slow breath in and let it out slowly several times. This works to lower the cortisol levels that increase in the body when it assumes it is under threat. I usually take deep breaths as I'm asking them to. Be aware that some students have heard "take a breath" so many times that they associate it with adults who are projecting stress at them—just the phrase can produce strong feelings and a desire *not* to take a breath. In this case, you might have to get creative. "Puff your cheeks out like a balloon and slowly press the air out with your fingers." "Breathe in a color that makes you feel good. Breathe out a color that you want to release."

Engage the senses. "Go wash your hands in warm water and take a moment." "Wash your face with some cold water." "Go stand at the window and see if you can spot one item for each color of the rainbow." "Grab a piece of peppermint candy out of the jar." Allow the student to bring in a calming scented oil they can rub on their temples.

Get physical. If a student's body is telling them to run away, and if you or another adult can keep an eye on them, let them run. This tells the body that it did what it needed to do. If there is a safe, soft object like a pillow to squish, squeeze, pinch, or punch, this may speak to some students' desire to fight without actually hurting anyone. If they can put headphones on and dance like nobody's watching, let them.

Another useful strategy is progressive muscle relaxation, which works well to help people relax when they have pent-up emotions or energy. Ask the student to squeeze their face as tight as they can and hold it for five seconds, then release. You can move through the body's major muscle groups one at a time, asking them to tense their muscles for five seconds and release, until they have reached their toes.

Other individuals experience relief when feeling their body squeezed. For younger students, you might provide access to a yoga mat. A student can lie down on the mat and roll themselves up in it like a burrito to help relieve physical distress.

Make some noise. Singing, humming, and chanting help activate the vagus nerve. Have the student pick a low note and see if you can match tones with them. This is also a way to connect, which will also help return them to a state of regulation. Have them put headphones on and listen to chanting or singing bowls.

Take a rest. Sometimes even a short rest can return the brain to a functional state. Let the student do what they need to do to get cozy. It's best if there's a place to stretch out on the floor and let go of all their muscle tension. If they only have their desk, allow them items like an eye mask or something soft to rest their head on.

Chapter 9: Trauma Awareness

KEY POINTS

- Trauma is the body's remembered physical and emotional state that occurred when something shocking or disturbing happened. Unresolved trauma can make it seem as if the traumatic event is in the present rather than the past. The body experiences it as real rather than a memory.
- Many types of events and experiences can cause trauma.
- Students may experience feelings of threat from school environments.
- When traumatic events occur, the brainstem is engaged to help a person survive. Reasoning, planning, and emotional processing are usually not functioning.
- Triggers can return a person to the state of threat they experienced during the trauma.
- The nervous system can get stuck in a state of immobilization (dorsal) or anxiety (sympathetic).
- Students who feel threatened may not be able to learn or take healthy risks.
- You can notice signs that your students feel under threat.
- You can initiate coregulation with your students by regulating your own nervous system.
- You can support deactivating students' fight-or-flight response through engaging the ventral vagal part of their parasympathetic nervous system. These actions—breathwork, sensory experiences, noise making, muscle relaxation, movement—tell the body there is no current threat.

For Teachers

NOTICING CUES

This activity is from the brilliant polyvagal theory proponent Deb Dana (2021). A body scan can help you get to know what feels safe and what feels scary to you. Everyone's nervous system is unique, and people may have different responses to the same things. And sometimes your nervous system tells you that something is dangerous when it might not be, like feeling afraid of a (benign) bug or having to speak in front of a group.

I recommend placing your hands on your heart, belly, and lungs when these parts of the body are referenced in the activity to better connect with the physical experience. Notice that this exercise moves you through danger and back to safety. During any given day, we all move through moments of danger (or discomfort) and back again—being human requires it. This activity builds flexibility in the nervous system and helps you learn to forge a recognizable path back to safety when you need it.

The following is an excerpt from Deb Dana's book *Anchored* (copyright 2021 by Deborah A. Dana, used with permission from the author and the publisher, Sounds True, Inc.):

- What are the cues of danger in this moment in your body? Start with a simple body scan. Is there any aching, tension, soreness, or numbness? Listen to your digestion, heart rate, and breath. Let your body show you cues of danger.
- What are cues of safety in this moment in your body? Listen to your body. Find the places of ease, warmth, and flexibility. Feel your heart and breath rhythms. Let your body show you cues of safety.
- What are the cues of danger in this moment in the immediate environment around you? Bring your awareness to the space you are inhabiting. Look around and see what is distressing to you.

continued

Chapter 9: Trauma Awareness   **155**

- Move your awareness out into the larger environment. As you look outside your space to the world around you, what do you find that feels distressing?
- What are the cues of safety in this moment in the immediate environment around you? Bring your awareness back to the space you are in. Look around you and see what brings you joy. Find what helps anchor you in regulation.
- And now move your awareness back out to the larger environment. As you look outside your space to the world around you, what do you find that feels nourishing?
- What are the cues of danger in this moment in your connection with others? Look for signs of warning that your social engagement system is sending or receiving from someone's eyes, facial expression, tone of voice, posture, and movements.
- What are the cues of safety in this moment in your connection with others? Look for the signs of welcome that your social engagement system is sending or receiving from someone's eyes, facial expression, tone of voice, posture, and movements.

For Students

GETTING TO KNOW MY NERVOUS SYSTEM

These activities support your students in increasing their own neuroception. Before beginning any of the following activities, you may want to explain that the nervous system is a messaging system between the brain and different parts of the body. It tells us when we are safe and can rest, eat, or play. It tells us when we are scared and need to run or fight. And it tells us when we are sad and need to stay in place. Most of the time, it does these things without us choosing it. Introduce the three nervous system states and provide examples of what each might look or feel like. If I am working with younger students, I avoid using terms like dorsal, sympathetic, and ventral, and instead provide basic feelings words, such as sad (dorsal), scared (sympathetic), and calm (ventral).

Activity 1: Visualization
To visualize the parts of the nervous system, you may ask students to depict each state with images. If you do this, ask them to divide their paper into three sections, like a ladder. At the bottom portion of the paper, have them create what dorsal vagal looks and feels like to them; above that, sympathetic; and finally, ventral vagal at the top. Or you may want to compare each state to a type of weather or other concept students can easily visualize. I've found that older students often enjoy very creative metaphors . . . dorsal is like pea soup, sympathetic is like Pop Rocks, ventral is like Jell-O.

Activity 2: Movement
Help students understand what movements or body language are associated with safety or danger. Exploring the nervous system through drama and movement can increase students' awareness of their own states and

continued

Chapter 9: Trauma Awareness   **157**

help them recognize ways in and out of them. Ask students to spread out around the room. The rules are no touching others and no talking during this exercise.

Ask students to move around the room in a way that feels relaxed. Tell them to notice the relaxation in every part of their body, from eyebrows to toes. This is ventral state, or safety. Give students a moment to really get into it.

Freeze. Now ask students to pose in a way that communicates feeling a little scared. Have them notice how it feels in their face, muscles, and breathing or heart rate. Hold it for a moment.

Now tell students to move slowly out of this pose of danger to a pose of strength. This is using the brave part of anxiety. Have them move about the room in a way that feels brave. (You may need to remind them here not to touch others. If it becomes too frantic, you can ask them to move in slow motion. If I'm working with a group that is a bit more reserved, I may join along and really amp up the drama, shoulders back, head high, maybe arms up.) Have them move in a way that feels good to them.

Freeze. Ask students to find a pose that communicates a big danger and notice what they feel in their body as they hold this pose. Then have them imagine a place they love where they feel safe—imagine the colors, temperature, sounds, smells. Tell students to ask their body to relax as they picture this place. Have them breathe slowly. Have them imagine a soothing color from the place washing over their entire body.

Finally, tell students to slowly come out of their stress pose to a more relaxed pose. Allow students to bask in this pose for a couple minutes. Have them come back into the room and begin stretching or rubbing their face or muscles to bring some energy back into their bodies. Form a circle for discussion of the following questions:

- What was the experience of moving from relaxed to scared like?
- Did your body do anything that surprised you?
- What were some of the themes or similar actions you observed in the group to show safety or feeling relaxed? For danger or feeling scared?

- How did your connection with others change when you moved from safety to danger? How did you feel when this changed?
- What was the difference in your body between relaxed and brave (or strong)? When in life might we need to move out of relaxed and into brave?
- Sometimes our nervous system tells us that something is scary and it really *is* something that could be dangerous—like a dog that is growling or trying to bite you, for example. But other times when we feel fear, it is our nervous system sensing danger where there may not be any, like when we're meeting a new person. What did you notice happened when you envisioned your favorite place and let it wash over you?
- What other ideas do you have to help your nervous system find a calm or a brave place?

Activity 3: Anchoring

Finally, you can support students in establishing their own anchor in the classroom. It could be as simple as explaining what an anchor is and saying that they can try to find one inside of themselves (as in picturing their favorite place) or outside of themselves. You could ask students if there is anything in the room or a small item that they can bring from home to anchor them, such as a nice-feeling rock or a small stuffed animal.

If bringing items to school seems logistically challenging, you can take time to make an anchor collage. Bring in magazines that have themes that are likely to increase regulation, such as nature, homes, food, or artistic photography. I suggest avoiding magazines that are full of images of people, as these can easily bring up insecurities in students. Ask students to select images that their nervous systems like—visuals that help them feel calm, peaceful, or pleasant. Glue these images onto cardstock and find eye-level places in the room to display the collages. Remind students that they can visit these anchors when they begin to feel distress.

continued

Chapter 9: Trauma Awareness   **159**

Post-Activity Check-In

You could conclude any of these activities by asking students to reflect on where on the ladder of nervous system states they were when they began the exercise and to notice where they are at the end of it. If you or your students are feeling stuck in a dorsal or sympathetic state, it's very likely that you will not find regulation through doing one activity. If this is the case, you can regularly check in with students about things they know can help them reach the top of the ladder, or the ventral state. What makes them feel calm and ready to be with people? You can also get to know individual students' cues that they are in distress. I knew one of my students was distressed if I noticed them ripping or folding paper or exhibiting repetitive tics such as twisting hair, picking skin, or tearing or biting nails. If you spot behaviors that indicate a student's distress, provide support in identifying what they can do to feel more regulated.

10

ALL ABOUT POWER IN SCHOOLS

*Literature teacher Mr. Wells was considered the most seasoned educator in his school. He was in his thirtieth year of teaching and had long ago reached the top of his school's pay chart. He was given his pick of which courses he'd teach each year, and he would spend the summer reading and creating a new curriculum based on his latest interests. His classes were known for being dynamic and challenging, which was equally fear-inducing and enticing to his students.

At lunch, students would vent to each other about how much they hated his class, but he had a 100 percent attendance and participation rate. He prided himself on the number of student photos he had pinned behind his desk, each representing an acceptance into an Ivy League school. He would occasionally drop a pin at the beginning of class, just to hear it land on the tiles in front of his silent and eager audience.

His favorite poem to teach was William Wordsworth's "I Wandered Lonely as a Cloud." He would recite it by heart for his students with perfect diction and tone. When he concluded, eager hands shot into the air from students hoping to contribute admiration and analysis.

After such a reading one fall day, a new student to the school, Tate, raised their hand. Mr. Wells nodded, waiting to hear the usual praise. "I think it's kind of a stupid poem," said Tate. "I mean, are clouds actually lonely? And why is the author so narcissistic? I mean, it's not a poem about nature, it's about him." Jaws dropped around the room. No one had ever heard of a student dissing Mr. Wells's choice in poetry. Mr. Wells, unblinking, turned to Sarah, who had her hand raised as well, and proceeded to ignore Tate's comment.

161

> The next day before class, Tate found a small card taped to their locker, embossed with the gold letters G.W. It was a note from Mr. Wells asking Tate not to attend lit class and instead to spend that period in the library for the next two days until analysis of the poem was finished. Mr. Wells concluded by saying that he looked forward to more constructive discourse from Tate in the future. Tate stared at the note in disbelief before tearing it up.

The day you were given your license and became a teacher is the day you were handed the rights and responsibilities of a profession with an immense amount of power. Though teaching salaries will never measure up to that power, it probably wasn't money that drew you to the profession anyhow. You're more likely a purpose-driven individual who, for some reason, was drawn to a tiny classroom packed with sweaty humans. Maybe you wanted to change something, to be something you didn't have as a student, to play a part you know is needed.

On our journey from wondering if teaching is the right profession for us, to our teaching program, and, finally, to our exams and licensure, we pass gatekeepers along the way who are often so thankful we are there with our big hearts and eager minds that they hate to slow us down with intricacies that might only be fully understood once we are actually teaching.

The Elephant in the Room

One of these invaluable missing lessons is about an awareness of your own relationship with and use of power. We assume a lot of things about our fellow humans, and when it comes to power, the assumption tends to be that "good" people with "good" intentions would not use their power to cause suffering for others. And from the beginning, we as teachers are given the badge of being "good, kind, caring, and thoughtful" people. No pressure! And yet . . . even teachers with the best intentions (including myself) can and do cause suffering for their students, especially when they are not aware of the power dynamic in the classroom and do not make conscious choices to account for it.

The Empathetic Classroom

Power as a Tool

When I was a young teaching aide in a behavioral learning room, I observed the power of Ms. B in action. First off, anyone who has taught in a room specifically for students who have instability at home and who struggle to find purpose in education knows that this is one of the most challenging environments in which to be an authority figure. Students often ran away, sometimes they hit, and no amount of kindness seemed to make a difference. These kids were there because they'd been hurting for most of their lives. Ms. B was there, I think, just to do her job. She had lots of rules, a domineering physical presence, and cupcakes.

When I was eighteen, I was hungry all the time. As Ms. B's aide, I watched, salivating, as she ate a cupcake each day very slowly in front of her students. The entire day, the students were told that they only got a cupcake if they were "well behaved." I now know that these students didn't know what "well behaved" even was. They had learned that survival with their primary attachment figures meant engaging in behaviors that got noticed: tantrums, running away, hitting. This got attention that ultimately helped them stay safe.

Now, here was this strange woman telling them the opposite: sit still, do what I say, and then you will be rewarded for your behavior. But if they sat still at home while abuse was happening, this could put their life in danger. And there were no cupcake rewards at home. This must have seemed like pure gibberish to them.

In practice, Ms. B decided on her own (sometimes inconsistent or even contradictory) standards for what warranted a cupcake. Billy only hit two students today instead of three, so he gets a cupcake. Marley cried all day; she doesn't get a cupcake. Maria is a substitute who earns more than I do in a day, so she definitely doesn't get a cupcake.

I remember going home at the end of those days feeling deflated and hungry. Those days seemed like a more exaggerated version of what I had often experienced as a child in school. The teacher was using a language with the students that they didn't know or understand and then handing out random rewards. While I felt quite peeved about Ms. B's behavior at the time, I can now see that she too was in survive-or-die mode. She used the only power she thought she had to try to condition her students into her version of good behavior. And it may have gotten her through each day, but the day-to-day mentality she was living in had to be exhausting.

Chapter 10: All About Power in Schools

Getting to Know Your Power

Often, if we come into this profession unaware of our own power, we soon are introduced to it through subtle and seemingly harmless teacher-student interactions. We learn which words or sounds can get command of the room. A dramatic pause with the right expression can be quite effective at getting the group's attention. Students learn to read their teachers, just as they read their primary attachments at home—*this look means he's in a good mood, this one means a storm is brewing, that one means I went too far!* Teachers also learn to read their students and use facial expressions, words, gestures, posture, and countless micro-cues to get things accomplished. Every classroom's ecosystem has its own language, as well as spoken and unspoken rules and expectations. In the chapter's opening story, Tate questioned the unspoken rules of Mr. Wells's classroom—which were to agree with Mr. Wells and like what he liked. In doing so, Tate seemed to embarrass Mr. Wells. And as a result, Mr. Wells felt he needed to communicate to the whole class what happened when anyone challenged his authority. Tate was banished from the classroom community lest their rebellious behavior become contagious.

Whether you like it or not, as a classroom teacher, you are the leader of a community. Some of your power may even go unnoticed to you via identities you inhabit. Race, gender, sexuality, class, religious beliefs, and ability are just some of the ways power operates in society. Plus, your personality, philosophies, passions, ideas about how things should work, and your own history of schooling are all present from day one when students enter with no prior knowledge of your unique language. In that moment, they are vulnerable.

Letting Your Students In

Thinking back to your own days as a student, do you remember having that teacher who you thought you could tease and then learned very quickly, nope!? Or the one who said you could write a paper however you wanted, and then graded you harshly for doing it "wrong"? These are all common missteps by students who have no idea what the rules are of the world they are entering. But as the teacher, you do know the rules, and you know yourself. It is in everyone's best interest for you to look at yourself honestly and help your students understand and learn about your classroom's world.

Power Through Assessment: Grading as Classical Conditioning for "Worth"

Assignments and grading are concrete examples of our power. And assigning homework and giving grades seem to be pillars of the classroom for teachers. But let's take a moment to really consider what this entails from a power perspective. Understanding this dynamic requires glancing back to the origins of assignments and grading. In their earliest form, assignments were a way for a philosopher's pupils to prove that they'd taken in the philosopher's teachings and now possessed that knowledge. The pupil could then become the philosopher and pass it on. Teachers today say you need to "show your work." These are variations of the same recipe. And at their core, they're all about worthiness. *If you can show me that you've understood me, I know I've done what I set out to do. I can die happy now.*

In other words, it's a little ego stroke for you as a teacher when your students do well on their comprehensive exams, or when parents tell you how proud they are of their student for getting an A instead of another B in math. (And if students do poorly, this also reflects on you.) But receiving an assignment is and can be a form of threat to students, especially if they don't understand your language and intentions.

Like assignments, grading began as a way to serve the teacher and the system rather than the student. Initially, in many institutions, students were not told their "marks" or rank so that the focus would not become competing for the best score. Instead, marks were a way for institutions like Cambridge University to evaluate their scholars from behind closed doors. So this mark had an impact on the scholar; they just weren't immediately aware of it. Fast forward to the 1900s in the United States, where compulsory mass education meant school systems had to figure out how to communicate with each other, and the A-to-F scheme was born. A university could now look at a piece of paper and determine if a student was fit for their institution. Again, the focus was on making it easy for institutions to assess student "worthiness."

Students, meanwhile, were and still are forced to play the guessing game of figuring out what output produces what response from their teacher. And because every teacher is different, every year students have to start all over again. Maybe by the end of last year they had finally learned what Mr. Becker deemed A-quality work. This year they're trying the same tricks with you but discovering they don't work the same way. Can you feel your students' nervous systems activating as you describe your first big project or assignment of the year? The hands shooting up with questions. The scribbling on paper. The student who is suddenly more interested in cleaning out their desk than listening to you. Someone breaks their pencil in half. This is them sensing threat.

In psychology, this is a case of classical conditioning. You remember Pavlov and the bell and the salivating dog? We as educators can easily fall into a role of conditioning our students without even realizing it. *If you do this, you get an A. I'm happy; you're happy. If you do this, you get an F. I'm not happy; you're not happy.* In the opening story, it's clear that Mr. Wells had conditioned his students, as it was out of the norm for anyone to question him. Whatever the specifics, students either comply with the conditioning and are "successful," or they don't comply and they "fail." After a while, some students—tired of the guessing game—would rather choose the familiar comfort of failure over the constant sustained effort to please you, along with every teacher before and after you for at least thirteen years of their life.

While we may say that grades don't matter in the long run, the truth is they can have a very real impact on a student's reality. Grades often group students into categories, essentially labeling them in ways that suggest unambiguous worth. I see many clients in my office who tell me they were a "straight-A student," or that they were a failure as an "F student." They look at me as if I should know what they mean by this. Grades can impact our sense of self-worth, our sense of capability, our decision-making, our friendships, our relationships with our families, the way our teachers view us, and the opportunities that come next. We don't want students to spiral into unhelpful panic about grades, but their fear is real and warranted. And when students are no longer afraid but apathetic, this too is the result of a system that isn't always upfront with its customers about how it works.

Power Through Communication: Direct Versus Indirect

In our attempts to consciously or subconsciously maintain a sense of power or control, we use verbal and nonverbal communication methods to convey meaning. We communicate many things to our students, coworkers, families, and friends, sometimes directly and sometimes indirectly. For instance, consider the note Mr. Wells left for Tate rather than having a conversation with them in the chapter-opening story. In our own lives, we might communicate indirectly to a loved one by leaving the dishwasher open to suggest that it is their turn to put dishes away. Or we might fear hurting a friend's feelings, so we do not respond their text. This is all indirect communication, and it is an attempt to maintain a sense of power or control when it feels like it's slipping away. You'll also hear some indirect communication referred to as passive aggressive communication, in that it is meant to express disapproval or dislike but is couched in a manner that seems "nicer." Many people do this without being aware that it's happening.

In psychotherapy, indirect communication is viewed as common yet highly problematic. The challenge with indirect communication is that it leaves a lot of room for personal interpretation, confusion, and hurt. The receiver of indirect communication will lack clarifying details that could help explain what the sender of the message means. Direct communication, on the other hand, is clear about the message and its meaning. It is not embellished, and the communicator does not claim to know things they do not. It does not need to be hurtful, though you cannot control what others might feel hurt by.

When I work on direct and indirect communication with clients, I often draw two dots on a marker board and explain that one dot is them and the other dot is the person they want to communicate with. Between them I draw a large circle to represent what needs to be communicated. I say, "When you communicate to your friend indirectly, it's like going the long way around the edge of the large circle, or the issue to discuss. It takes a lot longer to get the message to the other person and there are a lot of things that happen to the message on the way. Sometimes the message changes en route. The other option is to go from yourself right through the middle of the circle to the other person, or right through the heart of the issue." Usually, I see squirming when the client imagines this option—*you mean, just tell them?!*

When indirect communication is someone's preferred route, it usually means that they are afraid their message will imply that they are someone they do not want to be seen as or will hurt the other person. So they choose indirect communication—sometimes consciously, sometimes subconsciously—because they see it as an opportunity to soften the message, confuse the receiver, and appear as if they are not actively trying to affect the receiver. Guess what? Most recipients of indirect communication can still feel hurt, confused, or angry. And when we choose the indirect route, the message can end up being something very different from what we intended. Our attempts to avoid and obscure often result in a bigger mess. To get a

Chapter 10: All About Power in Schools

sense of when—and why—you may turn to this style of communication, try the Noticing My Communication Patterns activity on page 178.

Opening Up to Feedback

Power in classrooms can also take the form of students believing they need to agree with their teachers to succeed. (Just like the rest of us, they may struggle to communicate directly.) Educators are often drawn to teaching and emphasizing content we have a passion for—a certain book, a specific area of science, a type of writing, our favorite kind of math problem. It can be disheartening, then, when students give us feedback that they don't like or aren't as interested in something as we are. Sometimes it can be easier to assume that students "just don't get it" than to accept the reality that they truly don't like it or don't agree with us—and that we might need to consider making changes in response to that feedback. If your students believe that to do well in your class, they need to be in your good graces, they often won't tell you when they find something boring or disagree with your thoughts or feedback.

One school year, I was teaching a fifth grade writing class. I decided it was a good idea to bring in a piece of my own writing for a revision session before asking my students to be vulnerable and do the same with their writing. I thought it would be interesting to let them offer feedback before I told them who wrote it. They were excellent editors and found every issue in my work. *Cut this, change that, don't get that part, this doesn't make any sense!* When they felt the freedom to give real feedback, it was great. I had prepared myself for this and had my writer's ego in check. Then, when I told them I was the author, a look of dread crossed their faces. Suddenly they told me how amazing the piece was, and how they didn't really mean what they'd said about it. While I tried to reassure them that I really appreciated their honest feedback, it was clear they believed they'd crossed a line that they were not supposed to cross with their teacher. This was a lesson in how students have learned to fine-tune their responses to be accepted by their teachers, regardless of what they truly think and feel.

When You Give Feedback

Your power also runs the opposite way when you *give* feedback to students. It is important to be direct with your students and not shy away from feedback altogether, but you also need to consider the impact of your feedback.

168 *The Empathetic Classroom*

Teachers' comments on assignments are often accepted as fact: "My teacher said I'm not good at technical writing." A comment like this can alter a person's life course. The seeming authority and expertise of teachers means their assessment holds a lot of weight. Teachers' words, if not chosen with great care, can become part of an internal narrative that students hold and believe for a lifetime. For students like Tate, a negative association may begin to form around poetry analysis, literature in general, or participating in class—*unless* Mr. Wells actively repairs the conflict with them, or unless future teachers see what's happening with Tate and work to counter the association.

If a student does not have the skills to use the feedback as an opportunity to grow—skills that are fairly advanced and still difficult for many adults—even constructive feedback can be interpreted as a reason *not* to do something, as a reason to believe they will always be "bad" at something, or as a judgment on their very being. On the flip side, using your power to provide genuine positive or validating feedback can similarly change how a student views their capabilities. Many adults remember when they won a school award or received glowing praise for an accomplishment. This relatively simple recognition can lead to more engagement from students, including with content or tasks that are difficult for them. Even with this "good" form of power, it's important to raise our own awareness of how and why we are using it.

The Power Balance

What do we do with this power balance—or imbalance—inherent to our profession? One possible solution is to hand over those velvet reins of power to your students. You've seen this before, haven't you? Fearing becoming what they hated, a teacher may veer hard to the opposite side of the spectrum when it comes to power in the classroom. They sit back and let their students figure things out, emphasizing the lack of rules, boundaries, or expectations and leaning on natural consequences as the path to order. *If Sammy falls while hanging from the gym bleachers, I bet she'll never do it again.* This teacher does not have to be the bad guy. They might even be nurturing an ember of hope that they can be the friend. While I believe there's a place for anti-establishment educators and natural consequences, a *Lord of the Flies*–style classroom will inevitably lead to a student seeking and

Chapter 10: All About Power in Schools

assuming power. And this student doesn't have your training, experience, perspective, or goals.

The first step is to address the truth of our power as adults and as educators, not fool ourselves into thinking that we are somehow outside of it. We hold immense power and responsibility, and we should notice and question it daily. Begin asking yourself questions like the following:

- What are the ways in which I feel I must do something to get a response from my students? Do I take certain actions, have strategies, or use cues to elicit desired reactions? (For example, maybe you have "a look" that you give students when you disapprove of something.)
- What behavioral or emotional responses do my students have to these interactions?
- Have I addressed this power dynamic with them? If not, what is stopping me? (If what is stopping you is a feeling of vulnerability or a fear of the unknown, this is a sign that you might be coming up against something insightful about your relationship to power.)
- What might I be doing, intentionally or unintentionally, that could discourage students from challenging me or offering honest feedback?
- Do I have any methods for encouraging constructive feedback for my teaching?
- What would happen if my students were to challenge me?
- What do I fear as a teacher?
- How might this fear lead to relying on my sense of power?

You can dig further into these ideas using the My Power Associations activity on page 176. Exploring this concept can be challenging—but the good news is that the solution to the power imbalance is already as much of a part of you as the power itself is. You can accept and hold the natural power that comes through experience, training, and age, and also be both predictable and flexible to provide a sense of safety and well-being for your students.

Being predictable means you have your classroom policies ironed out before students arrive. You know how you feel about the tasks you are giving your students, and you have a sense of how much time and effort should go into them. There aren't surprise quizzes (which cause massive

The Empathetic Classroom

cortisol spikes) or constant changes after an assignment is underway. You don't change how you grade something after the fact—you provide clear grading rubrics, and you stick to them. You have thought through your classroom management policies, and you are able and confident in explaining the rationale behind them. You provide plenty of time for questions. You anticipate and speak to concerns you might have if you were a student in your classroom. Predictable can feel "boring" to the creative educator, but predictability for your students will reduce their feeling of being under threat, which will allow their brains to focus on more creative pursuits.

Being flexible means you are open to feedback and can make adjustments when warranted. If students explain to you that last night's homework took them five hours instead of the two you predicted, take heed! This does not mean you should immediately or rashly make a change—consistent responses are part of being predictable. Feedback can mean many things, and it is your job to collect more data to sort it out. Maybe students focused on something you didn't expect, misunderstood the directions, or aren't reading at the same level last year's students were. Letting students know that you have expectations but are also open to feedback will help them understand that giving constructive feedback is a way they can safely check your power. If you respect their check, they will tend not to abuse it.

You can also model offering positive and constructive feedback when you provide students with *support, context,* and some *choice.* In doing so, you convey that they are not alone (thereby turning off any abandonment alarms), provide clarity on what the feedback does and does not mean, and help them move toward or away from a threat. Nervous systems need these cues in order to regulate. Teachers are accustomed to giving feedback and may not think twice about doing it. Students, however, may perceive it as a really big deal. Providing context with your feedback is a way to say, *Hey, it's not a big deal*—because most things you are giving feedback on are *not* big deals in the grand scheme of life.

Your approach to feedback should also adjust based on *who* you are providing it to and what you know about them. For instance, if I have a second grader who is struggling with multiplication tables and their parents are reporting tantrums when they begin practicing them each evening, I may decide to offer support by reducing the pressure and not grading their assignments for a while so they aren't seeing a long string of low grades. I may meet with them individually to let them know I see them working hard

Chapter 10: All About Power in Schools

(context) and ask if they have ideas for making the learning less stressful (support and choice). I might provide empathy (support) for how difficult learning can be. (When offering empathy, if empathizing about a specific thing feels disingenuous or unnatural, imagine anything that has been a challenge for you, such as doing your taxes or having a difficult conversation with a friend. Remember that this may be the student's mountain, even if it seems small to you.) I would highlight what they are doing well and remind them that multiplication tables are like one fish in an ocean (context) and that it's okay if it takes time to learn them—I'd like them to get to know the other fish too! I would also remind their parents that it's okay to reduce the pressure at home.

If I were working with a student who is in middle school or above and wanted to ease them into what might be more challenging feedback on their work or classroom behavior, I would talk to them in person rather than providing written feedback. When we meet, I would take note of what cues the student is giving me as to the state of their nervous system. If they seem worried or scared, I may decide to connect with them first by talking about one of their interests or by checking in with them. When they have regulated—when I observe relaxed body posture, steady breath, engaged facial expressions—I would start by letting them know what I appreciate about them or their work. *I really appreciate how you always provide an unexpected angle to our class discussions. I think it encourages your classmates to try out new ideas too. Thank you for being so brave.* Then I would gently share that I noticed something that seemed challenging for them. Many older students will already know what you are referring to, and some may even feel relief at the direct communication about it. I would next ask if they are in a mindset today to talk about the situation. This is a genuine offer of choice! If they say no, I'd let them know that we'll touch base again soon. If the moment makes it more difficult to be ready to integrate feedback in a helpful way, neither of us is likely to benefit from the conversation.

With all feedback, it's essential to support students in identifying a path forward. If the feedback feels like a dead end, such as *you're not good at technical writing*, there is no opportunity for students to change this assessment or grow. Instead, try phrasing like this: *I noticed this type of writing assignment seemed challenging for you. I wonder if I could show you some of my tricks for getting through it.* This addresses the issue directly and truthfully, and offers support in trying a new approach. You can also take this opportunity to ask students if there is anything different you can do to better support them. Notice, I didn't tack on a lot of praise here. Older students, especially, tend to value supportive and direct communication rather than overt praise. You can show them you value who they are by how you treat them every day.

These examples of being present and flexible with your students are similar to a concept central to the therapeutic relationship. Existential psychiatrist Irvin Yalom confronted his own insecurities about power dynamics between therapist and client by working in what he calls the "here and now" (1980). He says, "Working on the here and now is working on the space . . . between me and patient" (Phillips 2021). He often will take the opportunity during a session to say to the client, "Let's take a look at how you and I are doing in this session. What's that like for you?" (Phillips 2021). This method doesn't avoid addressing the tough stuff, but it is unassuming and collaborative. It says we both get to work on things together. This can feel like a precarious position to situate yourself in as a teacher, but it gently adjusts the power dynamic to say, *I can handle some real feedback.*

Inviting Students to Challenge You

We can also work in the here and now with our students by encouraging students to disagree, challenge, or express distaste for something we teach. Students might need encouragement or practice to feel competent and safe in doing this. With my clients, I work on this skill by highlighting and praising times when they disagree with something I suggest. *I'm so glad you questioned that. Why don't you tell me more?*

I sometimes refer to the education system as a "game" to students or clients who feel they can't win at it. This is not to belittle an important facet of our society, but to introduce the perspective that navigating this system, with all its power dynamics, is not something we are innately born with. There are rules and strategies we must learn, and sometimes they don't come naturally or easily. We as educators can allow students to practice navigation strategies with low risk to their well-being. To help students build confidence challenging you in healthy ways, try the Role Cards activity on page 181.

One of our great strengths and privileges as educators is our perspective. We can see, hear, and understand a lot that might go unnoticed amidst the larger noise and distractions of life. Our perspective allows us to observe seemingly tiny details about our students—noticing the kid who doodles bees on every paper, for example. It also gives us information on a grander scale—such as when we notice how a student bravely sharing their autism diagnosis changes an entire classroom's outlook. Our students will come to us with their deepest concerns. They'll also come to us with remarks that make us laugh on the gloomiest of days. The perspectives we gain from our students and schools shape the way we interact with all humans and systems and may deepen our understanding of our own place in the world. This too is the result of power wielded with awe and care.

Using the gift we've been given by our students—this invitation to understand their thoughts and feelings—we can create a unique environment where everyone's individual rights are honored and uplifted. We set up our students to be responsible current and future holders of power by letting them in on ways that they can safely challenge power. We show them that we can handle it. We notice if we become defensive, scared, or numb when students question our power, and we examine those reactions. We invite conversations on how power functions in the education system and our society as a whole. The saying "speak truth to power" can have its debut in classrooms if we allow it.

KEY POINTS

- A power dynamic is present in every classroom.
- No matter how it feels to you, you are in a position of power.
- Classrooms are an ecosystem created initially by you, and only you fully understand your reasons for what you do. To students, the classroom can seem laden with land mines waiting to explode, which may lead them to feel vulnerable.
- Teachers have power in the form of grading; expectations and hopes; classroom policies; life experience; knowledge; the ability to remove privileges or impose consequences; the ability to impact others' opinions, thoughts, and feelings; and the ability to create a narrative about a student that can be broadcasted to others, to name a few.
- Many teachers use their power to gain control and affect student behavior.
- The feedback you give students can be very powerful and can have a great effect on their internal narrative. Lack of awareness of this power

The Empathetic Classroom

can lead to students feeling confused or engaging in a power struggle with you.

- You can reflect on how you use power in your classroom.
- You can provide direct and warm age-appropriate feedback to students by offering support, context, and choice.
- All feedback should have a path forward, not be a "dead end."
- You can let students in on why you have created the world you have by being predictable and flexible, working in the "here and now," and being open to power checks.
- You can invite opportunities for students to provide constructive feedback on your teaching.

For Teachers

MY POWER ASSOCIATIONS

This activity—which can be done alone or as a group exercise with other teachers—asks you to tap into your subconscious and explore your relationship to power. This can be a tricky part of our psyche to get at because it's often protected by our ego (the part of you that imagines yourself in a certain way), so I'm going to ask you to engage with visuals to allow for some free association. To gather these visuals, find some magazines you no longer want. It's ideal to have some variety, but it is also okay if you only have one magazine or one genre of magazines.

Set a timer for five minutes. I don't want you to overthink this, so we're going to move quickly! In your mind, focus on the word *power* and any variations of it (including *powerful*, *powerless*, *empower*, and so on). When you start the timer, begin tearing out magazine images that resonate with you when you think of power. When time is up, spread out these images before you. Notice what you see with curiosity. Then use the questions below to begin processing:

- Are any themes immediately visible?
- Do you have humans in your images? If so, are they young, old, or of specific genders, races, ethnicities, perceived income levels, or other identities?
- What are the humans doing?
- Do you have objects? What kinds of objects? Natural, human-made, large, small, with certain textures?
- What do the objects do?
- What colors are most common in your choices? Dark, light, multicolor, monochromatic?
- Do any of the images connect to your past? If so, how? Consider what power meant in your home, community, or school growing up.

176   *The Empathetic Classroom*

- Do you feel like you exhibit or inhabit the power you see before you? Do you feel like you are somehow beneath the power you see? Do you desire to have some of the experiences of power you see? Which ones?
- Which of these experiences of power show up in your school or classroom? How do they show up?
- Which of these experiences of power would you like to take with you? What would you like to leave behind?

For Teachers

NOTICING MY COMMUNICATION PATTERNS

You may turn to indirect or passive-aggressive communication styles for many reasons. This exercise asks you to identify and examine some of the common reasons why you might do so.

Begin by taking a look at the following list of common topics that can often lead to indirect communication:

- I want to give you **feedback**.
- I want to **apologize** or express regret.
- I **need** something from you.
- I'm **afraid of hurting you**.
- I don't want **you** to feel **embarrassed**.
- I don't want to feel **embarrassed**.
- I made a **mistake**.
- I want you to **change**.
- I want **distance** or no contact from you.

Choose one of these topics to focus on initially. On a sheet of paper, write it down with plenty of space around it, and then circle it. A little distance from the circle, write specific names or categories of the people in your life with whom you interact often. For example: *Sam, Mom, friends, students, coworkers, boss*.

Next, imagine you need or want to communicate something about the circled communication topic to each of these people. Think of a specific example of when this communication topic has come up or how you imagine it would look if it did. For example, suppose I've started with the topic of **change**. I might envision communicating to a close family member that I'd like her to try to work on changing her habit of interrupting me. Now I envision what I would most likely do if I were to try to communicate that to

178   *The Empathetic Classroom*

her. Maybe I would call attention to it next time it happens by saying, "Hey, I notice you tend to interrupt me when I'm sharing." That's **direct**! So I'd draw a *straight* line from the circled topic of communication to her name, indicating the likelihood that I would communicate with her directly on this topic. On the other hand, if I decide I'm more likely to gift her a book on communication skills, I'd draw a *zigzag* line to her name, indicating that I'd probably take an **indirect** route with her on this topic. Or maybe I realize I'd be most likely to just let her interruptions continue for fear of hurting her feelings. In that case, I'd draw *no line*, since I would avoid communicating at all with her on this topic.

Do this for each communication topic in the list, using a new sheet of paper for each one and writing the same names each time. Now look at all of your papers and notice what communication topics have mostly straight lines. Consider why it feels possible for you to communicate directly about these topics. What beliefs do you have about the topics that are driving your direct communication here? Next, look at where you have more zigzags, or no lines at all. Consider why it might seem challenging to use direct communication about these topics. Think about what beliefs you have about the topics that are driving your indirect communication (or noncommunication).

Next, look at other patterns, such as *who* among the people you named has a high number of indirect or no communication indicators. What beliefs do you have about these people that can make communicating with them directly seem difficult or impossible? Check in with what fears or concerns arise within you when you think about saying what you actually want to say to one of these people. Reflect on what has happened in the past if you *have* communicated directly with them (or have observed someone else doing so) and it has gone poorly. Sometimes we have good reason to avoid direct communication with people who respond reactively to it. For example, we might have a parent who yells when we share that we've made a mistake. But if you have not experienced or witnessed any harm, your fears that direct communication will go poorly may be unfounded.

Finally, look at the people in your life with whom you do not currently use direct communication and consider with which of them you might benefit from communicating more directly. Reflect on an issue you would

continued

Chapter 10: All About Power in Schools   **179**

like to communicate with them on, and write one sentence that directly states what you'd like to say to them. Resist the urge to mind-read their intentions around the issue. Instead, stick to explaining what the experience is like for you and stating if you need anything from them. For example, *I've noticed you tend to not call on me in meetings, and I feel ignored.* Read the sentence back, then try saying it aloud. Notice what happens to your nervous system when you do this. Reposition yourself so that you are sitting or standing with a posture that allows you to feel grounded and strong. Take a deep breath and say the phrase again, this time with more volume. Continue repeating the phrase until you notice you are feeling more comfortable saying it. If you do decide to say it to the person and you are still feeling really nervous, write it down and take it with you. Even if you feel silly reading from a paper, what you have to say is likely important enough to communicate that it is worth temporary discomfort.

For Students

ROLE CARDS

If I notice that students seem to need a bit more of a license to challenge me or even just be "challenging," I will hand out role cards at the beginning of a lesson or discussion. You can use these prompts to give students a chance to try on specific roles. Some of the roles ask students to play a part they may not be accustomed to playing and that they might feel uncomfortable with. I suggest being intentional about who you give what role to, to support stretching just outside their comfort zone. For instance, this can be a great activity for inviting quiet students to take a risk and be a bit more vocal, or for more talkative students to practice more listening or curiosity.

You'll find a starting point for cards on the next page. To create these prompts, I reflected on what types of interactions are part of a really interesting discussion. Feel free to add to the cards or to adjust them for the age, interests, and dynamics of your group. Note that there are duplicates of some prompts to accommodate larger class sizes. (These prompts are available for download at freespirit.com/empathetic.)

You can explain role cards to students by comparing them to roles in a play—these are their "parts" for the lesson. I usually tell students it is optional to play their role, and they are allowed to participate in other ways beyond roles if they would like. If you choose to offer participation points for playing roles, be sure to let students know ahead of time. After you pass out the cards, make sure students understand how their roles work before the lesson starts, and provide examples if needed. You'll see that I threw a few wild cards in to bring a bit of humor to the experience! The goal here is to build comfort with healthy risk-taking.

continued

Chapter 10: All About Power in Schools   **181**

Ask a someone a question.	Let someone know you appreciate something about a point they made.	Share something that is off topic!	Ask someone to offer an example to support their point.	Ask someone to repeat what they've said.
Agree with someone and say why you agree.	Disagree with something your teacher has said.	Tie what someone has said to something we have learned about in another subject recently.	Rephrase what someone has said to show you understand.	Add to what someone else has said.
Ask someone a question.	Rephrase what someone has said to show you understand.	Ask for more clarification on something you don't understand.	Agree with someone and say why you agree.	Disagree with something your teacher has said.
Ask for more clarification on something you don't understand.	Ask if you can further explain something by demonstrating on the board.	Rub your chin like a wise sage and say "hmm" after someone says something interesting.	Rephrase what someone has said to show you understand.	Let someone know you appreciate something about a point they made.
In three points, summarize what we talked about today at the end of the lesson.	Add to what someone else has said.	Raise your hand and then say you forgot what you were going to say.	Make eye contact and nod after someone says something.	Offer an example of a point that was made.

At the end of this activity, check in about what the experience was like for students with the following questions:

- What was it like to play your role?
- How did you feel before you played it? After?
- Would you try this role again without a role card?
- What surprised you during our discussion?
- What roles do you think would be the most challenging for you?
- What roles would you be willing to try?
- How does having all these roles during a lesson change the lesson or the way you experienced it?

11

HOW TO NAVIGATE BOUNDARIES

Doctoral student Jim Benes is a teacher of earth science and geography for first-generation students at the University of Nebraska-Lincoln. Jim's history is one that reaches far beyond the walls of the classroom you'll find him in today. He joined the US Coast Guard in his early twenties, was an aircraft mechanic for a time, and then became an interpretive guide in Yellowstone National Park. When he's not lecturing, he's working on his Ph.D. program and serving in the US Navy. He's curious about the stories our Earth holds, including what his neighbors are growing in their garden. He writes handwritten letters to his loved ones and held on to his flip phone until, well, it didn't work anymore. Like all teachers, there is more to Jim than what his students see each day.

Reflecting on his most recent school year, Jim recalls that his students were more inquisitive than ever. And not just about earth sciences but about him too. This felt new to Jim. *Why do you wear that bracelet? What did you do this weekend? Are you mad?* One student even asked, "You know what I like?" "What?" Jim replied. With all eyes in the room now on them, the student replied, "I like that your tie color matches your socks." An embarrassed Jim offered an awkward, "Thanks."

Jim knows that the role of educator carries responsibilities and a certain level of power, especially when it comes to grading, and it is important to him to maintain professionalism. So navigating these new interactions felt tricky for him.

"I can feel my face turning red when they ask personal questions," he says. One question that recently caught him off guard arose on the anniversary of 9/11. His students wanted to know what that day had been like for him. This is a deeply personal story for Jim, and one he decided to share with his students. He remembers feeling tears come to his eyes. Looking back, he was glad he'd chosen to let students in on this intimate part of himself.

As teachers, it can be difficult to know when, how, and if we allow different parts of ourselves to show up in the classroom. When talking about boundaries, there are typically two camps: the "I'm not good with boundaries" camp and the "these are my boundaries and I'm sticking with them no matter what" camp. Both camps exist as the result of real experiences that have led peopleto the conclusion that one approach is more manageable than the other. However, finding a flexible relationship with boundaries can allow us to be more active participants in our own lives and provide important cues to others about our unique needs or expectations.

Walls Down

Often, people who say they "can't do boundaries" have an internal narrative telling them that there's something innate within them that makes having boundaries really difficult. Rather than deal with that difficulty, they'd prefer to cope with the consequences—they'll answer that parent phone call outside of work hours, they won't mention the extra time they spent cleaning up another teacher's mess, they'll avoid telling the principal that they are actually allergic to her dog who wanders into their classroom each day. And they usually feel that they've gotten really good at dealing with the consequences, so why do anything different?

For several years, high school teacher Tony believed that establishing boundaries would result in being disliked by his students. He had grown up in a household of what seemed to be endless and rigid boundaries, so his response was to provide his students with something completely unlike his childhood experience. This meant his daily plans would often change on a whim—if a parent sent him an angry email about a book he was teaching, he stopped teaching it immediately, believing the parent's anger outweighed his own reason for choosing the text. If a student complained a task was too hard, he scrapped it, even when he saw value in it, and looked for something his students might find more palatable.

Chapter 11: How to Navigate Boundaries   **185**

At times, Tony's openness seemed to bring delight to both him and his students. But at other times, his saying *yes* led him to unexpected places—ones he then didn't know how to get out of. One day, he admitted to a colleague that he didn't think some of his students respected him as much as he did them. They often did not do what he asked them to, even though he didn't feel he wasn't asking for much. "And I'm so nice to them!" he exclaimed. Tony was bumping into a personal boundary—but admitting that he cared about (or even *had*) boundaries went against one of his old and deeply held beliefs.

Walls Up

On the other end of the spectrum, in the "boundaries or die" camp, we can find a different but similar story. Rose had been teaching for over twenty years, and boundaries were how she managed to keep going as a middle school math teacher for yet another year. She believed she had to keep a tight ship, or risk "losing her zip!"

Rose was predictable to the core—to the point that students knew which questions or needs were "appropriate" to express and which ones definitely were not. If a student ever tried to ask for something, they were greeted with a flat "nope" before they could even finish their sentence. Rose rarely, if ever, engaged in any comical banter with her students for fear they might take advantage of the situation should she get too silly.

And yet, anyone on the faculty who worked with Rose knew she had a brilliant sense of humor and an infectious laugh. Her students would never get to know this side of their middle school math teacher. As she once explained to a group of her peers, "There is a sharp line between professional Rose and private Rose, and it will not be crossed." Some of her students appreciated her predictability and hard lines. They never had to guess what math class was going to hold. Rose's class was always the same. Other students wondered if Rose was unhappy with her role as a teacher and questioned whether she even liked her students at all. They didn't feel like they knew her as a person and didn't feel attached to her in any way. After all her years of strict, by-the-rules teaching, Rose too wondered whether she was happy.

Boundaries Are About Control

Both of these approaches to boundaries are woven of similar cloth—*If I don't hold tight to my way of doing things, I will become something I am afraid of. I will lose control.* The examples we hold on to in our minds are often what motivate us to continue down the same path with our boundaries. We've known people who seemed too uptight or too loose. Or we tried being flexible once and got taken advantage of. Or we can't do boundaries perfectly, so why try at all?

A common myth about boundaries is that some people have them and some don't. Let's settle that right now: *Everyone* has boundaries. Everyone has experiences that feel like too much or aren't okay with them. Everyone has an opinion on their own experiences. The difference lies in whether a boundary will be listened to and upheld. So the question is not whether a boundary exists, but whether we're open to acknowledging it and listening to what it tells us about our own needs. And—you guessed it—we all have needs.

Another myth about boundaries is that upholding all boundaries is "good." Having this perspective is why feelings of shame can happen when we do not uphold a boundary. But if we think of boundaries as a metaphorical wall, we can more easily see why always having walls up isn't helpful to ourselves or others. Sometimes we need to lower our walls and let in other people and new experiences.

Types of Boundaries

There are three standard types of boundaries in the world of psychology: porous, rigid, and flexible. A porous boundary is one that lets in anyone and everything. A person whose boundaries are porous is often quick to trust others without any evidence that their trust is warranted. They are quick to forgo their own opinion in favor of others'. They often avoid conflict and communicate passively. You might be experiencing a porous boundary if you feel like you want to say no but can't for some reason. This was Tony.

The rigid boundary style is what we saw in Rose—she worked hard to keep her students at a distance, did not trust them, and was inflexible in her communication style. Rigid boundary holders avoid conflict too, but they do so by ignoring that there might even be the possibility of a conflict. The rigid

Chapter 11: How to Navigate Boundaries

boundary holder does not want to let others be just as they are because it might become too messy. Rigidity can give the illusion that life is orderly.

The person with flexible boundaries is in the boundary sweet spot. Having flexible boundaries means being able to hold both rigid and porous boundaries and knowing when each is needed. Sometimes this style is referred to as "healthy boundaries." Jim's openness to sharing a personal story, even though it was not typical of him, was an example of flexibility. He stepped out of his comfort zone to prioritize his connection with his students. But he probably won't choose to do this every day.

Someone taking this flexible approach to boundaries knows that they have to look at each situation and each person anew and assess what kind of boundary is needed. A person with flexible boundaries is selective about who and what they allow past their personal barriers. They are willing to trust others, but their trust takes time and evidence. They will share personal information, but they'll do so with an understanding of context and an awareness of potential consequences or benefits. This way, conflict is not avoided but is seen as a part of life. When it does occur, the flexible boundary holder communicates assertively to address it. To be flexible with boundaries means upholding values as important and also being willing to adapt when the situation calls for it. For instance, holding a rigid boundary with a student under duress may not be a sound or healthy approach to meeting their needs.

Flexible Boundaries Adapt and Change

In considering these boundary styles, you might notice that your own boundaries are flexible or that you tend to rely on one style more than another. Your boundaries also likely change according to the type of environment and relationship you are engaging in. My boundaries in home relationships are different than my boundaries in work relationships. If I hold the same boundaries with my husband that I do with my clients, our relationship would be unsatisfying. And if I hold the same boundaries with my clients that I do with my husband, I would not be practicing ethical therapy.

In education, the same can be said for our relationships with students, parents, and coworkers. When I was teaching, I initially had porous boundaries with parents and caregivers, because I came to the work with my own history of honoring and trusting parental figures. These porous boundaries

188 *The Empathetic Classroom*

resulted in parents finding me at restaurants on the weekend and talking to me about their child's challenges at school. They led to constant parent emails asking for adjustments to assignments and to me making changes based on what a parent believed their child needed. Because I was not a parent at the time, I also doubted my role as a teacher in conflict with parents. I would rather give in than face an angry parent.

After several years of teaching, feeling the initial symptoms of burnout and also having gained the confidence of knowing what I was doing, I became more rigid in my boundaries. I started to say no, and it felt good. It was like unleashing a power I never knew I had, and I became a bit tipsy on it. It started to spread into my personal relationships too, and some coworkers began to give me feedback on my lack of flexibility. At the time, though, as a formerly porous-boundary person, I was proud of my solid stance. I knew what I did and didn't want, and no one was going to get in my way. What I didn't take into account was how this actually worked in relationships with others.

Know Your Priorities

As educators, we can identify what our boundaries are in each situation by understanding our hierarchy of priorities. Some things will be higher on the list and will be more valued than others. These are essentially your values. Choosing a top priority can be difficult if you are used to valuing many things equally. And the organization of your priorities will not be identical to anyone else's; no two individuals' boundaries will be the same. You and your colleagues will have different boundaries, and that is okay.

So, how do you know if something is a priority for you? The What Are My Priorities? activity on page 192 will help you examine this question and gain clarity. In addition, try to get in the habit of noticing what happens within yourself when you have to put something on the back burner. Maybe it's your time, your money, or your health. What happens to your mood? How do you feel emotionally and physically? What do people you care about—and who care about you—say when you do this? How does saying no to something you care about impact the messages you send yourself about what you really *do* prioritize? Teachers are well known for putting personal needs on the back burner in the name of our students. Believe it or not, putting everyone else's needs first will ultimately harm your relationships with students. By giving your "all," you miss out on using boundaries to protect the parts of you that make relationships truly fulfilling.

Sometimes you will need to reassess, reorganize, and edit your priorities. They shift as you change and as your life circumstances change. Working full time changes priorities. Being in a committed relationship changes priorities. Having children does too. In midlife, I've come to prioritize the quality of my relationships, along with my mental and physical energy levels, so I look through this lens as I determine when to uphold and when to let down boundaries. I now know that equally prioritizing all relationships will not lead to quality interactions, so I pick and choose who I want to build relationship with and when to put forth that effort. I also have to be realistic with myself and acknowledge that I will not be able to do and have everything I want in relationships, even when I prioritize.

Later in my teaching career, after setting up those rigid boundaries, I decided to prioritize my students' mental well-being. How this changed my relationship to the boundaries I thought I knew! I became more flexible to addressing students' individual needs. I grew more trusting of my students. I worked on my assertive communication skills so that our relationship did not lead to confusion. I did share some personal experiences with my students when sharing was relevant and appropriate to the situation. Interestingly, I found that when I prioritized my students' mental well-being, I also noticed improvement in my own. I had worked so hard to protect my energy by keeping people out that I didn't realize that sometimes letting them in was good for my energy too.

When You Need Security, You Can Increase Your Boundaries

There will be times and places in life when you will need to protect yourself more, and when increasing the rigidity of your personal boundaries is the right call. If you are grieving a loss, feeling unwell, undergoing significant life changes, or needing space, you can remind yourself that instituting boundaries where they didn't exist previously might just be what is called for. Maybe you hold off on attending events where you know your boundaries will be pushed, like that after-work vent session at the local pub. Maybe you change your policy on students spending time in the classroom instead of going to recess. Maybe you have a conversation with the principal about parent behavior that needs addressing. Whatever the details may be, remember that people who care about you can support your critical

The Empathetic Classroom

boundaries by respecting them or by gently reminding you when you are considering doing something based on old beliefs instead of your current ones. For example, my husband now knows to remind me of my own client contact policy when I start to reply to non-urgent client communication over the weekend. Being reminded of our boundaries by people who love us can bring attention to our priorities and needs. From here, we can decide what is lost and what is gained by changing a boundary.

KEY POINTS

- Boundaries are a way of letting in or keeping out certain personal information and experiences and are often based on your past and your priorities.
- Everyone has boundaries and uses them in different ways. Three common approaches to boundaries are porous, rigid, and flexible.
- Having flexible boundaries with students involves actively deciding how to engage based on the person and the context. In general, flexible boundaries mean that communication is direct, you are adaptable when needed, you look for cues to build trust, and you know that conflict is an important part of life.
- There may be times when you need to employ more rigid boundaries to cope with life circumstances.
- You can identify your boundary needs by considering your hierarchy of priorities, based in your values.

Chapter 11: How to Navigate Boundaries

For Teachers

WHAT ARE MY PRIORITIES?

Even when you know what is important to you, it can sometimes be difficult to clarify *why* your values are what they are or to understand how they impact what you do, think, and feel. This activity is about identifying what you value, and, in turn, how to prioritize your time, energy, and resources. If this activity feels difficult to you . . . it should. It's designed to ask big things of you in order to get down to what really matters. After all, if everything matters, it becomes very difficult to prioritize.

Start by answering the following prompts in writing:

- Name five places that are important to you.
- Name five things that are important to you.
- Name five people who have had an important impact on you (good, bad, or neutral).
- Name five memories that are important to you.
- Name five goals that are important to you (personal or professional).

Now look at your lists. These are likely to be twenty-five of the most important aspects of your life. Next, imagine that five of them never existed. What would you choose to remove? (This will be hard!) Once you have done that, take a breather before removing five more. In this way, continue removing five things at a time until a total of only five are left.

Cutting any of these important parts of you most likely feels a bit painful. Or maybe there were a few that felt surprisingly easy to let go of. Plus, no one was watching, so hopefully you felt no judgment about what you cut. Take a moment to reflect using these questions:

- What items were the hardest to get rid of? Can I see why they were difficult? Did I feel any guilt or "shoulds" arise?
- Did any of my choices surprise me? Why?

192   *The Empathetic Classroom*

- Looking at the five items I have left, do I see any general themes or ways in which they are connected?
- If each of the remaining items says something about what I value, what might be the values I'd attach to them? (For example, relationships, creativity, money, time, home, beauty.)
- How have I been prioritizing these values—or not?
- Have any of my values changed over time? What is here that probably wouldn't have been in the past? Is anything *not* here that would have been in the past?
- How do I feel about what I have left on my list, or what I value?
- How am I supporting—or not supporting—these priorities with boundaries in my life? How could I do better at this?

Chapter 11: How to Navigate Boundaries   **193**

12

RESPONDING TO YOUR INTRUSIVE THOUGHTS ABOUT TEACHING

I have a vivid memory of sitting in a classroom full of teachers on a hot July afternoon. Everyone was tired. It wasn't just the heat; it was the exhaustion that comes after a year—and many years—of teaching. The type of tiredness that shows up the moment you get to slow down. You finally take a deep breath, and right away you get sick or sad, or you start to wonder how you'll be able to stand upright again come fall. This was us in that moment, and we all had to look each other in the eye. Janice, a teacher from a small Montana town north of where I lived, was taking her turn during a check-in. She was already starting to turn red with all eyes on her. Then tears welled up in her eyes.

"When I drive to school each day, I pass a field of cows. Several fields, actually. I must admit that every morning I have the thought that I would rather be a cow than have to go teach another day."

Thankfully, Janice was surrounded by people who could empathize with her longing for a life out to pasture. The quiet stillness of the land, the pure functionality of meeting one's most basic needs, the freedom to pass gas without a snicker. Even if not everyone felt the same way, no one berated Janice for her innermost thoughts or told her to go find a new profession. Janice seemed relieved to share this private burden she was carrying.

Years later, I ran into her while she was shopping for her daughter's wedding dress.

"That moment changed how I felt about myself," she said, pulling at the fabric of a gown. "Sharing my thoughts and realizing that other teachers didn't chastise me for having them really lessened the power those thoughts had over me."

Feeling less alone in her struggle to "turn on" every day to teach, Janice started to feel more compassion for herself. Soon that self-acceptance was also reflected in how she taught.

Internal Chatter

Teachers hold a unique role in society. They are often held up as if sacred and at the same time given little voice. In the work of teaching, a teacher's humanity can be whittled down and discarded. You want to go to the bathroom? You're going to have to learn to hold it. Want a free meal? Wrong career—that's tech. Here's time off, but we don't have enough substitutes, so it would be better if you just waited until summer. And remember, don't get sick. No one else can teach your eighth grade math lesson!

In many ways, you are told both that you matter enormously and that you hardly matter at all. Navigating challenging interactions with students and their caregivers can also contribute to an internal dialogue that can start to feel very lonely. All of these conditions are ripe for unruly internal babble. Sometimes you might be surprised by the thoughts that pop into your head.

Our brains generate all kinds of thoughts in a day—most of which we have zero control over. Often, the mind wants to experiment with an idea simply because it can. The mind is truly a wild frontier with no rules, and it's one of the few places where others can't constrain us. No one can tell you what you can and can't think. The mind knows this and sometimes takes advantage of it.

Typically, the way the brain works is that the more you try to suppress something, the more strength it will have. If I say to you, "Don't think about that cheesy pizza"—you're immediately going to have a thought about that cheesy pizza. Similarly, when you say no to a child, they will likely be more interested in doing whatever you've just asked them not to do. While this is natural, it can nevertheless be uncomfortable to feel as if we have so little control over our mind.

> *You'll notice that this chapter is all about you and your thoughts, not those of your students. Wading into your own cognitive territory is enough. If students report challenging thoughts of their own, it's best to refer them to a mental health professional.*

Intrusive Thoughts

In the world of psychology, the idea of automatic thoughts—or, as they are now more frequently called, intrusive thoughts—has been around for some time. Psychologist Aaron T. Beck, who made his name with cognitive behavioral therapy (CBT) in the '60s, coined the term *automatic thoughts* to describe thoughts that seem to arrive in our brain without going through the checks and balances that more ordinary thoughts do (Beck et al. 1979). These thoughts are typically sudden, strong, and brief—and they are usually more frequent when we are feeling uncertain, anxious, or depressed. And when we examine them from a distance, they might seem quite unhelpful. Beck learned about the presence of these thoughts by asking his clients to report to him the types of thoughts that occurred when they had challenging emotional experiences.

For example, a woman who was asked to speak in front of her peers at work was suddenly bombarded with the thought, *I'm stupid.* This thought then affected her feelings, sparking sadness and fear. Next it affected her behavior—she couldn't even open her mouth to speak. While we might believe these automatic thoughts to some extent, they are often distortions or exaggerations. And once she had some distance from the stressful moment, this woman was able to recognize that she wasn't, in fact, incapable or "stupid." She was an accountant who had worked hard to get where she was in her career. It just didn't make sense—why would her mind do that to her and trick her body into shutting down?

The Beliefs Beneath Our Thoughts

Beck was able to observe that these extreme thoughts are often driven by our underlying beliefs—something about ourselves that we conclude

The Empathetic Classroom

from previous experiences to be a truth, even if reality doesn't necessarily provide much evidence for it. For example, his client who was stressed by speaking in front of peers reflected on her beliefs about intelligence and was able to recall interactions between her parents in which her father would suggest that her mother wasn't smart enough. Even though this commentary wasn't about her specifically, she had taken on the belief that women weren't as smart as men. When she was standing in front of a room of mostly male peers, that old belief reared its head.

Intrusive thoughts usually fall into one of two categories: *ego-dystonic* thoughts and *ego-syntonic* thoughts. Ego-dystonic thoughts are ones that are *not* aligned with who you believe yourself to be. For example, if you believe it is important to be kind, an unkind thought will feel out of place. Alternatively, ego-syntonic thoughts *are* in line with who you believe yourself to be. For example, if you believe you are unworthy of someone loving you, a thought about being worthless will feel accurate. When an intrusive thought occurs, is important to ask yourself: Is this troubling thought one that I believe should be there (ego-syntonic) or one I believe should not be there (ego-dystonic)?

If you determine that a thought is *not* aligned with who you believe yourself to be (ego-dystonic), you can thank your mind's alarm system for alerting you to something that is out of character for you. This alarm system is often accompanied by emotions related to distress, and it's a sign that your mind is doing important protective work. On the other hand, if you believe a thought *is* aligned with what you believe (ego-syntonic), yet this thought causes you or people you care about distress, it's an indicator that you might benefit from the support of a mental health professional to explore your unique relationship to this thought.

One of the common distress feelings people experience with intrusive thoughts is shame or guilt. Many people feel shame about their intrusive thoughts because those thoughts are often critical of oneself, judgmental of others, or taboo in some other way. Voicing them aloud could put you on the acceptance "chopping block." Saying "I dislike or fear this student" to your boss could result in swift repercussions. Teachers, especially, often carry shame along with these thoughts because teachers aren't "supposed" to have anything other than positive, happy thoughts. I've had clients tell me, "But I shouldn't think that, I'm a _____!"

Chapter 12: Responding to Your Intrusive Thoughts About Teaching

Sometimes these self-judgments are about things we do. "I watch too much YouTube." "I should be cooking healthier meals." "I have a pile of laundry growing in my living room!" "I should be exercising." Yes, all of this might be true, and how nice it would be if it were not. But these behaviors are rarely the problem. Rather, they are symptoms of not having the time or energy to care for yourself. Your downtime behaviors are there for a reason, and attempting to replace or remove them without addressing the root of the problem isn't likely to result in long-term change. Your body and mind need to "check out" with these behaviors because they've been "on" too long.

While self-judgment might seem counterproductive, it is not without reason. There's often a part of us that believes we will change if we only judge ourselves hard enough. Judgment can pop up pretending to be a motivator. Many of us were raised with parenting styles that used explicit or implicit judgment to encourage behavior change. The issue with judgment as a motivator is that this motivation is based in fear. *I believe that if I watch too much YouTube, I'll become lazy. Therefore, if I despise myself for this behavior, maybe I won't watch so much.*

What to Do When It Happens

While we don't want to be ruled by our intrusive thoughts, we don't need to completely ignore them either. In mindfulness practices, the RAIN acronym, first coined by teacher Michele McDonald in the early 2000s, is an easy way to remember the process of accepting our thoughts (Vipassana Hawai'i, n.d.):

Recognition: See the thought for what it is. *I see you!*

Acceptance: Tell the thought it's okay that it is there and that you are not going to try to change it. Accepting a thought does not mean acting on it. *I accept you!*

Interest: Be kindly curious about it. *I want to learn about you!*

Not-identification: Let go of identifying with the thought. *I am not my thoughts!*

While using the RAIN process around my YouTube habits, I might think instead, *I see you, self-loathing! It makes sense that you are coming up for me. Yes, I watch YouTube after a long school day, and I wish I didn't. I think I feel bad doing it because I believe that reading or gardening are "healthy" activities, and that watching videos online is "unhealthy." Those beliefs are definitely from my past. When I start watching, I notice I feel relaxed for a while and then I just check out. I know this is my body telling me what it needs—a lot happened today, and checking out feels like the only way to cope. If I want to relax to YouTube, there is nothing wrong with me. And when I start to notice I'm no longer feeling relaxed, I know I can find other ways to take care of myself after a long day if I want. I recognize that I'm feeling some self-loathing, but I also know this is just one of many thoughts that will cross my mind. It is not who I am.*

In addition to the RAIN process, you can use the Working with My Intrusive Thoughts activity on page 205 to practice the skill of addressing intrusive thoughts, including using the strategy of reality-testing to explore how accurate—or distorted—they are.

Carl Confronts His Thoughts

Consider Carl, a second-year high school teacher who was passionate about teaching history. He'd thought history was boring when he was in high school himself—until he had Mr. Creighton. He wanted to do for others what Mr. Creighton had done for him. While he wasn't totally sold on every aspect of being a teacher, especially having to enforce rules in his classroom, he felt like it was the best fit for him compared to other careers that seemed less meaningful.

Carl's first year of teaching had gone pretty well. He was amped up on caffeine and adrenaline every day, and students and parents loved his energy, passion, and taste in music. But by his second year, he was in more of a routine and felt bored and restless at times, fearing he might become just like the teachers he'd hated in school. He started to have intrusive thoughts about a student who, in many ways, reminded him of himself as a kid. This student was always messing around and didn't seem to care. In his mind, Carl started to refer to the student as "that little jerk." While he knew the thought wasn't his finest, he didn't think anyone else could see it. One day, another teacher who was something of a mentor for him called him on it.

"I've noticed you've been on James's case in the halls lately. I don't hear you get after anyone else likc that. Do you want to tell me what's on your mind?"

It was only then that Carl could see how much his thoughts were impacting his behavior. He felt his face get red and an old tight feeling in his stomach. Working with his mentor after school that day, he was able to admit that he really struggled to accept this student, and he also acknowledged that this student reminded him of himself. As a student, he always believed his teachers thought of *him* as a jerk, so his brain dug up that old name when he encountered someone he saw as a version of himself. His mentor gently checked him on the distortion of these thoughts.

"What made you a jerk, in your eyes?" he asked.

Carl thought about it. "I didn't do what my teachers asked, so I assumed they didn't like me."

His mentor's eyebrows arched. "Do *you* not like James?"

Carl took a deep breath, and then said, "I actually admire him as a person, but he's tough to teach. I don't *not* like him. I just feel like we're always in a power struggle."

"Ah," said his mentor, "so *jerk* might be the wrong word. Let's find a better one."

After talking with his mentor and making his private thought known to someone he trusted, Carl felt the thought's power over him loosen up. It didn't immediately disappear, but when it occurred, he looked at it a little differently. *That's what you used to think about yourself, man. You don't believe that anymore,* he'd say to himself when it came to mind again. He'd also try to take note when James did something that didn't fit Carl's intrusive narrative of him being a jerk. For example, he started to notice that James was one of the few kids who thanked the lunch staff every day. Over time, he noticed his relationship with James improved. He even learned that they both liked to shoot hoops to de-stress and took the time to join James for a few minutes in the gym after school. It was a growth moment for Carl, one he was appreciative of throughout his career. He was grateful both for the mentor who gave him grace and guidance and for the student who allowed him to start over. Carl came to love, rather than fear, the challenges his students posed to him.

What If I Believe My Intrusive Thought?

Sometimes after doing this work, you will realize, *But I really do believe my intrusive thought. Now what?!* Let's say your thought is that your new romantic partner's cat is ugly, and the more you revisit it, the more you acknowledge that it is not a distortion—it is what you really think. But you also believe that it would devastate your partner to learn that Mr. Cuddlesworth is not your type. We often harbor guilt when we have intrusive thoughts, and even more so when we believe them—*something must be wrong with me.* It is distressing to imagine ourselves as someone who might have thoughts or beliefs like these.

200   *The Empathetic Classroom*

First off, you're not a "bad" person or wrong for accepting that you view a thought as a truth, even if it is taboo, unpopular, or literally untrue. At times, all humans have thoughts that feel simultaneously accurate and problematic. In psychotherapy, we might say there is likely a *part* of you that believes the thought, and that by getting to know this part of you better, you can understand why the thought has meaning or value for that part of you.

If this sounds like you, I invite you to look within yourself when you are feeling regulated. If you can set the thought or belief aside or put it in a container when it occurs—which will usually be when you experience a trigger and are unregulated—then you can bring it out again when you are in a more grounded mental and physical space. Write the thought on a piece of paper, envision it in your head, or say it aloud. Now consider these questions:

- How does having this belief impact my emotions?
- How does having this belief impact how I feel physically when I think about it?
- How does having this belief impact my relationships?
- How does having this belief impact my choices or behaviors?

Using your responses, reflect on the significance or impact of your thought. Is it a belief that causes distress to you or people you care about? If so, it's time to give this thought more attention and seek further support from a professional. If not, it might be a thought you can work with on your own.

Fear of Acting on a Thought

Simply knowing that intrusive thoughts will come to you unbidden, and that sometimes you will believe them, is a key step toward dealing with them in healthy ways. What you do with these thoughts is important. If it feels like your thought might cause you to *do* something, first remember that there is a big difference between having a thought and doing something because of it. While a thought might feel real, it is essential to acknowledge that it is not an action, just as a photo of a cat is not a cat. A thought is a mental image. Your intrusive thoughts do not need to dictate your actions. We frequently fear that if we think something, we will do or say it. Thankfully, because our systems are wired for survival, we often do *not* act on our thoughts even when they are powerful. However, if you find yourself feeling overwhelmed

Chapter 12: Responding to Your Intrusive Thoughts About Teaching

or as if your thoughts might prompt a problematic behavior, use the following strategies:

De-escalate: If you can, remove yourself from the immediate situation that is increasing your feelings of overwhelm. If you can't remove yourself, try cueing your nervous system to recognize that you are okay by changing your position in the room, your posture, or what you are doing. Just like your students, sometimes you need a break to regulate and reset.

Distract: Use distraction when you are unable to process your emotions in the moment. This could be thinking of a strong positive sensory memory, such as sitting by the ocean with the waves kissing your feet or smelling the aroma of baking cinnamon rolls. Revisit this same sensory experience each time the intrusive thought reappears. Distraction can also include reading something that is meaningful to you or looking at an image that is grounding or familiar.

Self-talk: Your internal narrative is likely to want to assign value or judgment to your intrusive thoughts. Rather than greeting your thought with shame-filled, angry, or unkind judgments, you can prepare specific phrases in advance that take a more neutral stance to the thought: *Huh, that's an odd thought*, or *That's my stress thought*, or *There's that annoying thought again*, or *There's my mind getting stuck again.*

When to Seek Help

We all hold ideas about who we should be or what we should be like. We may hold onto ideas about how we think *others* should be. Invariably, we experience confusion and distress when our minds tell us something that feels out of sync with ourselves or people who care about us. It can be challenging and ineffective to work with your intrusive thoughts by yourself. If you notice repetitive thoughts that are affecting your feelings and behavior, this is a signal to reach out to a mental health professional to talk about these thoughts. (For tips on finding a provider, see the guide on page 226.) A prospective client once asked me, "But what if my thoughts are angry and mean?" "Perfect," I say. Therapy is the place for uncomfortable thoughts and feelings. I am not here to tell you to stop being angry or mean. A therapist is not there to serve as judge, lawyer, or police.

The Empathetic Classroom

What a therapist *can* do is help you see your cognitions for what they are and what they are not. As a teacher, you work day in and day out with students who are complicated, messy fellow humans. And even if you *generally* love working with students, there will almost surely be those for whom you don't "feel the love." Those experiences can prompt a whole rainbow of thoughts and feelings—some more challenging and uncomfortable than others. Working with a mental health professional can provide you a safe place to begin the process of normalizing, identifying, and addressing intrusive thoughts so that you can feel better *and* show up in the classroom.

> *The limits to confidentiality for mental health professionals do include harm to self or others. So if physical, sexual, or emotional harm is an intrusive thought for you, know that your therapist will support you in working on this, and that they may have to break your confidentiality (usually looping you in first) if your thoughts seem to indicate an active idea rather than a passive idea.*

Our Brains Are Explorers

We can provide our brain with the freedom it craves by reminding ourselves that random, odd, or unwanted thoughts do come and go from time to time. Wonderfully so! Brains are explorers and there's no place they won't go. If our logical brain is online, and we are feeling regulated, security checkpoints in the brain stop us from saying and doing everything that comes into our mind. When we are less regulated, those checkpoints aren't always functioning at their best, and managing our thought-to-behavior reactions can be more challenging. If you feel your heart rate going up, your face flushing, or numbness in parts of your body, these can be signals that you are unregulated and that your internal checkpoints are down. Just as you'd advise for your students, this is a good time to take a pause, find your breath, see your thoughts as thoughts, and reset. Having a comfortable relationship with your own mind will allow you to be familiar with its habits and to address its needs when they arise.

Chapter 12: Responding to Your Intrusive Thoughts About Teaching   **203**

KEY POINTS

- The brain generates content outside of your control called intrusive thoughts.
- Intrusive thoughts are often private judgments about yourself or others.
- You might believe these thoughts are rooted in truth, even without evidence for it.
- Self-judgment sometimes arises as a way to induce shame or guilt and motivate new behavior, even though it usually isn't effective.
- Intrusive thoughts are usually based on old beliefs or things you've been told by others.
- Intrusive thoughts can be ego-dystonic (not aligned with who you think you are) or ego-syntonic (aligned with who you think you are).
- Most intrusive thoughts are an exaggeration or distortion of reality.
- You can use the RAIN acronym to see thoughts, accept them, and be curious about them but choose not to assign them value or give them disproportionate power over you.
- Sharing intrusive thoughts with a safe and confidential source can lessen their intensity.
- Reality-testing your intrusive thoughts can challenge their accuracy.
- When intrusive thoughts become overwhelming, you can de-escalate, distract, and use self-talk to reorient your nervous system.

For Teachers

WORKING WITH MY INTRUSIVE THOUGHTS

Changing your internal narratives takes effort. This activity provides a step-by-step approach to address intrusive thoughts just as Carl was able to do with his mentor. You'll choose one challenging intrusive thought to work through and write answers to the following questions for just that one thought.

1. **Identify the thought.**
   - What thoughts do you tell yourself about being unlovable, incapable, or worthless?
   - What do your thoughts tell you about others?

   Write one of your intrusive thoughts at the top of a sheet of paper. Once you've pinned down an intrusive thought, then you can work with it. It could be a thought about yourself, or it could be about others. For example: *No one likes me.*

2. **Notice the thought.**
   - How might this thought be functional? How is the thought serving you? How might it be trying to help you? For example: *If I remind myself daily that "no one likes me," that thought keeps me from taking part in uncomfortable social encounters, and I don't get hurt.*
   - How might this thought be dysfunctional? What problems does it contribute to—even if your mind keeps telling you it's true? For example: *When I think that no one likes me, I avoid social events and feel lonely.*

continued

Chapter 12: Responding to Your Intrusive Thoughts About Teaching   **205**

3. **Identify your old belief.** Do a rewind through your past. Identify old memories and beliefs that you may still be holding onto and that this thought may be tied to.

- When and where did the old belief start?
- Who was involved?
- What happened?
- Why might you have continued to carry this belief with you?
- What do you believe would happen if you stopped believing this? For example: *It probably started in grade school. I remember being bad at sports, and no one ever picked me for games on the playground. At the time I didn't think I wasn't being picked simply because I was not good at the sport. I thought it was because the others didn't like me. I still hold onto this because it really hurt, and I never want to forget it and get hurt again. I think I'd prefer to just believe I'm not liked than let people get to know me, find out they really don't like me, and get hurt.*

4. **Understand the distortion.** Once you've identified the old belief, you can start to unpack how and why it might be distorted. Identify which type of distorted thinking might be at work with your intrusive thought.

- **Polarized thinking:** These thoughts are framed as all good or all bad. They deal in extremes, rather than allowing potential for a middle ground. Example: *If don't do well in this interview, I'll never be a principal.*
- **Negative filtering:** These thoughts are seen through the lens of what's wrong rather than what's right. Example: *I stumbled through that entire lesson.*
- **Overgeneralizations:** These thoughts are telling you that what happens in one situation will always happen. Example: *The last time I gave this student more time, they just wasted it.*
- **Mind reading:** These thoughts occur when you think you know what someone else is thinking and draw conclusions based on that belief. Example: *That parent never looks me in the eye; she must hate me.*

The Empathetic Classroom

- **Catastrophizing:** These are worst-case scenario thoughts. Example: *My principal wants to meet with me. I must be in trouble.*
- **Personalization:** These thoughts tell you that everything is about you when it may not be. Example: *She doesn't come visit me during recess anymore. I bet she's mad at me.*

5. **Reality-test the thought.** Look at the thought you've identified, the belief behind it, and how it might be distorted. This perspective helps you see the story you've created about the thought to support it. Next, I'm going to ask you to reframe this thought by testing it against reality. This part can be difficult initially because you may *feel* that reality is telling you the thought is true. Sometimes it is, but most times it isn't— especially if this is a thought about yourself that was formed long ago.

- What evidence do you have for the basis of your thought? Is this evidence from the past or is it current? Remember, "evidence" does not automatically mean something is true. It just means we hold onto certain information that supports a story we have about ourselves or others.
- Consider the reliability of the source from which the evidence originated. Maybe some sources are people who said they loved you but were not always capable of showing it. Maybe the intrusive thought arose when a group of people were engaging in group dynamics rather than acting as thoughtful individuals, such as your classmates in grade school. Maybe your evidence comes from a time when someone was tired and frustrated and made a reactionary comment. For example: *When I think about it, I can see that I began to believe I was unlikable when the people picking teams were grade school kids with no supervision. I doubt they were thinking about much other than who would score the most goals. Today I sometimes believe that coworkers dislike me, but I'm not sure if this is true or if the reality is that they just don't know me.*
- It is not uncommon for our minds to tell us something that is false. Reflect on why your mind might want to keep telling

continued

Chapter 12: Responding to Your Intrusive Thoughts About Teaching

you that something is true, even when it might not be. Is there something about that thought that you never want to forget? What is it, and why is it important? What evidence do you have that supports the *opposite* of your thought? For example: *People smile at me quite often. I've had people confide in me. My school principal said how much he appreciates my creativity. And I do have friends, even if it is only a few.*

6. **Name a more accurate thought.** In naming a more accurate thought, you do not need to let go of all aspects of what may have been important to you about the intrusive thought. Maybe the thought was protective. If so, honor that. Or maybe the thought was partly true. Write down a reframe of the thought that is entirely true but that supports your self-worth or that of others. Sometimes a really positive thought will work for you, such as *I love myself.* But other times you just need something that is a stepping stone to more positive thoughts. For example: *I'm not sure how some people feel about me. In many cases, I think most people don't know me well enough to decide if they like me.*

7. **Address relapses.** As you work toward shifting your intrusive thoughts to something more realistic and more helpful, you will encounter your old ideas again—you can bet on it. When that happens, acknowledge the thought for what it is before moving on. For example: *This is an old belief. I'm working on a new one.*

CONCLUSION: FINDING SOLID GROUND

Several years ago, before I took a journey into my own mental health as a teacher, I received a phone call that would change everything about my life. It was my dad on the other end, calling from just five blocks away. With his big, soft hands cradling his old flip phone, he told me as calmly as he could that the doctor had found a spot on his lung. This was my dad who had just backpacked up a peak with my mom and then boogied to live music on Main Street that same evening. The guy who edited all my essays in high school and college, always catching my incorrect use of commas, and who made my peanut butter and jelly sandwich for school lunch for fifteen years. The same person who said I was a natural teacher and who visited my classrooms to talk with my students about astronomy. He was someone who could be silly when the situation called for it and serious as soon as someone scraped a knee. He was a significant and important presence in my life, one that no amount of time would replace.

It was a moment I had long feared as a teacher. At the time, I didn't actually know if I could continue teaching and grieve the loss of my dad at the same time. I didn't know if I could wear the heavy coat of suffering each day to school and still be all the things I thought a teacher should be. Most of all, I didn't want my students to see my sadness, because I did not want to pass it on to them. I also felt like it was something private and personal to me. Maybe I didn't want to deal with people's awkwardness around what to say when someone is sad or grieving. And I was so afraid of showing what I thought at the time was weakness.

It was my own counselor who challenged this thinking. He said, "What would happen if you cried in front of your students, even just a little?"

"I don't know. Maybe they'll laugh."

He looked at me, mildly incredulous. "Why don't you try it the next time you feel sadness come up and see what happens?"

Since we did regular check-ins at the beginning of class, I walked myself right into my counselor's trap. My turn came up in the check-in circle several days later, and an eighth grader asked, "How are you, Ms. Maria?"

Just being asked "How are you?" at this time pretty much guaranteed tears would form in the corners of my eyes. It happened, and I couldn't hide it. They rolled down my cheeks and formed a little puddle on my knee as I looked at the ground, hoping no one would notice. But eighth graders are very observant.

"Are you sad?" someone said.

"Yes," I finally admitted. "I found out last week that my dad has lung cancer."

To my surprise they did exactly what I had been doing for my students for my entire career. They gathered around me and reflected my hurt and sadness. They said things to comfort me. Of course, all of this made me cry more, but by that point the crying cat was out of the bag. I felt like I was playing some weird teacher version of the Grinch. I finally felt something real and personal in front of my students, and my little heart started to beat as I wondered, *What's this?!*

When we model empathy for our students, they can then give that empathy back to others—including us. If we only allow the caring stream to flow one way (from us to them), students miss out on chances to practice the skills needed for meaningful and balanced relationships going forward. As I have touched on throughout this book, care from students or children should not be *expected*, as there are many reasons a child may not be able to show care. And, as adults, it is our primary responsibility to provide care for children. But this reciprocal care can be *allowed*. The physical and mental well-being associated with giving are real, and genuine opportunities for students to play this role will arise in your classroom if you are attuned to them. At the same time, it's essential to care for yourself so that you can continue to extend care and support to your students.

Protecting Your Emotional Energy

As educators, we cannot ignore our students' mental health—and, in fact, we can create an environment that fosters mental health for all. There have been reminders throughout this book to notice when a student is sending cues that they need professional help. As a mandatory reporter, you have to know your state's reporting requirements on abuse or neglect. As part of a school, you must be aware of reporting policies around self-harm, suicidal ideation, substance use, or other harmful behaviors such as bullying. (For your reference, the National Institute of Mental Health's Warning Signs of Suicide infographic is located on page 225.)

At the same time, our perspective as teachers is, by its very nature, a limited one. We know a lot about our students, but we will never know their entire story. There are benefits to this limit! Knowing our students as they are right now allows us to meet and teach them where they are today, and not base our actions on where they've been or where they might be going. It allows us to focus on the momentous task of teaching valuable lessons that will allow them to gain new perspectives and experiences in life.

But even as we work to give students this time, care, and attention, there are also situations in which protecting our own emotional energy is critical to our continued success—and survival—in the profession.

So what are the limits to the emotional work you do in your classroom? Here are some indicators that you have found a limit:

- You think a lot about your students' issues during your time off. Taking home challenging emotional experiences that occur at school can have a significant impact on your home life and relationships outside of school.
- You are emotionally attached to an outcome for a student. You will encounter countless students who have painful histories and current challenges. Here, you can remind yourself that there is nothing that you can do that will take their story of suffering away from them. It is truly theirs, and the challenges and the triumphs that come out of it are theirs as well.
- You project your feelings, thoughts, or traits onto your students. This means you begin to believe your students are just like you, and that you have a solution or know how to handle their problems because you have been there.
- You play a role that's out of your scope of practice. It can be tempting to step into a social worker role and provide a family with assistance, especially when it seems in reach for you to do so. The issue in stepping outside of your role as teacher is that you enter legal and ethical territories that may have ramifications beyond your knowledge. In this case, when you choose to act, you could cause more emotional harm than benefit to your students.

Conclusion: Finding Solid Ground

When we encounter our own limits as educators, we often first experience this in our body. Perhaps we sense a headache coming on. We may be tired, or our body may feel so heavy that we're not sure we can get out of bed. Our balance might be shaky, and we may bump into people and corners. Or maybe we know something is off, but we can't quite put a finger on what it is. Meanwhile, our emotions are forming a little storm cloud over our head as feelings of impatience, irritation, frustration, anger, and depression set in for a good downpour. This is the mind and body saying, "Enough! Get me out of here!" They are staging a revolt because we are forcing them to exist in ways that are not in sync with what we need. And what we need is rest and recovery—but what does that look like while we continue to teach?

How Teachers Recover

Learning to better navigate your emotional landscape is an important step in cultivating a healthier and more sustainable experience in your classroom and at home. Remember back in the introduction when I said we're all in recovery? For educators, the road to recovery is constant and complex. On top of working to meet your students' needs each day, you exist in a school environment that exists in a district within a state and so on. And these entities hold their own ideas about how you should be or what you should or shouldn't do. Cultural, racial, political, and systemic issues in school systems can run deep. Everyone has an opinion. You might try to raise awareness to needs and concerns and not be heard. Or progress might be occurring, but at a glacial pace. Dedicating one's time, energy, and care to a system that may not prioritize human needs—yours or those of your students—can be traumatizing in and of itself. This trauma may not look as you expect it to, but it can be felt in the experience of burnout, silence, or anger. Teachers hold a lot of these traumas and experiences in their bodies.

Find Your People

American psychiatrist Judith Herman (2022), who has dedicated her life's work to understanding and teaching others about the realities of trauma, emphasizes the role of community in recovery. No one thrives alone on an island. Discovering a place where community is already engaged, or building our own community, is how we expand our sense of well-being. The more support structure you have beneath you, the more solid you will feel when challenges arise. I like to think of our communities as a basket we carry at our sides—we get to pick and choose what we put into our basket and what we leave out. While building community, you can decide what's supportive of your well-being. You do not need to take exactly what someone else has in their basket.

Take a look at your larger school community and assess its ability to be a part of your personalized community. Has your school community taken the time to truly address educators' concerns, harms, safety, or stress? Is there a way to raise these issues without fear of retaliation from administrators, parents, or fellow teachers? In a healthy school environment, school leaders serve as a secure base for their educators, students, and parents. Consider the Circle of Security graphic from chapter 6. Just as you offer your students this secure base and safe haven, you deserve to feel heard and cared for when you take concerns to leadership. You should then be encouraged to get back out to teach and take healthy risks. It is leadership's responsibility to actively work on their approach to recovery and regulation, not the educator's responsibility to adjust to school leaders' emotional needs for fear of their reactions. If your nervous system is giving you cues that there is danger in raising your concerns and needs even as you read this, then narrow your window of community to connect most with those who give attunement to you: people who listen empathetically, reflect accurately what you say, ask open-ended questions, and provide validation and encouragement.

If you are uncertain of your broader school community's ability to hear and accept teacher harms, big or small, finding just one trustworthy ally in your school is invaluable. This person will likely be another educator. Allies are those who show signs of having secure attachment traits. They exhibit the ability to handle challenges with calmness, compassion, and clarity. They can listen and collaborate. They work to maintain confidence in relationships. You'll see them connect and hold flexible boundaries with their students. You can always directly ask this individual if they have the time and mindset to listen to concerns. If the answer is no, keep looking! It is better to be aware that someone is not emotionally available than it is to jump right into sharing and then come away feeling unexpectedly empty.

Smaller groups of educators, who don't reply with judgments or cause you to feel shame or guilt for sharing your true thoughts, can be additional supports to fill your community basket. In the Discussion Questions activity on page 219, you'll find two sets of questions based on the concepts in this

Conclusion: Finding Solid Ground

book. You can use these to begin fostering a community of educators that is supportive of well-being. The first set of questions is more general and focuses on the practices in the classroom. These questions would be a good starting point for a new group. The second set of questions is more personal and may be better suited for a more established group or for a group that is looking to build deeper connection.

Seriously, What Is Self-Care?

The human-filled nature of the teaching environment is one in which our senses can often be overwhelmed. Our bodies grow tired. Our minds whirl. There are so many feelings, thoughts, beliefs, ideas, and needs all in one small space. Then, before we know it, that bell rings and then there is silence—*and* a stack of fifty papers waiting to be graded. Teaching is not for the faint of heart! And even when we have built and sustained strong communities, at the end of a long day or week (or month, or year), it's our own reflection we see in the mirror.

For teachers and mental health practitioners alike, *self-care* is often offered up as a solution to burnout—a condition that, itself, has almost become an accepted feature of these professions. While studying to become a counselor, I was often asked what I was doing for self-care. I was so unsure how to answer that it almost felt like a joke. Images came to mind of my fellow classmates and me sitting in a circle giving each other shoulder massages while listening to spa music, a lavender-scented candle sending relaxing wafts into the air.

Can you name a teacher or mental health practitioner who—given the budget and the time–would turn down the opportunity to go out to lunch, book a massage, take a cooking class, or coast along the water on a bike? Yet for many people in these lines of work, being told we should give ourselves some self-care can feel like an insult. No amount of self-care will help us recover from a fifty-hour marathon each week. This is not to say self-care is not needed—it certainly is. But the term's current use often seems to ignore the larger issue at hand: The systems in which humans work should provide opportunities for self-care as standard, not as an extracurricular activity.

If self-care is up to us for the moment while our schools and institutions are figuring themselves out, how can we make our well-being a priority every day? We begin by acknowledging the *self* within "self-care." For a moment, reflect on what comes up for you when I suggest that you be "self-ish." Anytime I recommend this to clients, I see their eyebrows raise. We imagine that being selfish is inherently problematic. And if that is *all* we are, it is. We envision selfishness as a developmental stage we must grow out of. To be self-*less*, though, is the equally problematic flip side of the coin. A more conscious version of selfishness is being aware of what brings you pleasure or joy.

Give Your Body a Voice

Consider this question: *What would make my school day—not my students' day—more pleasurable?* Points for honesty here. (And yes, I'm already imaging the wisecracks from you smarties out there!) If it's been a while since you've encountered the feeling of pleasure at school, this may be a sign that you haven't been selfish enough of late. Listen to your body. What is it telling you it needs? For example, if your back is hurting, what would it be like to lie comfortably on the floor for five minutes every period? Here are some ideas to consider to practice being a little more selfish during a school day:

- **Take back your time.** I know you have lots of things to get done and students to help and teachers to take a duty for, but try saying no for a change. You don't have to suddenly become a "no" person, but you *could* pick one thing that you do not want to commit to, even for one day. It's true that you might initially get a look of surprise or disappointment—and then everyone will get on with their life. There are teachers in your school who are already doing this, who still have their jobs, and who are doing those jobs well.
- **Don't give homework you don't want to grade.** Reassess what your homework assignments are actually doing—and not doing. There are ways to assess students' learning beyond lengthy homework that takes you four hours to grade. It might be as simple as having students write down three key ideas on small whiteboards after you teach a lesson, after which you walk around to look at the answers. You can see what concepts were missed or misunderstood and revisit these the next day. It doesn't mean you'll never assign something longer, but when you do, it will be for a good reason.
- **Insist on quiet time.** Every classroom has its own flavor and flow, but by building in an automatic period of quiet time in each

Conclusion: Finding Solid Ground

day or period, you will allow yourself and your students to reset. Talking is an important part of communicating and connecting, but quiet time is when learning is integrated. You can make this quiet time purposeful and productive, and you can also make it an opportunity to just *be*. You and your students don't constantly have to be accomplishing something!

- **Let loose!** We all need to let down our hair or roll up our cuffs sometimes. Play a game with your students and get silly. Maybe it's dodgeball, baseball, or soccer. Maybe it's finger painting, building with blocks, or making paper airplanes. Get in touch with your child self at least once a day.
- **Bring really good snacks to school.** Keep a personal stash stocked with food for your soul. These snacks should be more than simple fuel. They should look, smell, feel, and taste good. Get some of those fancy dark chocolate almonds, make a cup of loose-leaf tea, toast a slice of crusty bakery bread and top it with apple butter. Make a layered parfait in a jar and enjoy it on break. Make your acts of eating and drinking a ritual rather than a rush.
- **Play some high-quality tunes.** Nothing can change a mood quite like music can. Especially music you like. Not all music you like can be played at school, of course, but find something appropriate that is a mood shifter for you. Play it during class if students are open to it, or get it going during a break. If you play an instrument, bring it and share. There's something uniquely delightful for students about encountering their teacher immersed in listening to or playing their favorite music.

Guilty Pleasure

Now I want you to imagine actually *doing* some of these things that would bring you more pleasure. This is where the teacher guilt usually creeps in and the wagging finger of your past educators and parents may find you: *don't waste your time, get back to work, think about your future, quit messing around.* If this happens, remind yourself that the endpoint of conscious pleasure is not giving up, getting stuck, or failing. It is to reinvigorate your body and mind so that you can continue engaging in those pursuits that matter to you. If endless grading is grating on you, talk to the teacher down the hall who seems to have more free time than you do and ask how they assess their students. If you'd like to incorporate a read-aloud book into your class time, remind yourself of what is gained through the act of reading and being read to, and pick out that book. With some effort and creativity, you can experience pleasure in your school day.

Above all, remember that time taken for you, even in front of your students, is not time without value. In fact, I would argue just the opposite. Allowing students to see an adult actively engaged in totally selfish self-care is a valuable lesson. As a child, I remember watching my dad read each night after he cooked dinner. He would turn on his little lamp, kick his feet up, and ignore us kids for a while. I remember feeling cared for even though he was not playing with me. I now know that I was reaping the benefits of being in the presence of an attachment's regulated nervous state. If you can remember a time from your own childhood when you observed an adult doing something from which they clearly derived pleasure, and that did no harm, this likely stuck with you and maybe even changed your own sense of taking care of yourself.

Looking Back and Moving Forward

The relationships we have with our students are life changing for everyone involved. The impact you will have on countless individuals will never be fully known. When people recall those who have improved their lives, beloved teachers are often at the top of the list. I find my own mind returning to the teacher who first encouraged me to think outside of my comfort zone and the one who took time to sit with me as I cried over geometry that I didn't believe I could do. I often think back to the college classroom where my professor sat on her desk and led discussions that thrilled me. And I remember the science teacher who checked in on my mental health when I suddenly stopped participating. We are lucky when we have moments to encounter these people who literally change our world. Often, their influence lives on in our memories and in many of the little ways we express our humanity.

Now, as a former teacher myself, there is little I find more satisfying than encountering a student years later at the grocery store or a concert, out of the blue, and hearing them recount the years since they've been a student of mine. In those moments, I can see that they've grown, and at the same time I can see a spark of the child that they once were.

As I was finding my seat at my own graduation from my counseling program, in a stadium filled with tens of thousands, I turned around to smile at my fellow classmates and noticed a surprised look on the face of a young man behind me. Moments later, he said, "Miss Maria?" "Yes . . . ?" I said, surprised to hear this title. "I don't know if you remember me, but you taught me as a fourth grader. I'm Joey. I'm graduating with my master's degree today."

In an instant, I was transported back to the little boy who loved to be mischievous at any opportunity he could get. He stood up, taller than me now. With tears suddenly in the corners of both of our eyes, we clasped each other's hands. We were both students now, just two ordinary humans figuring things out, fortunate to pass each other twice on this wild adventure of a life.

For Educator Groups
DISCUSSION QUESTIONS

Reading *The Empathetic Classroom* alongside a group of fellow educators is an excellent way to encourage a more emotionally aware, curious, collaborative, and compassionate work environment— one that doesn't shy away from the tough stuff, and one in which colleagues are there for each other through the ups and downs of life. This book can provide a stepping stone for a shared outlook on how we think and feel about ourselves, each other, and our students. One hope I had in writing this book was to inspire discussion among your faculty about your internal experiences as educators. At its core, this hope is about normalizing some of the challenges we all face and learning from each other about what has worked and—importantly—what has not. Allowing for these real discussions to take place is essential to maintaining a strong heartbeat in our educational environments.

You may choose to read the book chapter by chapter as a study group and then gather to talk about the key points and work through the reflection activities together after finishing each chapter. Or you may find that another way works best for you and your colleagues. Regardless of your approach, after everyone has read the book I recommend gauging interest in further discussion of some of the concepts it addressed. The questions that follow provide starting points for this exploration.

It's vulnerable and uncomfortable work we're delving into here, so it's understandable if you have apprehension about opening up with colleagues. The first set of questions focuses on classroom well-being and is recommended for groups of educators who may not be ready to discuss personal experiences outside of the classroom but are comfortable discussing experiences within the classroom. Members of your group will likely have excellent wisdom and personal nuggets of advice, and these questions can get the ball rolling on sharing those ideas for improving classroom

continued

Conclusion: Finding Solid Ground   **219**

well-being. The second set of questions, focused on personal awareness, is for groups that have more experience discussing personal topics with safeguards in place. This means that everyone has an equal opportunity to share or not, discussion stays within the group, and skilled listening abilities are prioritized. When using either set, I suggest that group members review and reflect on the questions prior to meeting as a group.

Classroom Well-Being Discussion Questions

- How do you get to know your students? What does this look like? Was there ever a time when it felt difficult to get to know someone? How did you react?
- How have you made your classroom an environment that feels safe and welcoming to students? In what ways could you improve?
- Do you have any classroom rituals to help your students feel grounded?
- How have strong emotions (yours or your students') come up in your classroom? Can you name a specific example? What do you do when this happens?
- Describe a time when you felt vulnerable in front of your students. What was this like for you?
- Describe a time you felt triggered by a student's behavior. What do you see now, after reflecting on it?
- What lessons have you learned about power in your classroom? Share an example of power dynamics you've observed or participated in.
- Describe a time you had to talk with your class about something difficult. What was this like for you? How did your students react?
- What concepts from the book do you think you might try out in your classroom? What concerns do you have about doing so?
- What are ways your school could be more supportive of students' and teachers' emotional well-being?

Personal Awareness Discussion Questions

- Share a prominent memory from childhood. What do you remember feeling at the time? How do you feel looking back now? Why do you think this memory has stayed with you? How might aspects of your early experiences shape who you are today?

- What did discipline look like in your household? Who seemed to be in charge of discipline? How has this impacted your own current thoughts on discipline or power?
- What happened when someone in your family cried? How did your caregivers react? Did you feel safe or in danger when you cried?
- What did soothing look like for you as a child? Who was responsible for this and what types of behaviors elicited comforting responses from caregivers?
- How were feelings talked about in your home? Did anyone reflect your feelings to you? Were there any feelings that were encouraged or discouraged?
- What was valued in your home growing up? What values have you chosen to maintain today? What ones have you let go of?
- What is one new takeaway about yourself that you have learned from reading this book?

Conclusion: Finding Solid Ground

ACKNOWLEDGMENTS

Many thanks to those who were my early readers and whose responses gave me the fuel to go somewhere with my project. Dr. Katey Franklin, for her professional eye and stamp of approval as both an educator and counselor. My mentor, Stephen Davenport, who is not only an excellent educator but an excellent writer, and who spent hours really caring about the nuances of my examples and concepts. My mom, Theresa Nichols Schuster, whose editing expertise and writing work ethic are both gifts I am grateful to be the recipient of. My good friend and school psychologist, Steve Marty, for predicting my future and finding the details in my work that no one else would. Teacher and friend Marka Latif, an educator who isn't afraid to "do something different" and whose excitement for my work was essential.

There are many folks at Free Spirit Publishing and Teacher Created Materials who have dedicated significant effort toward seeing this book into being. Thank you all for being excellent collaborators and providing the highest levels of skills and expertise.

Writing can be a lonely and frustrating world, but my acquisitions editor at Free Spirit Publishing, Tom Rademacher, made sure it was anything but. Tom really made me feel seen as a new author and told me to "write the book I needed to write" anytime I was unsure. His positive support, professionalism, and humor made the decision to say yes to Free Spirit Publishing easy. I can't imagine a better person to introduce me to the world of book publishing.

In writing about the necessity of validation in our messy human experiences, I am grateful to have a person on my team who does just that: Alison Behnke, senior editor at Free Spirit Publishing, has allowed me to experience the benefits of genuine connection each step of the way in this process of book publishing—she gets excited along with me, knows when to take things seriously, and doesn't shy away from valuable feedback. The care she has for me as a person and my writing is ever-present and has allowed me to show up as myself in every aspect of this experience. Sitting down to a note from Alison is something I can only compare to the feeling of opening a gift.

I am grateful to the educators who allowed me to include their stories in this book: Eric Álvarez, Jacob "Buck" Turcotte, Melissa Barry-Hansen, James "Jim" Benes, and Stephen Davenport. Their natural care and ability to connect with their students is palpable, and I feel fortunate that they were willing to share personal experiences.

Several organizations and individuals kindly agreed to allow me to reprint their relevant and helpful materials so that I could expand on and clarify ideas in this book, including Jacob Martinez, LPC; Circle of Security International; Dr. Rebecca Koltz; Dr. Katey Franklin; The National Institute of Mental Health, Intermountain/ChildWise Institute; Deb Dana; and Dr. Janina Fisher.

Special thanks to my writing hero, author Janet Fox, for answering my questions about the ins and outs of nonfiction and pointing me to my publisher. The writing community is in a better place because of authors like her, who are not only highly skilled at their craft, but are believers in the power of kindness and knowledge sharing to see that writing continues to be a place for all voices.

I'm so appreciative of the clinicians who have sat with me in the "here and now" and who have guided my work with their insight, honesty, and humor—especially Justin Short, Ashton Snyder, Dr. Heidi McKinley, Mary Corelli, and Rebekah Patrick.

To my husband, Mark, who has supported my writing, teaching, and counseling in many forms and over many years of schooling, who encourages me to "go make the world a better place."

APPENDIX

WARNING SIGNS OF SUICIDE:
The behaviors listed below may be some of the signs that someone is thinking about suicide.

TALKING ABOUT:

- Wanting to die
- Great guilt or shame
- Being a burden to others

FEELING:

- Empty, hopeless, trapped, or having no reason to live
- Extremely sad, more anxious, agitated, or full of rage
- Unbearable emotional or physical pain

CHANGING BEHAVIOR, SUCH AS:

- Making a plan or researching ways to die
- Withdrawing from friends, saying goodbye, giving away important items, or making a will
- Taking dangerous risks such as driving extremely fast
- Displaying extreme mood swings
- Eating or sleeping more or less
- Using drugs or alcohol more often

If these warning signs apply to you or someone you know, get help as soon as possible, particularly if the behavior is new or has increased recently.

988 Suicide & Crisis Lifeline
Call or text 988
Chat at 988lifeline.org

Crisis Text Line
Text "HELLO" to 741741

  National Institute of Mental Health

www.nimh.nih.gov/suicideprevention

NIMH Identifier No. OM 22-4316

How to Find Your Own Mental Health Professional

Searching for a mental health professional can be an overwhelming and scary process. This is someone with whom you intend to share deep personal stuff, so you want to be sure you can trust them. It can seem like there are so many people to choose from and so many different styles of therapy. How do you ever choose? Here's my guide, as counselor, for connecting with a provider who works for you.

First, it is important to be aware that there are many names for mental health professionals, including psychotherapists, counselors, psychologists, social workers, family therapists, child therapists, couples' therapists, addiction counselors, and career counselors. In addition, each state has its own licensing requirements, and this also dictates what clinicians can call themselves. You do want a licensed provider. You'll see their license type after their name: LCSW, LCPC, LPC, LMHC, Psy.D., or Ph.D. An unlicensed provider might use the term "life coach" and claim to treat mental health disorders. While a life coach or mentor may be the right fit for your needs, it's important to recognize the potential limitations of this relationship.

There are numerous benefits to seeing a licensed provider. One is that you, as the client, are offered many protections, including HIPAA, an explanation of your privacy and rights, and the ability to consent for services. In addition, treatments are more effective due to these providers' extensive qualifications (including meeting degree requirements, training, supervision, and following profession-specific ethical standards). Licensed providers must also meet certain standards to maintain their license. If you are unclear about what a provider's specific title and licensure mean, you can always ask. If you want to ensure that a provider you are interested in is currently licensed, you can view their license and practice information by looking up their credentials at npiregistry.cms.hhs.gov using their National Provider Identifier (NPI) number.

However, before you jump onto a provider database for your area and start looking at profiles, answer these questions:

- Why am I seeking the support of a mental health provider right now?
- What am I expecting from the experience?
- Do I have any identity requirements/preferences for my provider? (For example: gender; age; racial, ethnic, or cultural

background; religion; sexual orientation; or explicit support for experiences or lifestyles.)

- Do I have any ideas about what type of personality would be helpful for me? (For example: more direct, good listener, uses humor or not, challenging, supportive, interactive, and so on.)
- What time, money, or location constraints or preferences do I need to consider? Do I want to meet in person or online? If in person, do I want (or not want) to meet close to work? After school? Do I want the ability to meet outdoors?
- What are my goals for therapy?
- When will I know I no longer need therapy?
- Is there anything that would be helpful for my provider to know to best work with me?

Now is, hopefully, the fun part. Get on one of those provider databases, such as Psychology Today or GoodTherapy. Start talking to people you know who have gone to therapy. If you do like the sound of a friend's therapist, be sure to alert the provider that your friend sees them before you begin working together. The therapist won't be able to confirm or deny that they see your friend, but they should be aware so they can determine if there will be a conflict of interest. If you're using a database, use filters to narrow down your options. It will be of central importance that you find a provider who accepts your insurance or offers a sliding fee scale that works for you. Next, look at the answers to the questions you asked yourself earlier, and filter options further based on these needs. Before getting invested in the idea of a specific provider, I strongly suggest looking at what they treat or specialize in. Most providers specialize in treating specific disorders. The more complex the issues you're seeking help with, the more essential it is to find a provider who will offer reliable treatment.

Also, look at photos! This may sound shallow, but in this case, appearance matters. Because of your own history, some faces will appear friendly or safe, and some may appear scary or untrustworthy. This has been well studied. It's how we choose friends and mates and how we determine an enemy. You probably know this assessment of a person may not be accurate, but for therapy to start off on the right foot, your provider's appearance needs to provide you with cues of safety. Say a provider reminds you of your father—maybe that is a good thing, or maybe not. To feel comfortable with the topics you want to talk about, you might prefer someone who appears

How to Find Your Own Mental Health Professional

older than you—or someone who resembles a peer. Avoid providers you find sexually or romantically attractive. That dynamic will not result in effective therapy and can be very challenging to address in the therapy room.

Providers usually write their own bios, and you can learn a lot from this little nugget of text. What is their tone like? What do they focus on? Do you feel invited to work with them based on what they are saying? Do they talk about things in a way that clicks for you? What does other text on the page tell you about this person?

Using all these guidelines, try to put together a list of five providers you like. Now, a big step . . . reaching out. You can usually do this through email or by phone. Many providers have full days, just like you, so try to keep your initial communication to the point. Here's what they're generally looking for:

Hi, my name is _____. I'm _____ years old. I have (type of insurance)/I (would need a sliding fee scale/can pay directly). I'm seeking therapy for _____. This has been affecting me for (amount of time). If you have an opening, I would like to set up a consultation. I would (need, want, or prefer) (time and/or day of week) for regular sessions. My phone number or email is _____. I am (okay/not okay) with a voicemail or email reply.

Be prepared for it to take a while for providers to get back to you. And unfortunately, some may never respond at all. If you do not hear back after three days, it is okay to reach out again. Some providers have a waiting list that you can be added to if they are full. You may have to reach out to more providers than you expected to find your match.

A consultation meeting is how you and your provider will determine if you are the right fit for each other. This can bring up fears of rejection, but it is key that you find someone who you want to work with and who wants to work with you. There are many reasons the fit may not be right, including ones that you will likely have no knowledge of, such as the provider's own history and triggers. Or a provider may feel that someone else has more appropriate experience for what you are seeking therapy for.

It's ideal if you can go the provider's office for a consultation rather than doing it over the phone. These meetings are usually shorter than the average length of a therapy session, and they give you a chance to assess your surroundings. What do you think of their office? How does their furniture feel? Do you need natural light? Also notice what it feels like to be with the counselor. Do you notice yourself feeling dysregulated—sweating,

The Empathetic Classroom

breathing hard, heart racing? Is this because you're nervous or because something about the interaction feels off? Do you sense this person is genuine and that you can trust them? You might want to bring the questions you answered on page 226. Just as the provider is wanting to learn about you in this meeting, you are also interviewing them—so feel free to ask questions. They always have the option to answer as they wish. I've had some surprising things matter to clients, and I was so glad they asked. *Are you married? What happens if I feel angry while at therapy? Do you have any pets? What do we do in therapy? What does it cost? What kinds of things do you need to report?* Great questions!

I always ask my clients to reflect on their time with me for a day or two before deciding if they want to move forward together. I tell them to think about how it felt to talk with me. I ask them to notice how being in the room felt. I ask them to reflect on whether they felt safe. I let them know that if they decide to not go with me, it's okay—my feelings will not be hurt. I encourage them to shop around. I want them to have a good experience with therapy.

Another thing to know is that one of the most common fears my clients have about the therapy relationship is how to go about ending it. This is an important aspect of being in therapy (and life), and you can ask your provider for information about it upfront. There are many reasons to end therapy, including feeling better, feeling stuck, feeling disconnected or misunderstood by your provider, a change in finances, ethical concerns, or just feeling you've outgrown your provider. Providers are trained to transition clients out of therapy, so I recommend you be brave and always let your provider know if something has shifted for you and you would like to conclude your work.

Now you have a few guidelines for getting started in this therapy world. If you decide to work with someone, congratulations! I hope this relationship will provide you with benefits beyond the therapy room for years to come.

How to Find Your Own Mental Health Professional

RECOMMENDED RESOURCES

Books

Adult Children of Emotionally Immature Parents: How to Heal from Distant, Rejecting, or Self-Involved Parents by Lindsay C. Gibson. New Harbinger Publications, 2015.

Anchored: How to Befriend Your Nervous System Using Polyvagal Theory by Deb Dana. Sounds True, 2021.

Attached: The New Science of Adult Attachment and How It Can Help You Find—and Keep—Love by Amir Levine and Rachel S. F. Heller. TarcherPerigee, 2010.

Be Child Wise: A Dynamic Approach to Raising and Caring for Emotionally Distressed Children by Intermountain and ChildWise Institute, 2016.

Far from the Tree: Parents, Children, and the Search for Identity by Andrew Solomon. Scribner, 2012.

How to Navigate Life: The New Science of Finding Your Way in School, Career, and Beyond by Belle Liang and Timothy Klein. St. Martin's Press, 2022.

No Bad Parts: Healing Trauma and Restoring Wholeness with the Internal Family Systems Model by Richard C. Schwartz. Sounds True, 2021.

Trauma and Recovery: The Aftermath of Violence—from Domestic Abuse to Political Terror by Judith Herman. Basic Books, 2022.

The Whole-Brain Child: 12 Revolutionary Strategies to Nurture Your Child's Developing Mind by Daniel J. Siegel and Tina Payne Bryson. Delacorte Press, 2011.

Under Pressure: Confronting the Epidemic of Stress and Anxiety in Girls by Lisa Damour. Ballantine Books, 2020.

Organizations and Websites

Child Mind Institute. childmind.org.

DonorsChoose. donorschoose.org.

National Council for Mental Wellbeing. thenationalcouncil.org.

REFERENCES

Ainsworth, Mary D. Salter, and Silvia M. Bell. 1970. "Attachment, Exploration, and Separation: Illustrated by the Behavior of One-Year-Olds in a Strange Situation." *Child Development* 41 (1): 49–67. doi.org/10.2307/1127388.

Baggerly, Jennifer N. 2004. "The Effects of Child-Centered Group Play Therapy on Self-Concept, Depression, and Anxiety of Children Who Are Homeless." *International Journal of Play Therapy* 13 (2): 31–51. doi.org/10.1037/h0088889.

Barrett, Peter, Fay Davies, Yufan Zhang, and Lucinda Barrett. 2015. "The Impact of Classroom Design on Pupils' Learning: Final Results of a Holistic, Multi-Level Analysis." *Building and Environment* 89: 118–133. doi.org/10.1016/j.buildenv.2015.02.013.

Beck, Aaron T., A. John Rush, Brian F. Shaw, and Gary Emery. 1979. *Cognitive Therapy of Depression.* The Guilford Press.

Brown, Elizabeth Levine, Kate L. Phillippo, Karen Weston, and Susan Rodger. 2019. "United States and Canada Pre-Service Teacher Certification Standards for Student Mental Health: A Comparative Case Study." *Teaching and Teacher Education* 80: 71–82. doi.org/10.1016/j.tate.2018.12.015.

Centers for Disease Control and Prevention. 2024. *Youth Risk Behavior Survey Data Summary and Trends Report: 2013–2023.* U.S. Department of Health and Human Services. cdc.gov/yrbs/dstr/index.html.

Cooper, Glen, Kent Hoffman, and Bert Powell. 2018. "The Circle of Security: Teacher Attending to the Child's Needs." Image, Circle of Security International. Accessed February 15, 2024. circleofsecurityinternational.com/cosc-approach-an-overview.

Dana, Deb. 2021. *Anchored: How to Befriend Your Nervous System Using Polyvagal Theory.* Sounds True.

Doan, Sy, Elizabeth D. Steiner, Rakesh Pandey, and Ashley Woo. 2023. *Teacher Well-Being and Intentions to Leave: Findings from the 2023 State of the American Teacher Survey*. RAND Corporation. rand.org/content/dam/rand/pubs/research_reports/RRA1100/RRA1108-8/RAND_RRA1108-8.pdf.

Feeling Wheel. Accessed January 7, 2025. allthefeelz.app/cc/feeling-wheel.

Feldman, Ruth. 2007. "Parent–Infant Synchrony: Biological Foundations and Developmental Outcomes." *Current Directions in Psychological Science* 16 (6): 340–345. doi/10.1111/j.1467-8721.2007.00532.x.

Fisher, Janina. 2011. *Psychoeducational Aids for Working with Psychological Trauma*, 10th edition. janinafisher.com.

Franklin, Cynthia G. S., Johnny S. Kim, Tiffany N. Ryan, Michael S. Kelly, and Katherine L. Montgomery. 2012. "Teacher Involvement in School Mental Health Interventions: A Systematic Review." *Children and Youth Services Review* 34 (5): 973–982. sciencedirect.com/science/article/abs/pii/S0190740912000503.

Franklin, Katey T. 2022. "The Classroom System" and "Visualizing Change" [class exercises]. *Child and Adolescent Counseling*. Montana State University, Bozeman, HDCO 525.

Gibson, Lindsay C. 2015. *Adult Children of Emotionally Immature Parents: How to Heal from Distant, Rejecting, or Self-Involved Parents*. New Harbinger Publications.

Harris, Judith Rich. 1998. *The Nurture Assumption: Why Children Turn Out the Way They Do*. Free Press.

Herman, Judith. 2022. *Trauma and Recovery: The Aftermath of Violence—from Domestic Abuse to Political Terror*. Basic Books.

IFS Institute. n.d. "What Is Internal Family Systems?" Accessed January 6, 2025. ifs-institute.com.

Intermountain and ChildWise Institute. 2016. *Be Child Wise: A Dynamic Approach to Raising and Caring for Emotionally Distressed Children*. ChildWise Institute.

Jones, Elizabeth Murphy, and Garry Landreth. 2002. "The Efficacy of Intensive Individual Play Therapy for Chronically Ill Children." *International Journal of Play Therapy* 11 (1): 117–140. doi.org/10.1037/h0088860.

Kennedy, Becky. 2022. *Good Inside: A Guide to Becoming the Parent You Want to Be*. Harper Wave.

Kohut, Heinz. 1984. *How Does Analysis Cure?* University of Chicago Press.

Koltz, Rebecca L., and Katey T. Franklin. 2012. "Goals of Behavior: Part 1: What You Can Do to Redirect Your Kid!" *Montana Parent* November 2012: 54–55. Media Mavens, LLC.

Landreth, Garry L. 2002. "Therapeutic Limit Setting in the Play Therapy Relationship." *Professional Psychology: Research and Practice* 33 (6): 529–535. doi.org/10.1037/0735-7028.33.6.529.

Lin, Yung-Wei, and Sue C. Bratton. 2015. "A Meta-Analytic Review of Child-Centered Play Therapy Approaches." *Journal of Counseling & Development* 93 (1): 45–58. doi.org/10.1002/j.1556-6676.2015.00180.x.

Martinez, Jacob. n.d. "Updated ACT Wheel." ACT Naturally. Accessed January 7, 2025. actnaturally.net/actmaterials.

Moon, Jungrim, Anne Williford, and Amy Mendenhall. 2017. "Educators' Perceptions of Youth Mental Health: Implications for Training and the Promotion of Mental Health Services in Schools." *Children and Youth Services Review* 73: 384–391. doi.org/10.1016/j.childyouth.2017.01.006.

National Council for Mental Wellbeing. n.d. "Mental Health First Aid." Accessed January 7, 2025. thenationalcouncil.org/our-work/mental-health-first-aid.

National Institute of Mental Health. 2022. "Warning Signs of Suicide." NIMH Identifier No. OM 22-4316. nimh.nih.gov/health/publications/warning-signs-of-suicide.

Nummenmaa, Lauri, Enrico Glerean, Ritta Hari, and Jari K. Hietanen. 2014. "Bodily Maps of Emotions." *Proceedings of the National Academy of Sciences* 111 (2): 646–651. doi.org/10.1073/pnas.1321664111.

Perl, Ofer, Or Duek, Kaustubh R. Kulkarni, Charles Gordon, John H. Krystal, Ifat Levy, Ilan Harpaz-Rotem, and Daniela Schiller. 2023. "Neural Patterns Differentiate Traumatic from Sad Autobiographical Memories in PTSD." *Nature Neuroscience* 26: 2226–2236. doi.org/10.1038/s41593-023-01483-5.

Phillips, Lindsey. 2021. "Yalom Discusses Power of Therapeutic Relationships at ACA Virtual Conference Experience." *Counseling Today*. ctarchive.counseling.org/2021/04/yalom-discusses-power-of-therapeutic-relationships-at-aca-virtual-conference-experience.

Porges, Stephen W. 2022. "Polyvagal Theory: A Science of Safety." *Frontiers in Integrative Neuroscience* (16): 871227. doi.org/10.3389/fnint.2022.871227.

Prochaska, James O., and Carlo DiClemente. 1983. "Stages and Processes of Self-Change of Smoking: Toward an Integrative Model of Change." *Journal of Consulting and Clinical Psychology* 51 (3): 390–395. doi.org/10.1037/0022-006X.51.3.390.

Steiner, Riley J., Ganna Sheremenko, Catherine Lesesne, Patrica J. Dittus, Renee E. Sieving, and Kathleen A. Ethier. 2019. "Adolescent Connectedness and Adult Health Outcomes." *Pediatrics* 144 (1): e20183766. doi.org/10.1542/peds.2018-3766.

Schwartz, Richard C. 2020. *No Bad Parts: Healing Trauma and Restoring Wholeness with the Internal Family Systems Model.* Sounds True.

Vipassana Hawai'i. n.d. "R.A.I.N. ~ D.R.O.P." Accessed January 7, 2025. vipassanahawaii.org/resources/raindrop.

Walker, Robin. 2011. "Making Child Therapy Work." Psychotherapy.net. Video, 1 hour, 35 min. psychotherapy.net/video/walker-child-therapy.

Yalom, Irvin D. 1980. *Existential Psychotherapy.* Basic Books.

INDEX

f denotes figure.

A

abuse, 4, 142, 163

acceptance and commitment therapy (ACT), 36, 37*f*, 38

acknowledging feelings, 75

action stage of change, 119

ACT Method, 74–78

Ainsworth, Mary, 99–100

"alarm systems", 34, 197

allies, 213

alternative behaviors, 70*f*, 71*f*, 72*f*, 75, 76, 77–78

Álvarez, Eric, 89–90, 97–98, 103

American Counseling Association, 14

American Foundation for Suicide Prevention, 6

amygdala, 2, 140–141, 144

Anchored (Dana), 155–156

anchors, 41, 42–43, 149–150, 156, 159, 202

anger
  anchoring as response to, 41, 42–43, 149–150, 156, 159, 202
  "caring for", 23
  in goals of student behavior, 71*f*
  helping students through, 27, 56, 58, 75
  physical sensations from, 62
  protective role of, 38, 40
  self-awareness of, 8, 39–40, 53
  as suicide warning sign, 225
  in sympathetic nervous system state, 146, 149
  triggers and, 151

anxiety
  anchoring as response to, 41, 42–43, 149–150, 156, 159, 202
  automatic thoughts in, 196
  "caring for", 23
  in COVID-19 pandemic, 139
  environment and, 84, 85, 88
  helping students through, 27
  physical sensations from, 63
  play therapy in, 126
  self-awareness of, 25–26
  as suicide warning sign, 225
  in sympathetic nervous system state, 146, 147–149
  See also fear

anxious attachment style, 100, 101, 110–111

artwork, 65, 82–83, 93, 122–123, 130–131, 157

assignments, 165–166, 168–169, 171–172, 215

attachment, 97–112
  history of psychology behind, 99–100
  relationship-building with students in, 98–99, 103–107, 112
  in-school manifestations of, 101–103, 102*f*, 110–111
  in structural dissociation, 37*f*

attention-seeking behaviors, 70*f*, 77–78, 100
  attunement, 19–31
  in building community, 213
  cues of connection in, 21–22
  self-attunement in, 22–24, 25–26, 31*f*
  to a system, 24–26, 29–30, 31*f*
  wanting to be wanted in, 20–21
  to your past, 26–28

automatic thoughts, 196

autonomic nervous system (ANS), 143–144

avoidant attachment style, 100, 110, 111, 205–208

awards ceremonies, 129

B

babies, 99–100

Barry-Hansen, Melissa, 82–83, 90, 103–104

Beck, Aaron T., 196–197

behavior, 66–81
  attachment styles and, 101–3, 102*f*, 107
  "behavior train" approach towards, 67
  guidelines for intervention in, 74–78, 80–81
  power dynamics in, 36, 38, 71*f*, 72*f*, 161–162, 163
  self-judgment in, 198
  teachers' intrusive thoughts on, 199–200
  trauma in, 141–143, 144, 163
  in triggering teachers, 33, 34, 35–36, 38, 39–40, 42, 45–48, 50, 70*f*–72*f*, 73
  understanding emotions behind, 61, 68–69, 70*f*–72*f*, 73–74, 80–81

beliefs
  behind student behavior, 70f–72f, 73
  in communication, 179
  in intrusive thoughts, 196–198, 199–201,
    205–208
  in risk-taking, 72f, 144
Benes, Jim, 184–185, 188
Benji (student), 141–142, 143
Best, Charles, 90
Bill (teacher), 32–33, 36, 39–40
the body
  in nervous system regulation, 146, 149, 150,
    155–156, 157–160
  physical sensations in (see physical sensations)
  in self-care, 89, 215–216
  triggers and, 34, 151, 153
body language, 21, 151, 152, 157–158, 164
boundaries, 184–193
  as control, 187
  in discussing emotions with students, 57, 58
  flexibility in, 188–189, 190
  overuse of, 186
  priorities in, 189–191, 192–193
  types of, 187–188
  underuse of, 185–186
brains
  calories for, 88
  intrusive thoughts in, 195, 203
  in nervous system, 157
  play and, 125
  sadness in, 52
  triggers in, 34, 140–141, 143, 144
  See also nervous system
brainstem, 140, 144
bravery, 158, 159
breathing, 41, 80, 134, 152–153
bullying, 32, 66–67, 69, 73–74, 75

C

calmness and relaxation
  anchoring in, 41, 42–43, 149–150, 156, 159, 202
  in cues of connection, 21
  environment in, 84–85, 92
  in exploring playful side, 134
  muscle relaxation in, 153
  nervous system in, 147, 148, 149, 158, 159
care, 3, 33, 98, 210
  See also self-care
caregivers. See parents
Carl (teacher), 199–200
catastrophizing, 207

Centers for Disease Control and Prevention (CDC),
  3
change, 113–123
  direct communication in, 178–180
  habit and, 114–115
  healing fantasies in, 115, 116
  inward basis of, 115–116
  stages of, 116–120
  Visualizing Change activity for, 122–123
choice, 77, 89, 128, 171, 172
Circle of Security, 102–103, 102f
classical conditioning, 166
classroom environment, 82–96
  attunement to, 24–26, 29–31
  daily rituals in, 87, 95–96
  environmental psychology and, 83–84
  importance of, 84–86
  power dynamics in (see power)
  qualities of great, 86–90, 92–94
Classroom System activity, 29–30
cognitive behavioral therapy (CBT), 196
collaboration, 70f, 76–78, 173
colors, 23, 65, 92, 149, 153, 158
communication
  in attunement, 20–22, 23, 27–28
  in behavioral intervention, 75–78, 80–81
  boundaries in, 184–85, 186, 188, 190, 191, 211
  in change, 114, 116–120
  in classroom environment, 84, 87, 88
  emotion-oriented language in, 12
  in feedback (see feedback)
  indirect vs. direct, 166–168, 172–173, 178–180
  with mental health professionals (see mental
    health professionals)
  on observations of others' emotions, 53–54,
    55–59
  with parents, 120, 148, 171, 172, 185, 188–189
  in relationship-building with students, 90,
    103–107, 211
  about student behavior, 66–67, 68–69
  about triggers, 42, 43, 49–50
community, 212–214
conditioning, 166
connection. See relationship-building
consequences, 66–67, 68, 76–77, 169
consistency, 105–106
contemplation stage of change, 117–118
context, 171, 172
control. See power
co-regulation, 125, 145–146, 152–153, 217
corners, 89

238   *The Empathetic Classroom*

corrective emotional experiences, 21
Council for Accreditation of Counseling, 14
COVID-19 pandemic, 139
cues of connection, 21–22

D

D, Ms. (teacher), 19–20, 25–26, 27
Dana, Deborah A., 147, 149, 155–156
danger. *See* triggers
Davenport, Stephen, 105
de-escalation, 42, 202
defensiveness, 36
dentists, 84–85
depression
    in COVID-19 pandemic, 139
    natural elements in, 88
    nervous system in, 149
    play therapy and, 124, 126, 130–131
    prevalence of in students, 3
    in teachers, 7
    visualizing change in, 122–123
detachment, 107
developmental age, 142
DiClemente, Carlo, 116
digital natives, 2
direct communication, 167, 172–173, 178–180
disgust, 63, 71*f*
dissociation, 36, 37*f*, 149
DonorsChoose, 90
dorsal vagal state, 146, 147, 148, 149, 151, 157, 160
drawing, 65, 93, 122–123, 130–131, 157

E

ecotherapy, 83–84
ego, 176, 197
emotional detachment, 107
emotional mapping, 61–65
    See also feeling wheels
emotions
    in attachment styles, 100, 101–102, 107
    attunement to, 20–24, 25–28, 29–31
    in behavioral intervention, 74–78, 80–81
    behind student behavior, 61, 64, 68–69, 70*f*–72*f*,
        73–74, 80–81
    boundaries and, 184–85, 187, 192–193
    in change, 113–114
    communication on observations of others',
        53–54, 55–59
    as data, 52–54, 61–65
    in direct and indirect communication, 178, 179,
        180
    environment in, 84, 85

intrusive thoughts in, 194–195, 196, 197–198
in mental health mindset for teaching, 3, 4–5,
    7–12, 209–212
nervous system in, 143–144, 145–150, 155–160
play and, 125, 126
in power balance, 170
regulation of (*see* regulation)
in relationship-building, 3, 7–11, 21–22, 104, 105,
    107, 184–185, 210
as shared experience, 55–57
in suicide warning signs, 225
in teacher exodus, 7
in trauma, 139–40, 142, 143, 145, 146–150,
    151–153
triggers in, 34, 37*f*, 38, 39–40, 45–50, 49*f*
visualizing change in, 122–123
empathetic attunement. *See* attunement
The Empty Chair activity, 80–81
entrance and exit rituals, 87, 95–96
environment. *See* classroom environment
environmental psychology, 83–84
Explore Your Playful Side activity, 134–135

F

fear
    in behavior management, 67, 72*f*, 198
    of change, 113–114
    of classroom emotional expression, 56
    environment and, 84, 85
    intrusive thoughts and, 196, 201–203
    in nervous system, 37*f*, 158, 159
    in passive aggressive communication, 178, 179
    past experiences in, 26, 39–40, 143
    self-awareness of, 26, 39–40, 53, 170
    in triggers, 37*f*, 39–40
    See also anxiety
feedback
    from students, 8, 88, 98, 106, 168–169
    from teachers, 81, 171–173
    See also grading
feelings. *See* emotions
feeling wheels, 25–26, 31*f*, 61, 64
    See also emotional mapping
fight, flight, freeze, submit, or attach response, 36,
    37*f*, 140, 143–144, 147, 148, 151
"firefighter" emotions, 38
flexibility, 54, 56, 155, 171, 173
flexible boundaries, 188–189, 190
focus, 120
food, 88–89, 216
free writes, 105
Freud, Anna, 125

Index **239**

Freud, Sigmund, 20
frustration, 25–26, 27, 58, 70*f*, 75–77
fun, 128
   See also play

G

Gabe (student), 113–114
Genuine Experience of Self, 16
Getting to Know My Nervous System activity, 157–160
Gifting Improv Game, 136–137
giving up, 72*f*
Goals of Behavior charts, 69, 70*f*–72*f*, 77
Good Inside (Kennedy), 43
Gracie (student), 143
grading, 165–166, 171, 215
   See also feedback
gratitude, 39, 49*f*, 135
Grayson (student), 77
greetings, 84, 87
guilt. *See* shame and guilt

H

habit, 114–115
happiness, 23, 52, 53, 63, 134
healing fantasies, 115, 116
helplessness, 72*f*
Herman, Judith, 212
hide-and-seek, 128
homework, 165–166, 168–169, 171–172, 215
hopelessness, 3, 72*f*, 149

I

Identifying My Attachment Tendencies at School activity, 110–111
Identifying My Triggers activity, 45–48
indirect communication, 166–168, 178, 179
individuality, 86
infants, 99–100
Insight Survey, 104–105, 112
inspiration, 132
Internal Family Systems (IFS), 36, 38
intrusive thoughts, 194–208
   beliefs behind, 196–198, 199–201, 205–208
   brains as explorers in, 203
   internal chatter in, 195–196
   origins of as concept, 196
   responding to, 198–200, 201–203, 205–208
irritability, 53–54, 57, 70*f*, 151

J

James (student), 199–200

Janice (teacher), 194–195
Jason Flatt Act, 6
Johnny (student), 97–98
journaling, 50, 135
judgment, 197–198
Julie (student), 66–67, 68, 69, 73–74

K

karaoke, 128
Kendra (therapy client), 51–52
Kennedy, Becky, 43
Kohut, Heinz, 20–21
Kylie (student), 75

L

Landreth, Garry, 74–75
licensure, of mental health professionals, 226
life coaches, 226
lighting, 87–88
limbic system, 125, 140, 144
limit setting, 74–78
listening, 23, 50, 213
lying, 33, 36, 39–40, 41

M

Maddie (therapy client), 124, 130–131
maintenance stage of change, 119–120
mandatory reporters, 4
marks, 165
McDonald, Michele, 198
memories. *See* the past
Mental Health First Aid, 6
mental health mindset
   need for in classrooms, 3–5, 16
   relationship-building in, 3, 7–11, 15–16, 210
   risks of, 11–13
   teachers' mental health in, 6–7, 10–11, 210–217
   teacher training for, 5–7
   theoretical foundation for, 14–15
mental health professionals
   attunement with, 20–22
   child clients and, 15, 124, 125–127, 130–131, 141
   how to find, 226–229
   nature-based therapy with, 83–84
   power dynamics with, 173
   reflection on emotions with, 51–52
   in teachers' roles, 4
   when to seek support from, 10–11, 112, 196, 197, 202–203
Meyers, Principal, 66, 69, 73, 74
mind reading, 206
monoamine oxidase A (MAO-A), 52

mood. *See* emotions
movement, 125, 129, 153, 157–158
muscle relaxation, 153
music, 128, 129, 153, 216
My Power Associations activity, 176–177

N

natural consequences, 77, 169
naturalness, 86, 87–88
nature-based therapy, 83–84
nature-nurture debate, 100
negative filtering, 206
neglect, 4
nervous system, 143–144, 145–150, 155–160
    See also regulation
neuroception, 146
Noticing Cues activity, 155–156
Noticing My Communication Patterns activity, 178–180

O

The Observation Point activity, 49–50, 49*f*
ocean waves, 24
open doors, 113–114
overgeneralizations, 206

P

painting, 65, 105
parasympathetic nervous system, 146, 147
parents
    in attachment styles, 99–100
    beliefs from, 197
    in co-regulation, 145, 217
    in developmental age, 142
    in healing fantasies, 115
    lack of empathetic cues from, 21
    mismatch between words and actions in, 55
    students taking on responsibilities of, 69
    teacher communication with, 120, 148, 171, 172, 185, 188–189
    yelling by, 143, 179
passive aggressive communication, 167, 178
the past
    in attunement, 26–28
    beliefs stemming from, 197, 199–200, 206
    in emotional mapping, 64, 65
    in exploring your playful side, 134–135
    importance of self-awareness regarding, 8
    triggers stemming from, 38, 39–40, 141
pencil nubs, 129
performances and presentations, 1–2, 25–27, 113–114, 196

personality
    getting to know students', 103–105, 112
    nature-nurture debate on, 100
    parts of, 36, 37*f*, 38
    showing students your, 89–90, 127–128, 216
personalization, 207
philosophers, 165
physical sensations
    in emotional mapping, 61, 62–63
    negative emotions stemming from, 57–58
    nervous system in, 146, 149, 155–156
    in suicide warning signs, 225
    triggers and, 153
    See also senses
plants, 88
play, 124–37
    communication and connection through, 124–127, 130–133
    in daily schedule, 127–128
    in self-care, 134–135, 216
    teaching through, 128–129, 132, 136–137
play therapy, 125–127, 130–131, 141
pockets, 89
polarized thinking, 206
polyvagal theory, 143–144, 145, 146–147, 155–160
Porges, Stephen, 143–144, 146
porous boundaries, 187, 188–89
post-traumatic stress disorder (PTSD), 83–84, 141
power, 161–183
    attachment styles and, 101–102
    balance of, 169–173
    boundaries and, 187
    feedback and, 168–169, 171–173
    indirect vs. direct communication in, 166–168, 172–173, 178–180
    letting students in on, 77, 164–168, 172–173, 181–183
    student behavior and, 36, 38, 71*f*, 72*f*, 161–162, 163
    subconscious conceptions of, 176–177
    teachers' awareness of own, 162, 164, 170
praise, 169, 173
precontemplation stage of change, 116–117
prefrontal cortex, 140, 144, 151, 152
pregnancy, 145
preparation stage of change, 118–119
presentations and performances, 1–2, 25–27, 113–114, 196
priorities, 189–191, 192–193, 215
Prochaska, James, 116
progressive muscle relaxation, 153

Index   **241**

protection
in Circle of Security, 102*f*, 103
environment in, 84, 92, 94
"firefighter" emotions in, 38, 40
as goal of student behavior, 71*f*, 73–74
psychoanalysis, 20–21
psychological flexibility, 54, 56
pulling, 36, 38–39, 49*f*, 50, 70

Q
quiet students, 74, 113–114
quiet time, 215–216

R
RAIN process, 198–199
RAND State of the American Teacher (SoT) survey, 6, 7
reality-testing, 207–208
rebellious behaviors, 71*f*
Re-Envisioning Our Spaces activity, 92–94
regulation
anchoring in, 41, 42–43, 149–150, 156, 159, 202
co-regulation in, 125, 145–146, 152–153, 217
in de-escalation, 202
nervous system states in, 143–146, 147, 148, 149–150, 152–153
relapses, 119, 208
relationship-building
with allies, 213
attachment in, 98–99, 103–107, 112
boundaries in, 184–185, 188–190, 211
cues of connection in, 21–22
getting to know students in, 103–105, 112
intrusive thoughts in, 199–200
long-term impact of, 217–218
mental health mindset in, 3, 7–11, 15–16, 210
play in, 127–128, 130–133
showing students your personality in, 90, 128, 216
relaxation. *See* calmness and relaxation
repair, 43, 106–107
rest, 153
retaliatory behaviors, 71*f*, 73–74, 75
re-traumatization, 141
rewards, 163
rigid boundaries, 187–188, 189, 190–191
risk-taking
classroom environment in, 85
in goals of student behavior, 72*f*
nervous system and, 148
in Role Cards activity, 181

as suicide warning sign, 225
trauma and, 143, 144
rituals, 87, 95–96
Role Cards activity, 181–183
Rose (teacher), 186, 187–188
Ryan (therapy client), 84

S
sadness
anger in protecting from, 38
"caring for", 23
chemical basis for, 52
helping students through, 56
intrusive thoughts in, 196
in nervous system states, 149
physical sensations from, 62
self-awareness of, 53, 61, 62, 63, 65
showing students your, 209–210
as suicide warning sign, 225
in withdrawal behaviors, 72*f*
See also depression
safe haven, 102*f*, 103
Sammy (student), 33, 36, 39–40
school community, 213
Schwartz, Richard, 36, 38
seating, 89, 128
secure attachment style, 100, 105–107, 111
secure base, 102, 102*f*
self-attunement, 22–24, 25–26, 31*f*
self-awareness
of attachment style, 110–111
of beliefs (*see* beliefs)
of communication patterns, 178–180
in healing fantasies, 116
identifying specific emotions in, 22–24, 25–26, 31*f*, 51–54, 61–66
importance of, 8
of nervous system, 149, 155–60
of one's past (*see* the past)
of power, 162, 164, 170
of triggers, 39–40, 45–50, 49*f*
self-care
in classroom rituals, 87, 95–96, 215–217
definition of, 214–215
for emotions, 23, 39, 43
play in, 134–135, 216
snacks in, 88–89, 216
Self-Care Jar, 87, 95–96
self-harm, 151, 203
self-talk, 43, 202

senses
- in calming and anchoring oneself, 41, 149–150, 153, 159, 202
- classroom environment and, 87–88
- imagining emotions as, 23
- in Observation Point activity, 49f
- in trauma, 140–141, 146
- *See also* physical sensations

shame and guilt
- boundaries and, 187
- from intrusive thoughts, 197–199, 200–201
- physical sensations from, 63
- in self-care, 216–17
- student behavior and, 70f, 75, 130
- in suicide warning signs, 225
- in teacher exodus, 7
- trauma and, 37f, 143

shoeboxes, 93
silliness, 127, 128, 129, 136–137, 216
snacks, 88–89, 216
somatization. *See* physical sensations
songs and singing, 128, 129, 153, 216
space, 21–22, 42, 56, 78, 152
- *See also* classroom environment

stimulation, 86
stones, 88, 122, 123
structural dissociation, 36, 37f
structure, 106, 127, 128, 169–170
subconscious, 176–177
submission, 37f
suicide, 3, 5–6, 225
sympathetic state, 146, 147–148, 149, 150–151, 157, 160
systems, 24–26, 29–31, 36, 38

T

Tate (student), 161–162, 164, 166, 169
teacher training programs, 5–6
tension, 29–30
therapists. *See* mental health professionals
thoughts
- in change, 113, 116–118
- as data, 52–53
- in emotional mapping, 61
- intrusive (*see* intrusive thoughts)
- in Observation Point activity, 49f, 50
- psychological flexibility in, 54

threats. *See* triggers
thrill-seeking behaviors, 72f
time, 215
Tony (teacher), 185–186, 187

trauma, 138–60
- in behavior, 141–143, 144, 163
- learning difficulties and, 143–144
- limits to teachers' emotional work in, 211–112
- nervous system in healing from, 145–50, 155–160
- neurological impact of, 140–141
- teacher recovery from, 212–217
- triggers and, 36, 37f, 38, 140–141, 143–144, 150–153

triggers, 32–50
- body's alarm system in, 34
- finding your footing in, 40–43
- in nervous system, 143–144, 147, 148
- noticing patterns in, 40, 45–50, 49f
- personality in, 36, 37f, 38
- recovery from, 38–40
- in teaching, 35–36, 70f–72f, 73
- in trauma, 36, 37f, 38, 140–141, 143–144, 150–153

trust
- boundaries and, 187, 188, 190
- in change, 113–114
- in discussing emotions with students, 56, 152
- past experiences in, 39–40
- repairing broken, 106–107

tug of war, 36, 38–39, 49f, 50, 70
Turcotte, Jacob "Buck", 87, 138–139, 145

U

universities, 165

V

values, 192–193
ventral vagal state, 146–147, 149, 152, 157, 158, 160
Visualizing Change activity, 122–123

W

Walker, Robin, 15, 16, 124
wanting to be wanted, 20–21
water, 88
waves, 24
Wells, Mr. (teacher), 161–162, 164, 166, 169
"What are My Priorities?" activity, 192–193
withdrawal, 72f, 151–152, 225
Working with My Intrusive Thoughts activity, 205–208
wounded parts, 38, 39, 43

Y

Yalom, Irvin, 173
yarn, 29–30
yelling, 34, 74, 143, 151, 179

ABOUT THE AUTHOR

Maria Munro-Schuster, M.A., M.S., LCPC, is a Montana counselor and educator. Growing up on the Fort Peck Reservation, she became interested in how education issues impacted her community. She began her exploration into the gray area between education and psychology as a sixteen-year-old presenting her two-year research study on type-2 diabetes prevention using psychology-based teaching methods at the International Science and Engineering Fair.

After earning her bachelor of arts in education, she taught in a variety of settings including public and independent schools, spent time at a groundbreaking school in India featured in the documentary *Daughters of Destiny*, and has worked with students from kindergarten to college. She went on to earn a master of arts in English, writing her thesis on how student grief plays out in the college writing classroom.

Her publications include works in *The Lascaux Review, The Whitefish Review, Graze,* and *Montana Quarterly*. She was a finalist for the William Van Dyke Short Story Prize and the Big Snowy Prize. She was mentored by Lan Samantha Chang at Tin House Writers Workshop. Her curiosity led her to work as a social-emotional educator and presenter for a Nordic digital media company, which opened her eyes further to the mental health crisis occurring out of sight of caring adults. She was selected as a Hatch North America honoree for teaching. She's served as an associate head of school and board member at a place-based middle school, where she taught English with a mental health focus. She received her master of science in counseling, and now works as a counselor in Bozeman, Montana, where she lives with her husband.